PEOPLE ARE TALKI

2012

"Geezumpiece! This is the best book I've ever seen in my life! It's so professional and well put together." -- **Troy O'Neil**

"This is long overdue! I love that finally we have a book that encapsulates all of our Cayman sayings. Unna really need ta read dis book!" -- **Dara Flowers Burke**

"I think this is a brilliant mode of capturing, preserving and transcending our linguistic culture which is unique but constantly changing. As a pivotal document in the literary arts it can be utilised as an educational tool, tourist/cultural guide and a historical manuscript for us to reflect and reminisce of our yesteryears. Well done!" -- **Anthony Ramoon**

"As we grow up and educate our children, we should always remember what makes us uniquely Caymanian, and what better way than to have a reference within our reach. I love it!" -- **Tania Ebanks**

"This document brings forward a lot of our culture that has been overlooked for quite some time. My hope is that it will be used in the schools as a cultural tool for future generations." -- **Brainard D. Watler**

"At last! Great insight! Exactly what Cayman needed. This will cement and further showcase a very important piece of our unique culture locally and worldwide. What better way than through our local dialect?" -- **Merta Day**

"This is the perfect book to help us understand dem older Caymanians when they get to telling their old time stories. It's an absolutely essential educational tool for the younger generation to learn their linguistic history." -- **Devon Edie**

"I am excited about the Cayman Islands Dictionary! Now my children can look up all the 'crazy' words and expressions that I use and I might actually start to make some sense to them! -- **Delores Thompson**

"This is definitely a wake-up call for those who take our heritage for granted. Hopefully it will inspire our people to delve into things Caymanian instead of recycling other cultures." -- **Cara Anderson**

"In today's society it seems like each of our generations are losing pieces of our culture. This dictionary is an invaluable tool that preserves our culture and proves to be a real eye opener." -- **David Goddard**

"At Last! Cayman has its own first illustration of spoken word, culture and identity, in the Cayman Islands Dictionary. A must read for Caymanians, as well as anyone who wants to be 'in the know' about being a Caymanian." -- **Kim Wallace-Watler**

"It's amazing that someone would think about writing a dictionary just for Cayman! What a great legacy to leave for our children." -- **Victor Thompson**

"A Caymanian Dictionary? Why didn't I think of that?" -- **Morris Martin**

"Spoken word is an integral component of any culture. To that end, this Dictionary takes a stab at truly defining that component which is Caymanian culture!" -- **Daniel Reid**

"This dictionary should be taught in all of the schools, both private and public. Our children need to learn more about our heritage so that they may pass it on to their children." -- **Marcia Finnikin (Watler)**

"Awlehkipitins! It's about time we had our own dictionary. This is the perfect marriage between Cayman's traditional past and its contemporary future." -- **Maxwell Linwood**

"Finally, a way for the older people to understand the current generation. Now they don't have to ask "wah dis mean?" and "wah dat mean?" -- **Carla Martin**

CAYMANOLOGY™

EDUCATE. ENTERTAIN. INSPIRE. **EMPOWER**.

Traditional Caymanian occupations such as Thatch Weaving and Basket Making are still being practiced by artists and traditionalists today.

The Cayman Islands Dictionary is the flagship product of
The Caymanology Collection

published by: **GapSeed**

GapSeed
P.O. Box 1142
Grand Cayman KY1-1101
Cayman Islands
Email: info@caymanology.com
Official Website: www.caymanology.com

The Cayman Islands Dictionary©
A Collection of Words used by Native Caymanians
(from the Caymanology Collection)
Design and Layout by Kevin M. Goring
Compiled and Written by Kevin M. Goring
Chief Editor: Sarah V. Goring
Copy Editors/Proofreaders: Kurt Goring, Leticia Goring
Contributors: Tania Ebanks, Avons Ebanks,
Inez Goring, Ted Goring
Copyright registered 27 April 2007 and updated 8 July 2008
Printed in the USA
First Printing November 2011
ISBN: 978-0-9570951-0-6

THE CAYMAN ISLANDS DIC·TION·ARY

A COLLECTION OF WORDS USED BY NATIVE CAYMANIANS

Compiled and Written by

KEVIN M. GORING

WWW.CAYMANISLANDS.KY

Welcome to the Cayman Islands

HE HATH FOUNDED IT UPON THE SEAS

Ackee (ah-kih) *Noun* – **1.** *Blighia sapida;* a tropical Caribbean evergreen tree having leathery red and yellow fruits. It is naturalized and cultivated in the tropics and in Florida. **2.** the edible, fleshy, ripe aril of this tree, especially popular as a food in the Cayman Islands. **Eg.** *"Anytime yah waugh sump'm good ta eat, juss try some Ackee n' Codfish from Miss Vivine Kitchen. She kin cook good y'see!"*

Ackee Stick (ah-kih stik) *Noun* – **1.** a long stick designated for picking Ackees. **2.** a fruit-picking instrument which is generally shorter than a *breadfruit stick* and much thinner than a *mango stick.* **Eg.** *"Henry go find my ackee stick so I kin pick sum fa dinna nah?"*

Ackee Tree Garage (ah-kih tree gah-radj) *Noun* – **1.** a 'small-time garage'. **2.** a private business which involves one or two mechanics working on cars under an actual ackee tree, or similar trees. **3.** the poor man's alternative to using a professional mechanic. **Eg.** *"Doon' mek nobody from ah ackee tree garage touch yoh car unless you know fah sure dey know wah dey doin'."*

Acks (Ahks) *Verb* – **1.** to solicit (ask). **2.** to make a formal or informal request. **Eg.** *"I hate hawin' ta acks my boss fah anyting cuz he always be in ah bad mood."*

Agouti (ah-goo-tee) *Noun* – **1.** the Cayman jackrabbit. **2.** any of several short-haired, short-eared, rabbit-like rodents of the genus *Dasyprocta* of South and Central America and the West Indies; destructive to sugar cane. **Eg.** *"If you tink you fass, try ketch ah agouti wit yoh bare hands."*

Agriculcha Field (ahg'reh kull-chah feel) *Noun* – **1.** the property on which the current Cricket Field is located. **2.** the venue for the annual Agricultural Show during the 1980s and early 1990s. **3.** a popular site for football games during the 1980s. **Eg.** *"Maannn, I kin rememba when I used ta watch Renard Moxam n' Dale Ramoon shiffin' up all kinda man up by Agriculcha Field."*

Aa

Ah Good Lil' While (ah guud lill wyle) *Slang* – **1.** some time ago. **2.** a pretty long time, but not too long. **Eg.** *"I doon' know wah Kurtis be doin' in dah bahtchroom but he bin in deh fah ah good lil' while n' I needa get ready fa work."*

Ah Lil' (ah -lill) *Interjection* – **1.** a non-specific reference to something large or small, depending on the object and the occasion. **3.** a common expression of amazement. **Eg.** *"Look yah! Ah lil' car he gah deh. Dah ting barely look like it gah ah engine!"*

Ah Pretty (ah prih-deh) *Adverb* – **1.** silly. **2.** ludicrous, foolish, goofy. **3.** ridiculous. *Noun* – **4.** a type of marble. **Eg.** *"Cuzzy, hear wah I tell you, if you go up in dah Maiden Plum Bush, when you come out you gah look ah pretty, n' I nah tennin' ta ya nydah"*

Ahn (aah'n) *Noun* – **1.** one's aunt. **2.** the sister of one's father or mother. **3.** the wife of one's uncle. **4.** someone to love or fear when your parents are not around. **Eg.** *"Lisa, go so acks ya Ahn Dean if you kin sleep ova her house t'night cuz I gah go church."*

Ahn'deh (aah'n-deh) *Noun* – **1.** one's aunt. **2.** the sister of one's father or mother. **3.** the wife of one's uncle. **4.** someone to love or fear when your parents are not around. **Eg.** *"My ahn'deh always say if I be good she gah take me Tampa n' go shoppin'!"*

Ah Wah (ah-wah) *Suffix* – **1.** or what. **2.** the end of a question. **3.** yes or no. **Eg.** *"Morris, you goin' back home now ah wah?"* or; *Dah you ah wah?"*

Aie! (eye) *Interjection* – **1.** wow!; woah! **2.** ouch! **3.** oh my gosh! **Eg.** *"Aie! Watch way ya goin' nah? You jess step on my toes wit dem big ol' hoofs you gah deh!"* or; *"Daddy, Daddy, No! please doon' lick me wit dah switch again, aie!"*

Aingh! (eyenghh) *Interjection* – From West Bay; **1.** take that. **2.** yes. **3.** its about time. **4.** good for you. **Eg.** *"Aingh! Tek daah! You waugh run chrew people grass piece? Ah know ya look ah pretty now wid dah horse dung all ohwah yoh new school shoes."*

Aa

Air Condition (ere kun-dih-shun) *Adjective* – **1.** having holes or full of holes. **2.** allowing passage in and out. **3.** old or tattered clothing which are full of holes, resembling a/c vents. **Eg.** *"When Clinton had rip he pants, errybody say it wah air-condition cuz it wah rip from front ta back."*

Ajiculcha Show Ground (ah-jih-kul-chuh sho groun) *Noun* – **1.** the former Agricultural Field, currently known as the Cricket Field which is located on Thomas Russell Way; near Owen Roberts International Airport. **2.** the first official venue of the annual Agricultural Show. **Eg.** *"I doon' know how come u doon' rememba goin' ta Family Fair Day up by Ajiculcha Show Ground. Dah wah so much fun!"*

Aloe Wera (ah-loh-wear-ah) *Noun* – **1.** any aloe of the species *Aloe Vera*, the fleshy leaves which yields a juice used as an emollient ingredient of skin lotions and for treating burns. **2.** a leafy plant bearing a sap that is often used to correct children from using foul language. (also known as: **semper vivie, simpa wiwie,** or **alloways**) **Eg.** *"I try nah ta cuss too much in school or else Teacha McField gah put aloe wera in my mout again."*

Allawow (ah-lah-wow) *Interjection* – From Old People Times; **1.** to express one's surprise or dismay. **2.** to become excited. **3.** caught off guard. **4.** to be amazed. **Eg.** *"Allawow! Ya almost mek me jump outta my skin!"*

All Channels (awl chah'nulz) *Noun* – **1.** one of Cayman's early movie rental facilities which specialized in pre-recorded Beta and VHS tapes. All Channels was located at Merren's Plaza near the Watler's Road area of George Town. **Eg.** *"Erry Satday my whole family used ta go All Channels n' rent one whole pile ah moowiz boy."*

All Deck Out (awll dek owt) *Adverb* – **1.** dressed more formally or elaborately than necessary. **2.** dressed up. **3.** impressively adorned with clothing. **4.** very dapper. **Eg.** *"When MC Hammer wah popula I used ta go by Faces Niteclub all deck out in my parachute pants n' ting."*

All Now (awl now) *Slang* – **1.** for all time, up until now. **2.** even until now. **3.** to this day. **4.** to this instant. **Eg.** *"Ol' Al had promise me ah Foster's bag full ah mangoes from long time, 'n all now I nah see nuttin' yet."*

Aa

Alloways (ah-loh-waze) *Noun* – **1.** *Aloacae*; any aloe of the species *Aloe Vera* which originated in the Canary Islands. **2.** a puss-like liquid from the aloe vera plant which is sometimes used to reprimand children who use foul language. (also known as: **semper vivie, simpa wiwie,** or **aloe wera**) **Eg.** *"Ya bedda try hush yoh mout in church t'day or else daddy gah mek ya drink ah whole bottle ah alloways."*

American Football (ah-mear-ih-kun Futboll) *Noun* – **1.** an Americanized version of the sport of Rugby. **2.** Cayman's way of distinguishing the American sport from the world-standard sport of 'Football'. **3.** a word that is openly disputed by many Caymanians for causing unnecessary confusion. **Eg.** *"Wheneva Robert be down in he American Football he doon' pay nobody mind."*

American Twang (ah-mear-ih-kun twaingh) *Adverb* – **1.** to imitate or formulate an American accent. **2.** to speak with an American accent knowingly, but without regard. **Eg.** *"Lass week, Carson went Miami fa tree days n' come back wid ah American twang."*

Americanized (ah-mear-ih-kun twaingh) *Adverb* – **1.** assimilated to the customs and institutions of the United States. **2.** in accordance with everything that is seen on American t.v. **3.** conformed to the culture and fashion of America. **Eg.** *"It's ah wonda how come tourisses still comin' Cayman cuz deez days errytting becomin' so Americanized it like dey nah even leave home."*

And Odd (in awd) *Conjunction* – **1.** and more. **2.** more than the current figure. **3.** the prime number plus an unknown number. **4.** an unknown figure. **5.** into the unknown. **Eg.** *"Really n' truly, if I had know dah private dentist woulda charge me five hundred and odd dollas fah ah fillin', I woulda jess gone hospital."*

And Someting (in sum-teeng) *Conjunction* – **1.** and whatever else. **2.** more than what is currently known. **3.** the prime figure plus an unknown amount. **4.** an unknown figure. **Eg.** *"Me n' my wife just paid 'bout ah tousin' and someting dollas fah uwah plane tickets ta Disney World."*

Aa

Annex (ah-nix) *Noun* – **1.** Cayman's most popular football arena, located between School House Road and Eastern Avenue. **2.** the George Town playing field. **3.** the football pitch adjacent to the George Town Primary school. **Eg.** *"I 'memba dah Sundeh affanoon when Scholars had beat Strikers down by Annex."*

Any n' Errybody (eh-neh-in-eh-reh-baw-deh) *Noun* – **1.** any person at all; anybody. **2.** anyone. **3.** whomever. **Eg.** *"I doon' know how some people kin still put dey clothes on da line fa any n' errybody ta see."*

Any Ol' How (eh-neh-ole-hou) *Adverb* – **1.** any how. **2.** any way whatever. **3.** in any case; at all events. **4.** in a careless manner; haphazardly. **5.** at any rate. **Eg.** *"I cyah teck da way dem mobile car wash people do my car yih'see? Dey juss like ta wipe it up any ol' how n' expeck people ta satisfy wit waheva dey ghee um."*

Architeck (arr-chih-tek) *Noun* – **1.** an architect. **2.** a professional building designer. **3.** the deviser, maker, or creator of anything. **4.** one who designs and supervises the construction of buildings or other large structures. **Eg.** *"I rememba dah time when Delroy tell me he had waugh be ah architeck. All now he cyah eeab'n draw ah dog house tah save he life."*

Areckleh (ah-reck-leh) *Adverb* – **1.** later. **2.** the not-so-distant future. **3.** a future time to come. (also pronounced: **'ereckleh'**, **'dereckleh'**, or **'tereckleh'** in some areas) **Eg.** *"Sometimes it bedda ta know wah ya dealin' wit right now dun tah fine out 'areckleh'."*

[Ol'] Arnold (ole ar-null) *Noun* – **1.** a local crow, bearing dark-coloured feathers and parrot-like features. **Eg.** *"Dah ol' Arnold cyah stop mekkin' nize while I tryin' sleep ah wah?"*

Awleh (awe-leh) *Interjection* – From West Bay; **1.** a startled reaction to a particular situation. **2.** a verbal demonstration of surprise. **3.** another way of saying "oh my gosh!" **4.** reference to a group of individuals. **Eg.** *"Awleh! I didd'n know you could fishin' like dah."* or; *"Awleh unna come less go wid me ta da supamahkit."*

Aa

Awlehkipitins (awe-leh-kipp-eh-tinz) *Interjection* – From 'Old People Times'; **1.** a general expression of excitement or dismay. **2.** another way of saying 'Are you serious' or; 'Really?'. **Eg.** *"Awlehkipitins! I cyah believe I didd'n rememba ta bring my false teet ta church! I cyah sing widdout 'um yih'nah."*

Awlehmillikins (awe-leh-mih-lih-kinz) *Interjection* – From 'Old People Times'; **1.** a general expression of excitement or dismay. **2.** another way of saying 'Oh my gosh!' **3.** wow! **Eg.** *"Awlehmilikins! Deez people newah learn how ta drive before dey get dey license a wah?"*

Aw'right (awh-rite) *Adverb* – **1.** without doubt (used to reinforce assertion); *"aw'right nah, jess lee me alone"* **2.** an expression of agreement normally occurring at the beginning of a sentence. **3.** expressed approval. **Eg.** *"Da new Turtle Farm dat juss build look kinda aw'right, but it cost too much money man."*

Awh-Awh! (Augh-Auwwhhh) *Interjection* – **1.** an expression of disappointment or unexpected surprise. **Eg.** *"Awh-awh! Boy look yah. If you doon' get outta my room I gah tell daddy on you."*

Aye (aay) *Interjection* – **1.** hey. **2.** you. **3.** a verbal gesture or signal to attract attention. **4.** the first word in an angry sentence. **Eg.** *"Aye you lil' boy, you cyah hear stay outta people yard ah wah?"*

Ayegah (aay-gah) *Adjective* – **1.** feverish. **2.** pertaining to, of the nature of, or resembling fever. **3.** cold chills. **4.** excited, restless, or uncontrolled, as if from fever. **Eg.** *"Boy I dunno if I kin go movies wid unna t'night. I feel kinda ayegah n' dah a/c gah mek it worse."*

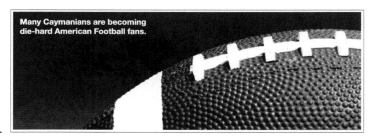

Many Caymanians are becoming die-hard American Football fans.

Aa

Babbecue (bah-beh-kyue) *Noun* – **1.** a meal, usually in the open air and often as a political or social gathering, at which meats are roasted over an open hearth or pit. **2.** to cook by barbecuing or to entertain at a barbecue. **Eg.** *"Afta Ivan we hadda use babbecue grill ta cook cuz we nehwa had no stove."*

Babes (baybz) *Slang* – **1.** one's sweetheart; dear. **2.** a young woman or man. **3.** either of a pair of lovers in relation to the other. **4.** a term of endearment for one's lover. **5.** a generous, friendly person. **Eg.** *"Babes, you juss goin' bade now? We gah be late fa da movies yih'nah?"*

Bachelah Party (bah'chih-lah) *Noun* – **1.** a party or event which is severely lacking in female attendants. **2.** a particular situation whereby both men and women were invited to a party, concert, dance or gathering, but only men show up. **Eg.** *"Christopher muss be doon' know much gyals, cuz errytime he have sump'm by he house, it juss be ah bachelah party wit pure man n' 'bout tree woman."*

Backhand Slap (bak han slahpp) *Noun* – **1.** a strike to the face using the rear of one's hand. **2.** a stroke, slap, etc., made with the palm of the hand turned toward the body and the back of the hand turned in the direction of the stroke, slap, etc. **Eg.** *"If you doon' stop yoh fassniss, I gah ghee you one backhand slap so hard yoh mama gah feel it."*

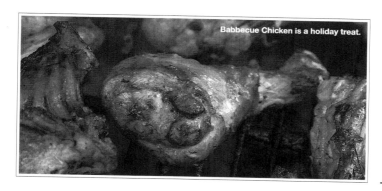

Babbecue Chicken is a holiday treat.

Bb

Back House (bak howce) *Noun* – **1.** a small tool shed or storage facility which is usually located at the rear of a dwelling home. **2.** an old Cayman-style bathroom made of wood, built over a large pit, which houses one or more crudely made toilet seats. **Eg.** *"I used ta hate goin' down by my granny's cuz all she had wah ah back house n' I always use ta get stuck in deh wit no tylit paper."*

Backside (bak-syde) *Noun* – **1.** the buttocks; any part of the lower half of the human body from the spine to the hamstrings. **2.** reference to the entire body stemming from a single part of the anatomy. **3.** a non-sexual reference to the female body part most attractive to Caribbean men. **Eg.** *"I keep havin' ta tell my sista ta hurry her backside or else we gah miss da play."*

Backin' News (bak-in nyuwze) *Verb* – **1.** gossiping. **2.** engaged in idle talk or rumor, esp. about the personal or private affairs of others. **3.** to share in small talk, hearsay, palaver, chitchat. **4.** chattering, prattling, palavering. **Eg.** *"Erry election time people be backin' all kinda news 'bout dem MLA's yih'see."*

Bad Accident (bah'd ak-sih-dent) *Noun* – **1.** a really terrible accident. **2.** an unfortunate catastrophe. **3.** an undesirable or unfortunate happening that occurs unintentionally and usually results in harm, injury, damage or loss; casualty; mishap. **Eg.** *"Anytime ya see traffic back up on Harquail Bypass, I betcha anyting its ah bad accident someway 'bout."*

Bad Boy (bah'd boi) *Noun* – **1.** a young man who lacks proper upbringing. **2.** a mischevious individual. **3.** a cruel and uncouth child. **4.** one who displays a lack of manners, obedience and restraint. **Eg.** *"My lil' niece say she 'fraid ah walk home from school cuz one bad boy always be fassin' wid 'er.'"*

Bad Luckid (bah'd luh-kidd) *Adjective* – **1.** cursed; damned; doomed. **2.** stricken with misfortune. **3.** unblessed. **Eg.** *"Lemme hold dem eggs cuz you so bad luckid you gah drop um fah no reason."*

Bb

Badness (bah'd-niss) *Noun* – **1.** the opposite of goodness. **2.** full of or exhibiting faults or errors. **3.** full of lies, deceit. **4.** having the character or disposition harmed by pampering or oversolicitous attention. **Eg.** *"Mummy, come so deal wit R.J. nah? I know he only four but he be goin' on wit pure badness n' I cyah deal wid im right now."*

Bad Up (bahd-upp) *Verb* – **1.** to vex or agitate the mind or emotions of; upset; scare. **2.** to get the ball rolling. **3.** to encourage progress through upset. **Eg.** *"Anytime I orda food from Ricey Restaurant I always gah bad up da place cuz dey too slow man!"*

Bad Wedda (bad-wed-ah) *Noun* – **1.** a disturbance of the normal condition of the atmosphere, manifesting itself by winds of unusual force or direction, often accompanied by rain, thunder and lightning. **2.** a Tropical Storm or Hurricane. **Eg.** *"My mama say we cyah go outside n' play kite til dah bad wedda hole up lil' bit."*

Baff Room (bahf-roome) *Noun* – From George Town; **1.** bathroom; a room equipped for taking a bath or shower. **2.** any room which includes a toilet and sink. **3.** the most important room in a nightclub. **4.** an unofficial conference room for women. (see also: **Bahtchchroom**) *Noun* – From George Town. **Eg.** *"When Champion House used tah stay open till tree'clock, errybody used ta be fightin' ta get in ta da baffroom"* or *"Da bess way ta scare somebody in da bahtchroom is ta tell um da tylit nah flushin'."*

Baila (bay-lah) *Noun* – **1.** 'bailer'; a small or medium-sized bucket used to remove water from a boat. **2.** one who subjects to the job of bailing water from a boat or house. **3.** a small bucket used to remove sand, fish and water from homes after Hurricane Ivan. **Eg.** *"If ya ehwah get ta see one mooweh neem 'Old Man and the Sea', yih gah see why dem fisha man always need ah baila in da boat."*

Baiyk (baiyck'h) *Adverb* – From West Bay and Cayman Brac; **1.** back. **2.** to return or retreat. **3.** the opposite of forward. **Eg.** *"I cyah wait ta go baiyk Kimmin' Braiyk so I can see my granny."*

Bb

Balboa (bal-boh-ah) *Noun* – **1.** a 375 foot freight ship, which sank on November 10, 1932 during the '32 Storm. **2.** a ship which lies in approx. 50 feet of water directly off the George Town harbour. **3.** a popular diving site for tourists, which has been featured in Skin Diver magazine. **Eg.** *"I always used ta wonda wah da Balboa is tell Teacha McField explain it ta us in History class."*

Bald Forrid (ball-foh-rid) *Noun* – **1.** *bald forehead*; a large and hairless area of the forehead which recedes into the hairline. **2.** lacking detail; bare; plain; unadorned. **3.** open; undisguised (see also: **peel forrid**). **Eg.** *"Dey say if ya wear hats too much yih get bald forrid early n' look like ah ol' man."* or; *"Henry gah one piece ah bald forrid deh. It look like ah avacado upside down wit two lil' piece ah hair on da top."*

Ball Plate (bawl play't) *Noun* – **1.** the Cayman wild pigeon. **2.** a wild fowl which scavenges on scraps of food, grain and insects. **Eg.** *"Uncle Alison had cyar me n' my brudda shootin' wid one 12-guage one time n' all I hit wah ah Ball Plate."*

Ball Up (bawl up) *Verb* – **1.** to coil. **2.** to wind into continuous, regularly spaced rings one above the other; to ball up a fishin' line after use. **3.** to wind on a flat surface into rings one around the other. **Eg.** *"Hurry so ball up dah hose so we kin rake da yard nah?"*

Bammy (bah-mih) *Noun* – **1.** a bitter species of the Cassava root, which is commonly used to make cakes. **2.** a must have for traditional Caymanian families as it is often eaten with fish and other dishes. **3.** a Cassava bread which is generally baked and eaten with meat during Christmas time. **Eg.** *"Wheneva my Granny fix bammy n' conch stew it taste like angels had cook it."*

Bananas (buh-nah-nuzz) *Noun* – **1.** a popular ice cream stand which was located in the Anchorage Centre during the late 1980's and most of the 1990's. **3.** a popular venue for teenage battle during the 1990's. **Eg.** *"I remeba when dem bad boys had clot dah boy in he head out by Bananas."* or *"Bananas used ta have da bess ice cream n' sorbet y'see?"*

Bb

Banana Bird (buh-nah-nah berd) *Noun* – **1.** a small tropical bird which feeds on the banana. **2.** a tiny yellow-chested bird of the genus *Certhiola*, allied to the creepers. **3.** a common victim of slingshot fire. **Eg.** *"Daddy say when he wah my age, dem banana birds wah tick like ants n' dey used ta eat up all da fruits."*

Banga Langa Langa (baing-ah laing-gah laing-gah) *Interjection* – **1.** you're gonna get it. **2.** you're in deep, deep trouble. **3.** you're in for a beating. **4.** a song of impending doom for a child. **Eg.** *"When I wah small my sistas always use tah sing 'banga langa langa' when I drop someting, cuz dey know my mama wah goin' beat me."*

Barba Grain (bahr-bah greene) *Noun* – **1.** a paved road made of asphalt. **2.** a large patch of black-top tar. **3.** any paved street, including side roads, parking lots and residential neighborhoods. **Eg.** *"If you fall down on barba grain, you goin' be well skin-up when ya done."*

Bar Bay (bahr bay) *Noun* – **1.** a former name for the area of George Town waterfront where the beachside fish market is located. **2.** the sandy area off of North Church Street, located next to Hammerheads Bar. **Eg.** *"I nehwa know it wah name Bar Bay till my daddy tell me 'bout it."*

Barra (bah-rah) *Noun* – **1.** the great, fearsome, Barracuda; ray-finned fishes notable for their large size and fearsome appearance. The body is long, fairly compressed, and covered with small, smooth scales. **Eg.** *"Gillis tell me det one time when he wah spear fishin' one Barra had chase im right out da wadda; all up on one reef in East End, yih'nah."*

Barriss (bah-riss) *Adverb* – **1.** an abbreviation of the word 'embarrassment'; to cause disrespect or unkind attention. **2.** to highlight a person's faults. **Eg.** *"I see one time Harry had get barriss when he acks one gyal fah her phone numba n' she tell im she had ah boyfriend."*

Basley (baz-leh) *Noun* – **1.** *Basil*; any of several aromatic herbs belonging to the genus *Ocimum*, of the mint family, as *O. basilicum* (sweet basil), having purplish-green ovate leaves used in cooking. **2.** an aromatic shrubby plant. **Eg.** *"I usually doon' like how basley taste unless my mudda cook it."*

Bb

Batabano (bah-da-buh-noo) *Noun* – a word linked to Cayman's history in 'turtling'. **1.** the name of the second-most popular Caribbean festival held in the Cayman Islands. **2.** the tracks left by turtles when they drag themselves onto the beach to nest in the sand. **3.** the name of a main street in West Bay. **Eg.** *"I lowe Batabano so much det I eewin tinkin' 'bout buyin' ah house on Batabano Road."*

Bath Pan (baht pan) *Noun* – **1.** a large metal bathtub. **2.** a broad, round, open, metal container used for bathing. **3.** an open, flat-bottomed vessel, usually round and typically wider than it is deep, used for washing, packing or storing. **Eg.** *"Afta Iwan we hadda go back ta bath pan n' chimmy days like my granny use tah talk 'bout."*

Baw-Baw (bawh bawh) *Slang* – **1.** a baby's bottle. **2.** a bottle with a teat (or nipple) to drink directly from. **3.** the easiest way to satisfy a young baby when one is tired of breastfeeding. **Eg.** *"My sweetums, ya waugh ya baw-baw now nah? Doon' worry, mummy soon have it ready."*

Baya (bay-ah) *Noun* – **1.** an individual who was born in the district of West Bay. **Eg.** *"If yah waugh know 'bout good fishnin' juss acks any Baya n' dey kin tell ya way ta go."*

Bawlin' (baw-lin) *Verb* – **1.** crying, weeping or pleading. **2.** any utterance of inarticulate sounds, esp. of lamentation, grief, or suffering, usually with tears. **Eg.** *"I wah bawlin' my eyes out when I see all ah dah wadda from Iwan messin' up my pretty liwin' room."*

Bawl Out (ball-owt) *Verb* – **1.** to accelerate while driving to a speed which results in smokey tires due to friction. **2.** to spin tires in place, causing a loud screeching noise. **3.** a way to bring attention to oneself while driving. **Eg.** *"I rememba when Troy used ta bawl out in he Iroc-Z down by Champion House."*

BBC (bee-bee-cee) *Noun* – **1.** the British Broadcasting Company. **2.** the most popular shortwave radio station among older Caymanians. **3.** a reason for young children to keep quiet to avoid punishment. **4.** a news-carrying person. **Eg.** *"Erry time my daddy use tah lissin' tah BBC we hadda keep quiet or else he wah gah beat us."*

Bb

Beady Head (bee-deh hed) *Noun* – **1.** having small beadlike hair clusters in one's head due to lack of grooming. **2.** short curly hair that is nearly impossible and extremely painful to comb. **Eg.** *"Erry Sundeh when Arnold come from baydin' in Hog Sty Bay, he gah use half ah bottle ah shampoo n' two condishionah's ta get rid ah dah beady head."*

Beast (bee'ce) *Noun* – **1.** a very strange, ugly, repulsive person or thing. **2.** an object which is untrendy and therefore unattractive to modern cultures – especially teenagers. **3.** obsolete technology. **Eg.** *"Wheneva my nephew look at my ol' Nintendo, he always gah say "look ah dah beast, man!"*

Beef (beef) *Noun* – **1.** one's counterpart. **2.** a word used to define ownership or affiliation to an individual of the opposite sex. **3.** a girlfriend or boyfriend. **Eg.** *"Harwell tell me I mussin' mess wid Molly-Anne cuz dah Otis beef."*

Beggin' Bread (bay-gin bred) *Adjective* – **1.** torn apart, ragged, open, exposed. **2.** having a huge gaping hole in the front of an old shoe which exposes the toes to onlookers. **Eg.** *"One time when Ornel had wear he church shoes ta football, afterwurds he shoes wah all tear up n' beggin' bread."*

Beliewe (bah-leewe) *Adverb* – **1.** *believe;* to have confidence in the truth, the existence, or the reliability of something, although without absolute proof that one is right in doing so. **2.** to suppose or assume; understand. **3.** to have faith. **Eg.** *"Yeah, dah wah you beliewe but I nah no edieyut doh yih'nah."*

Bell Bell (behl-behl) *Noun* – **1.** a George Town neighborhood located off Crewe Road, approximately between the Esso service station and Jacques Scott. **Eg.** *"I used to have fun wit dem boys from Bell Bell on Sundays when we use ta jump in da sea at Hog Sty Bay."*

Ben Up (beh'n upp) *Adverb* – **1.** not straight; bending; curved; crooked. **2.** bent; deformed; disfigured. **3.** not straightforward and often moved to one side. **Eg.** *"Dah time when I had fall offa my bicycle people say I wah walkin' all ben up aftawurds."*

Bb

B.E.T. Baby (bee-ee-tee bay-beh) *Adverb* – **1.** a product of the music video age; the current generation of Caymanian youth. **2.** one who is raised by music videos, hip-hop and other foreign cultures. **3.** one who lacks knowledge, understanding and/or allegiance to Caymanian culture. **Eg.** *"If I wah born deez days I woulda probleh turn out tah be ah B.E.T. Baby too."*

Big Accident (big ack-zih-den't) *Noun* – **1.** a huge crash. **2.** a stockpiling of damaged vehicles. **Eg.** *"Doon' go chrew by Jose's afta work cuz ah big accident up deh. Police, Fiyah Truck, Ambulance n' errybody hadda come see wah happen."*

Big Buhind (big buh-hyne) *Noun* – **1.** having a large pair of buttocks. **2.** a large behind. **3.** a big person. **4.** oversized hips. **Eg.** *"Took-eh, you 'memba wah dah big buhind gyal det use tah go school wid us wah name?"*

Big Face (big fayce) *Noun* – **1.** one's face. **2.** a portrait or other picture. **Eg.** *"Yeow! Wah yah sayin' man? I juss see ya big face up in da newspaypah still."*

Big Finga (big fee'ng-gah) *Noun* – **1.** one's thumb. **2.** the short, thick, inner digit of the human hand next to the forefinger. **1.** the finger most commonly used to hitch rides. **Eg.** *"Mahma, I juss jam my big finga in da door. You gah any ban-daids?"*

Bigga (bih-gah) *Noun* – **1.** an affectionate nickname for a large or husky person. **2.** an overweight male who is usually friendly to all. **Eg.** *"Yeah Bigga, wah ya sayin', errytin cool ah wah?"*

Big Hard Back Man (big hah'rd bak-mahn) *Noun* – **1.** a grown man of 30 years or older who is generally hard-working and respected for being independent; inspirational. **Eg.** *"Come now, you know ah big hard back man like you nah suppose tah live up in bar room."*

Big Head (big hed) *Noun* – **1.** conceit; egotism. **2.** one who is stubborn and head strong. **3.** an annoying person. **4.** an obstruction. **Eg.** *"Aye, moo yoh big head out da way nah?* or; *"We coulda get ta sleep ova by Lisa house lass week if ol' big head Charlotte diddn' tell mama we wah goin' party."*

Bb

Big Joe (big joh) *Noun* – From Old People Times; **1.** a popular fruit-flavoured candy on a stick measuring approx. 6 inches. long and having a striped, multi-coloured body. **Eg.** *"Boy I wish I could juss taste ah piece ah Big Joe right now yih'see?"*

Big Lick (big lik) *Adverb* – **1.** a sudden, hard stroke with a hand, fist, or weapon; a blow to the head. **2.** a sudden shock, calamity, reversal, etc. **3.** to make fatal contact with a blunt object or person, resulting in pain or embarrassment. **Eg.** *"If you don't hush yoh mout, I gah ghee ya one big lick wit diss fryin' pan."*

Big Odd (big awd) *Conjunction* – **1.** a huge unknown amount. **2.** more than what was expected. **3.** a lot more than one should have to pay for anything. **4.** too much. **Eg.** *"I wonda if dem people expeck yah ta walk rong bare foot, cuz dey chargin' ah hundred n' big odd dollas juss fa ah pair ah keds."*

Bine Up (byne upp) *Verb* – **1.** to become constipated after eating too many fruits, especially guineps. **2.** to cause constipation in; make costive. **3.** to clog or make sluggish; obstruct. **4.** affected with constipation. **Eg.** *"Geee! Terry! how come you eat out all ah my guineps man? I hope ya get bine up n' cyah walk tomorrow."*

Bird Chest (burd chess) *Noun* – **1.** the upper torso area of a lean-bodied Caymanian male which often lacks muscularity . **2.** the unmuscular or underdeveloped chest area of a growing teenage boy or young man. **Eg.** *"I doon' like changin' afta football practice cuz errybody always say dey doon' waugh see my bird chest."*

Bird Legs (burd lay'gz) *Noun, Pl.* – **1.** really skinny legs. **2.** long, slender legs with knobbly knees and very little hair. **3.** legs which resemble a bird's. **Eg.** *"If ya ehwah waugh ah good laugh, jess go down by Annex n' watch Hayman runnin' rong in football shorts wit he bird legs."*

Birtday (birt-dey) *Noun* – **1.** *Birthday;* the day of a person's birth. **2.** the annual celebration of the day one was born. **Eg.** *"I always gah send flowas tah my mama fa her birtday."*

Bb

Bitin' Ants (byt'n ahn'tz) *Noun, Pl.* – **1.** large black ants which tend to bite when disturbed. **2.** stinging ants. **3.** really annoying ants. **Eg.** *"Aieee!! I jess step in one bitin' ants ness n' dey all dong in my shoe."*

Blackeh (blak-ih) *Noun* – **1.** a person of dark-skinned complexion. **2.** an antonym for a clear-skinned or Caucasian person. **Eg.** *"I went gym d'udda day n' I see Blackeh liffin' one whole heap ah weight!"*

Blackuh (blak-ah) *Noun* – **1.** a person of dark brown complexion. **2.** an antonym for a deeply tanned *Caucasian* person. **Eg.** *"If ya waugh know 'bout rims juss check Blackuh. He know erryting 'bout cars."*

Black Cow (blak-kow) *Noun* – From Old People Times; **1.** a creamy, chewy, chocolate candy bar which closely resembled a **Sugar Daddy**. **2.** a chocolatey caramel candy. **3.** a popular candy among children of the 1950s and 60s. **Eg.** *"I know all yih get is Sugar Daddy deez days, but if ya show me ah Black Cow – I would ghee ya $10.00 fa one right now. "*

Bleech (bleech) *Verb* – **1.** to stay up late at night. **2.** to succumb to insomnia. **3.** to prowl the streets until the wee hours of the morning. **Eg.** *"Cayman so small det when it get borin' we juss bleech cuz it nah nuttin' else tah do."*

Blie (bly) *Verb* – **1.** to give leeway or special pardon to another person. **2.** to relax certain rules or policies in favor of another. **3.** to perform a charity for one who is in need. **Eg.** *"Wheneva I used tah go by Sharkey's da security guard used tah gimme ah blie n' lemme in chrew da back."*

Bloods (bludz) *Slang* – **1.** brethren, friend, brother. **2.** an informal handle that is often used among teenage males. **Eg.** *"Wah goin' on bloods? You cool ah wah?"*

Bloomin' (blu-min) *Adverb* – From 'Old People Times'. **1.** an annoyance **2.** an annoying object or person; "gimme the bloomin' ting." or **Eg.** *"Mama said dah man is ah bloomin' eediot cuz he wah drivin' on da wrong side ah da road."*

Bb

Blow Holes (bloh-holez) *Noun* – **1.** one of Cayman's feature tourist attractions. **2.** a stretch of iron shore in East End, which features large waterholes that produce a geyser-like water spout. **3.** a popular place to take pictures and watch the sun rise. **Eg.** *"One touriss man tell me det when he went up by blowholes, he figget he camera n' when he went back it wah full ah wadda."*

Blue Iguana (bloo ee-gwawh-nuh) *Noun* – **1.** *Cyclura nubile lewesi*; the indigineous species of iguana which has become endangered due to the growth and development of the Cayman Islands. **2.** a large, arboreal lizard, native to the Cayman Islands, having stout legs and a crest of spines from neck to tail. **3.** a large herbivorous lizard. **4.** one the Cayman Islands' many National Symbols. **Eg.** *"Bobo, try so doon' mek National Trust ketch you wit dah Blue Iguana cuz dey gah lock ya up n' chrow way da key."*

Boatbuilding (bote bill-din) *Adverb* – From Old People Times; **1.** the process of designing, constructing, maintaining, and refining vessels for commercial and private martime use. **2.** a popular trade among early Caymanian men which earned the country worldwide acclaim. **3.** the process of creating ships and boats from salvaged wood and other parts, as well as, from local hardwood trees (such as Mahogany). **Eg.** *"Dey say Captain Rayal Bodden was bouk da bess one tah come outta da boatbuildin' times n' I tink dass da chroot."*

Bobo (boh-boh) *Pronoun* – From West Bay; **1.** a close personal friend. **2.** the object of one's affection. **3.** a woman's pet name for a boyfriend or close male friend. **Eg.** *"I gah plenty guy friends but Derrick is my bobo, boy."*

Bodda (baw-duh) *Noun* – **1.** bother; to cause frustration by way of hinderance or constant badgering. **2.** to get on one's nerves. **3.** to interrupt. **4.** to invade the personal space of another. **Eg.** *"Lissin' yah man. Doon' bodda me no more or else I gah tell my mama on you."*

Boddaration (baw-dah-ray-shun) *Noun* – **1.** the act or state of bothering or the state of being bothered. **2.** something or someone that causes trouble; a source of unhappiness. **Eg.** *"Aye look yah. Stop ghee'in me all diss boddaration fah I send ya go get dah switch."*

Bb

Bodden Tong (baw-din tawng) *Noun* – Bodden Town; **1.** the first capital district of Grand Cayman. **2.** the district which received the most catastrophic damage during Hurricane Ivan. **3.** the area starting from Sawannah to Breakas; including, Low Walley, Pedro and Nortwurd. **Eg.** *"I rememba when I used ta ketch Bodden Tong bus from Kirk Plaza."*

Bogga Boo (bawg-ah boo) *Noun* – **1.** hardened nasal fluid or mucus. **2.** cold in the nose. **3.** particles or projectiles which originate in the nasal passage or nostrils. **Eg.** *"Sandra say she hate da way her brudda always pick he nose n' try put da bogga boo on her."*

Boggy Sand (bog-eh san) *Noun* – **1.** the Boggy Sand area of the District of West Bay. **2.** the area behind Four Winds Esso. **3.** a long, narrow road on the sea side behind Heritage Square. **Eg.** *"I always taught Boggy Sand Road wah da road way da Wess Bay Police Station on."*

Boilers (bie-luhz or boi-luhz) *Noun* – **1.** the original name for the neighborhood currently known as 'Windsor Park'. **2.** the name of the road on which 'Merengue Town' is located. **Eg.** *"My mama always used ta tell me doon' walk chrew Boilers afta sun come down cuz dey nehwa had no street lights."*

Boney (boo-neh) *Adverb* – **1.** a nickname for an unusually skinny person. **2.** one who is apparently malnutritioned or lacking in musculature. **3.** 'skinny'. **Eg.** *"I can't believe Robert tried ta set me up wit one ol' boney gyal."*

Booby Key (boo-beh kee) *Noun* – **1.** a small body of land off the coast of South Sound, near the South Sound Civic Centre. **2.** one of the many habitats of the Red-footed Booby. **3.** a very scenic location to take pictures. **Eg.** *"It's ah wonda how Booby Key still standin' afta all ah dah damage det Sout Sound get durin' Ivan."*

Boo Narrow (boo-nah-row) *Noun, Pl.* – **1.** *bow* and *arrow;* a two-piece weapon or hunting tool consisting of arrows and the bow to shoot them. **2.** a Caymanian hobby, usually made from Birch or other similar trees, fishing line, twine and sticks. **Eg.** *"I betcha anyting I kin still mek boo narrow bedda dun you."*

Bb

Borden's (bor-dinz) *Noun* – **1.** *Borden's Pizza* - a popular restaurant located next to Morgan's Harbour in West Bay for years. **2.** the best local pizza on the island for more than 20 years. **3.** a family business which specialized in pizza and local food. **Eg.** *"When I had work at Hurley's in Eden Centre I used tah go by Borden's erry day fa lunch n' dinna."*

Bore (bohre) *Verb* – **1.** to create a hole in an inanimate object. **2.** to cause interference or obtrusiveness. **3.** to clear a path. **Eg.** *"People call me tattle-tale cuz I had tell on Franky when he had bore ahead ah me in da lunch line."*

Borry (baw-reh) *Verb* – **1.** *borrow*; to take or obtain with the promise to return the same or an equivalent. **2.** to use, appropriate, or introduce from another source or from a foreign source. **Eg.** *"Kin I borry one ah yoh pencils ta do my homework?"*

Bottlah (bawt-lah) *Noun* – **1.** *bottler*; an angular shaped vegetable from the banana and plantain family of fruits and vegetables. **2.** a triangular-shaped plantain. **Eg.** *"Yuck! Mama how come you always gah buy so much bottlahs when you know I lowe bananas bedda?"*

'Bout (bowt) *Adjective* – **1.** about; from one place to another; in this place or that. **2.** on every side; in every direction; around. **3.** in or somewhere near. **Eg.** *"When I bored, I like walk 'bout da place lookin' in shops and stores, fassin' wit people n' hailin' up my friends."*

Bowsin' Bay (Bow-sin Baye) *Noun* – **1.** Boatswain Bay; an area within the district of West Bay which earned its name after a boatswain of the pirate ship 'Scourer', who was killed and gave his name to the area. **2.** the birthplace of many West Bay fishermen. **3.** the area encompassing everything from Fountain Close to the Goat Yard area. **Eg.** *"My mama say she might liwe in George Town but she still from Bowsin' Bay all da way."*

Box Dat (bawx daht) *Verb* – **1.** encouragement to defend one-self. **2.** to avenge. **3.** to return an insult. **4.** to engage in a fistfight or brawl over a disagreement. **Eg.** *"Marlon tell Burney ta 'box dat' when Lowell call im ah fraud fa nah comin' movies wid us."*

Bb

Boyfriend n' Gyalfriend (boy-fren n' gyal-fren) *Collective Noun* – **1.** an intimate relationship involving a male and a female. **2.** man and woman. **3.** a teenage relationship. **Eg.** *"Willy jess tell me dat he bin boyfriend n' gyalfriend wit Felicia fah tree munts now."*

Boys Home (boiz hoom) *Noun* – **1.** a shorthand reference to the (reform or) foster home for boys in Grand Cayman. **2.** a professional facility for assisting displaced boys or those with special challenges. **Eg.** *"I rememba when my mama n' daddy used tah tell me dat if I doon' keep still, they wah gah send me Boys Home."*

Bracka (brah-kah) *Noun* – **1.** any person who is native to the island of Cayman Brac. **2.** a proud individual from one of Grand Cayman's two Sister Islands. **Eg.** *"Dah time when Mona Lisa had win Miss Cayman, it made me proud ta be ah Bracka boy."*

Brackish Wadda (brah-kish wauh-dah) *Noun* – **1.** *brackish water;* water which has a salty or briny flavour. **2.** distasteful; unpleasant water. **3.** salty fresh water. **4.** the type of water found in most freshwater wells. **Eg.** *"Daddy say doon' drink brackish wadda or else it gah hurt ya stomach."*

Breadfruit (brade-froot) *Noun* – **1.** a large, round, starchy fruit borne by a tree, *Artocarpus Altilis*, of the mulberry family, native to the Caribbean islands; used, baked or roasted, for food. **2.** the tree bearing this fruit. **Eg.** *"You don't eat yoh breadfruit wit salt on it ah wah?"*

Breadfruit Stick (brade-froot-stik) *Noun* – **1.** a long stick used for picking breadfruits. **2.** a stick that is often too long for picking mangoes and too big for picking ackees. **Eg.** *"Norman usually use he breadfruit stick ta fix he satellite dish when it nah workin good."*

Breadfruit Walk (brade-froot wohk) *Noun* – **1.** an area in Lower Valley; located on the corner which bends to the right. **2.** the area directly to the west of the Lower Valley water reservoir . **3.** an area where cows are currently kept. **Eg.** *"Come less go up by Breadfruit Walk n' teck some pitchas ah dem pretty cows nah?"*

Bb

Brand-New-Second-hand (brahn-n'yoo-seh-kun-hahn) *Noun* – **1.** previously used by someone else, but still in excellent near-perfect condition. **2.** recycled; refurbished. **3.** just as good as something new. **Eg.** *"I hear dem deportee cars people be gettin' from Japan be brand-new second-hand, but people still love um cuz dey cheap."*

Bread Kind (brade-kine) *Noun* – **1.** starchy vegetables. **2.** side orders in a traditional Caymanian meal which include; breadfruit, sweet potato, yam and cassava. **Eg.** *"My mama always say we muss eat da bread kind before we touch da meat."*

Breakas (bray-kuhz) *Noun* – **1.** Breakers; the eastern district located between Bodden Town and Frank Sound. **2.** a peaceful locale bearing beautiful sunrises and sunsets. **Eg.** *"Afta Ivan wah da first time I meet somebody from Breakas when I had went lookin' ta see if Lighthouse Club wah still deh."*

Bret (bret) *Noun* – **1.** one's breath; the air inhaled and exhaled in respiration. **2.** life; vitality. **3.** an intake of oxygen to fill one's lungs. **Eg.** *"The best way ta train fah Flower's Sea Swim is tah make sure ta ketch ah bret erry few strokes."*

Breezeway (breez waye) *Noun* – **1.** a porch or roofed passageway open on the sides for connecting two buildings such as a house and a garage. **Eg.** *"I hate havin' ta sweep da breezeway wheneva it rain cuz all kinda leaves be mix up wit wadda n' dirt."*

Breezy Castle (breez-zeh k'yass-ul) *Noun* – **1.** a small housing community located near the Owen Roberts International Airport. **2.** the area across from the George Town Fire Station. **Eg.** *"My breddren say when he wah livin' Breezy Castle all he hear is planes landin' all da time."*

Breddren (breh'drin) *Noun* – **1.** a close friend, cousin, or family member. **2.** a trustworthy friend that is supportive and genuine. **Eg.** *"Sometimes when I bored I juss go down by my breddren house n' cool out."* or; *Yeow! Breddren! Wah goin' on man? You still goes up by Norwell house n' play Nintendo?*

Bb

Bresh (bresh) *Verb* – **1.** to brush. **2.** to sweep, paint, clean, polish, etc., with a brush. **Eg.** *"Before I go ta my bed I gah mek sure ta bresh my teet first."*

Brights (bryt'z) *Noun* – **1.** the bright light function on one's automobile. **2.** the high beam. **Eg.** *"I rememba when ya used ta have drive wit ya brights on when dey had first build Harquail Bypass cuz it wuz'n no street light yet."*

Bring Up (bring up) *Verb* – **1.** to strike one another or one against the other with a forceful impact; to come into violent contact; crash. **2.** the happening of a funny accident involving one person and an inanimate object. **Eg.** *"Daddy, Mista Harley say tell you it wah two cars det bring up in front ah Sunny yaad lass night."*

Broke (broh'k) *Verb* – **1.** to break. **2.** to destroy or interrupt the regularity, uniformity, continuity, or arrangement of; interrupt. **3.** to disable or destroy by or as if by shattering or crushing. **Eg.** *"Curtis! If you doon' fine yoh backside in dis house, I gah broke off dah tamarind switch on yoh behind!"*

Broughtupsy (brot-up-seh) *Adjective* – **1.** having good manners as a result of a positive upbringing. **2.** civilized and well behaved. **3.** a clear understanding of how to behave in public. **Eg.** *"I hate takin' Willie anyway wit me cuz he nah gah no broughtupsy."*

Bruck-a-dum-bram (bruk-ah-dum-brahm) *Interjection* – From 'Old People Times' **1.** an expressive sound effect used to illustrate (by mouth) a loud crash or accident. **2.** a vocally illustrated fatality. **Eg.** *"Dah time when Spurgeon fall offa he bicycle, all ya hear is bruck-a-dum-bram!"*

Brudda Man (bruh-dah mahn) *Noun* – **1.** a close friend or acquaintance. **2.** a way of referring to someone when you can't remember their name. **Eg.** *"Aye brudda man, wah goin' on?"*

Bubbies (buh-biz) *Noun, Pl.* – **1.** the chest or upper torso area of the female anatomy. **2.** a pair of instruments used for feeding young babies. **3.** an area of the female anatomy that is attractive to the opposite sex. **Eg.** *"Mama, tell Roy stop teasin' me 'bout I nah gah no bubbies..."*

Bb

Buck Toe (buk-toh) *Noun* – **1.** the result of a painful collision between one or more toes and an inanimate object. **2.** the most popular injury among young children. **3.** a legitimate reason to wear slippers to school. **Eg.** *"When I wah small, my granfadda used ta mek me wear shoes in he grass piece so I diddn' get no buck toe."*

Buff Teet (buff teet) *Noun* – **1.** large protruding front teeth. **2.** a pair or more of the front teeth which are usually oversized, disfigured and crooked. **3.** funny looking teeth. **Eg.** *"Roy had look like one rabbit wit buff teet before he get braces."*

Bug (buhg) *Adverb* – **1.** of; concerning; in regard to. **2.** connected or associated with. **3.** here or there; in or on. **4.** on every side; in every direction; around. **Eg.** *"Tee-Dee, if you doon' stop pesterin' me bug which boy like you, I gah tell yoh mama yih'nah?"* or; *"Devon always say bug he needa be mekkin' more money but all he do is spend it on foolishness."*

Bug Eye (bug-eye) *Noun* – **1.** huge bulging eyes. **2.** very round eyes. **3.** flared eyes resulting from irritation or amazement. **Eg.** *"When Suzette fine out dat Greggy wah messin' rong wit one bug eye gyal name Rosey Ann, she went n' pong up all two ah wum."*

Bugga (bug-ah) *Noun* – **1.** one who surrounds him or herself with controversy. **2.** a person deserving great misfortune, simply for being in or around mischievious company. **3.** an idiot. **4.** the center of mischief. **5.** a despicable or contemptible person, esp. a man. **Eg.** *"Hear wah I tell you. If I ketch dah bugga runnin' chrew my yaad again it gah be me an' him."*

Buggage (bug-idge) *Noun* – **1.** a species of Trigger fish, closely related to the 'Old Wife'. **2.** a dark-coloured fish with a coarse hide and no scales, which measures at least one foot long. **Eg.** *"When Tenisha cry, she always long out her mout like one ol' buggage."*

Buggerin' (bug-er-in) *Verb* – **1.** creating frustration or discomposure. **2.** vexing. **3.** perplexing. **3.** exhausting the full length of one's patience. **Eg.** *"Dah boy ah mine is really buggerin' me wit dem bad grades he gettin'"* or; *"Keisha say Mista Atlee be buggerin' her 'bout keepin' her desk neat."*

Bb

Buggin' (buh-gin) *Adjective* – From 'Old People Times'. **1.** an annoyance **2.** an annoying object or person; **Eg.** *"gimme da buggin' ting."* or; *"Olice say dah man is ah buggin' eediyut cuz he wah drivin' on da wrong side ah da road."*

Bun (buhn) *Verb* – **1.** to catch afire. **2.** set ablaze. **3.** burn or singe. **4.** to cheat on one's relationship. **Eg.** *"I saw Lucy Ann at cinema lass week with Roydell. She muss be ghee'in Michael bun."* or *"Errytime Steven cook bacon it always come out all bun up."*

Bun (buhn) *Noun* – **1.** hair gathered into a round coil or knot at the nape of the neck or on top of the head in certain coiffures. **2.** a favourite hairstyle among local Christian women. **3.** a common hairstyle to use after washing one's hair (female). **Eg.** *"I keep tellin' Hannah she gah really pretty hair, but all she do is wash it n' roll it up in ah bun."*

Bun Up (buhn upp) *Verb* – **1.** to burn completely or utterly. **2.** to cease functioning because something has been exhausted. **3.** to damage through excessive friction, as in grinding or machining. **Eg.** *"I hear one time Darwin car had get bun up by Nineteen Hole Restaurant n' all now dey nah find out wah happin' yet."*

Bung Eye (bung-eye) *Noun* – **1.** huge swollen eyes. **2.** large round eyes which protrude from the skull. **3.** eyes which are swollen excessively due to crying or as a result of being punched [in the eye] by someone. **Eg.** *"Tee Cee be runnin' rong wit one bung eye deez daze cuz her brudda accidentally pelt her in her face wit ah Playstation control."*

Bung Over (bung ova) *Verb* – **1.** to lean or bend forward until the buttocks are at full eye level. **Eg.** *"Jim hadda bung ova so errybody could root im in he bunkey cuz he get salads while we wah playin' 'Salad-ah-Kick.'"*

Bung Up (bung-up) *Verb* – **1.** the act of bending over while exposing the buttocks to unsuspecting viewers. *Noun* – **2.** a swelling of the eye. **3.** injury to the face which results in swelling and bruising. **Eg.** *"Dah time when Bruce had get sting by bees he face wah all bung up."*

Bb

Bunkey (bung-kih) *Noun* – **1.** *gluteus maximus;* the buttocks; either of the two fleshy protuberances forming the lower and back part of the trunk. **2.** the rear pelvic area of the human body. **3.** the female body part which is most attractive to Caribbean men. (also spelled: **Bonkey**) **Eg.** *"Erry time I try do gymnastics, I always fall down on my bunkey."*

Bunkey Cheeks (bung-kih) *Noun* – **1.** the fleshy extension of one's backside, used primarily for sitting or resting. **2.** the target area of weight gain in most females. **3.** the butt. (see also: **Bunkey**) **Eg.** *"Aye man, moo yoh bunkey cheeks outta my face!"*

Bunkey Chin (bung-kih ch'inn) *Noun* – **1.** a cleft in one's chin. **2.** a cloven chin. **3.** a split chin. **Eg.** *"Gee! look ah dah piece ah bunkey chin da new Supaman gah nah?"*

Bun' Up (buh'nr-uhp) *Verb* – **1.** to consume by fire or heat. **2.** to use up. **3.** to exhaust all usefulness. **Eg.** *"Aye man' get offa my phone. All you wah do is bun' up my credit n' ya doon' waugh buy none back."*

Burnin' Heap (bur-nin heep) or **Bunnin' Heap** (buh-nin heep) *Noun* – **1.** the act of disposing one's trash (leaves, papers, bottles, etc), by piling it all into a heap and setting it afire. **2.** to create a make-shift incinerator in one's yard. **3.** a great way to dispose of leaves and other organic debris. **Eg.** *"Up until dey say yah cyah doo it no more, people wah bunnin' heap erry week."*

Burr (buhr) *Noun* – **1.** a small, prickly spore which is generally attached to a long, straw-like plant. **2.** a prickle-carrying plant found in most grasspieces. **3.** a soft pod with protruding prickles which sticks to clothes and irritates the skin; can be painful to the touch. **Eg.** *"Don't walk chrew Mista Harley yard on da way ta school or else you gah get burrs on yoh pants."*

Bush Jacket (bush jah-kit) *Noun* – **1.** a short-sleeved cotton shirt bearing four or more front pockets; two on either side of the chest and two lower down. **Eg.** *"Mista Miller always wear ah bush jacket ta school so he kin keep he chalk in da pockets when he teachin' class."*

Bb

Bush Med'sin (bush med-sin) *Noun* – From Old People Times; **1.** *Bush Medicine*; any series of medical concoctions or homemade remedies made from plants or vines.

Some excellent examples are:

Tea Banker – applied to boiling water to improve the appetite

Leaf of Life – leaves roasted and squeezed to produce a juice to treat coughs.

Fever Grass – tea for colds and fever

Jennifer – bark will deaden toothache

Eucalyptus – hot baths for fever

Fine Leaf Mint – tea for upset stomachs

Worry Vine – tea to clear skin from heat rash or loss of appetite

Coconut Water – to cleanse the kidneys

Mulberry & Almond Leaves – wrapped around the feet to alleviate rheumatism

Speak Nut – for increased appetite

Birch Tree Leaves, Pear and Breadfruit buds – made into a tea and taken to alleviate high blood pressure and related symptoms

Providence Mint & Dash-a-Long – made into a tea for hearing ailments

Periwinkle Leaf – made into a tea for coughs and diabetes

Eg. *"Granny always used ta have some kinda bush med'sin ta cure any pain or sickness I had when I wah small."*

Bushy Head (buh'sheh hed) *Noun* – **1.** the state of one's hair which closely resembles a bush; thick and shaggy. **2.** unkempt hair. **3.** full or overgrown, thick and poorly groomed hair. **Eg.** *"You shoulda see dah bushy head man det came tah my door acksin' fah money. Boy he wah frowsy!"*

Bushy Theatre (buh'sheh tee-yay-dah) *Noun* – **1.** one of George Town's first movie theatres (circa 1970's). **2.** a movie theatre which was located on North Church Street, where the Bush Centre is currently located. **Eg.** *"Me n' my friends use ta hawe ah time up in Bushy Theatre boy."*

Bb

Source: Cayman Islands National Archive

Buss (buh'ce) *Verb* – **1.** to burst. **2.** to put into action. **3.** to do. **4.** to speak or deliver verbal correspondence. **5.** to strike one's person; inflicting pain and discomfort. **Eg.** *"If you doon' hurry up n' buss dah gapseed you gah fah me, I gah kunk you in yoh head wit diss curlin' iron."*

Buss Head (buh'ce-hed) *Noun* – **1.** an injury to the skull which results in separation of the skin and minor bleeding. **2.** a major insult or embarrassment. **Eg.** *"I went ta go use da women's bathroom awhile ago n' I juss got ah 'buss head' – it wah locked!"*

Buss Lip (buh'ce lipp) *Noun* – **1.** a busted lip. **2.** an injury to the mouth which involves an open wound on either lip. **3.** the result of having been punched in the mouth. **Eg.** *"You bedda try so hush yoh mout or else you gah get ah good buss lip yah t'night."*

Buss Out (buh'ce-owt) *Verb* – **1.** to explode in a violently emotional way, especially with noise, laughter, violent speech, etc. **2.** to exceed a reasonable level of containment. **3.** to expand with force and noise because of rapid chemical change or decomposition. **Eg.** *"One day Shelly jess buss out laffin' fa no reason n' errybody taut she wah goin' off."*

Buss Tree Hill (buh'ce tree hill) *Noun* – **1.** the *Birch Tree Hill* area of West Bay. **2.** the area stretching from Rev. Blackman Road to Barkers. **3.** the area encompassing the Ed Bush playing field and Scholar's Park. **Eg.** *"My ahn'deh always use ta mek me go dong Buss Tree Hill ta get fish from one ol' woman house."*

Buyed (bye-d) *Verb* – **1.** past tense of the word 'buy'. **2.** bought **3.** to have accepted. **4.** to have acquired by exchange or concession. **Eg.** *"I had like da way dah car had look when Jimmy had it, so I buyed it from im lass year."*

'Burnin' heap' is an age old tradition.

Bb

Caboose (kah-buce) *Noun* – From 'Old People Times';
1. a make-shift wooden stove filled with sand and rocks
to hold pots and frying pans. **2.** a traditional Caymanian
stove, which is similar to a modern concrete barbecue
grill found at most public beaches and parks. **Eg.** *"Granny
say when she wah growin' up, it wah hard ta fix breakfast on
ah caboose cuz errybody had waugh see wah ya wah cookin'."*

Cabinet (kyah-bih-nette) *Noun* – **1.** a governmental body
comprised of three official members and five elected
members, called Ministers. **2.** the board of elected
Members of the Legislative Assembly which oversees all
major government departments, subsidiaries, and
statutory authorities. **Eg.** *"I really waugh get ah job in da
Cabinet Office when I graduate from UCCI but it hard ta get
in ta gowament."*

Cah-Cah (kah-kah) *Noun* – **1.** waste matter discharged
from the intestines through the anus; excrement. **2.** stool.
3. number two. **4.** solid excretory product evacuated from
the bowels [syn: **fecal matter**]. (also called: **doo-doo** or
dee-dee) **Eg.** *"Dah movie wah so funny, I almost cah-cah
up myself."*

Cake-Up (kayke up) *Noun* – **1.** excessive make-up. **2.** an
abundance of facial cosmetics, as eye shadow or lipstick.
3. make-up which appears to have been applied using a
spray gun and a trowel. **Eg.** *"Errytime I see dah gyal, her
face always be cake up even when she up in da gym."*

Calabash (kal-ah-bash) *Noun* – **1.** *Crescentia cujete;* the
large fruit from the Gourd Tree, which remains green
when ripe but cannot be eaten. **2.** a large, melon-like
fruit, similar to pumpkin featuring a smooth outer hide.
3. a fruit, bearing a skin/rind which was often used to
make bowls, dippers, water containers and other utensils
during Old People Times. **Eg.** *"I doon' know if it chrew or
not, but I hear some people used ta put calabash on dey head
and use it to line up dey hairstyle ta get ah cleaner cut."*

Cc

Calalu (kaugh-lah-loo) *Noun* – **1.** a local dish, made from a series of plants and leafy vegetables such as the water spinach. **2.** a local weed. **3.** a vegetable which is the primary ingredient in the thick soup also known as 'pepperpot'. **Eg.** *"I cyah stand da way Calalu smell when it bein' cooked sometimes, except when my ahn'deh cookin' it."*

Calavan (kal-ah-van) *Noun* – **1.** a large box made of twigs and sticks woven together, and string (the trigger) - used to trap chickens and other game. **Eg.** *"I hear dey gah all kine ah tings up in dah museum deez days, even one ah dem ol' calavan dat Mr. Early used'ta mek."*

Calipea (kah-lih-pee) *Noun* – **1.** the part of a turtle next to the lower shield, consisting of a yellowish gelatinous substance that is considered a delicacy. **2.** an edible flesh lying beneath the lower shell of a turtle. **Eg.** *"Most people seem ta like da calipea from turtle betta dun da ress ah da meat."*

Callie (kah-lih) *Noun* – **1.** a 220 foot, four-masted schooner which was built in the year 1900 by skilled Caymanian shipwrights. **2.** a ship which sank in 1944 carrying a cargo of grain; as the grain absorbed water, it quickly expanded and caused the doom of the ship. **Eg.** *"My pahpa used ta tell me da Callie wah so beautiful ta look at."*

Can Can (kyahn-kyahn) *Noun* – **1.** a stiff mesh petticoat or half slip which lines a woman's skirt, forming an umbrella-like shape. **2.** a hoop skirt. **Eg.** *"Aunt Julia might still hawe ah ol' Can Can in her closet from long time ago."*

Cane Piece (kayne peece) *Noun* – **1.** a former name for the area in George Town which includes the current George Town Hospital property as well as the Templeton Pine Lakes community. **Eg.** *"I doon' know how dem people coulda live down in Cane Piece when it wah first developin'! It wah so swampy n' fulla ah pile ah miskittas."*

Cane Row (kayne row) *Noun* – **1.** a hairstyle which involves hair being plaited into rows stretching from the forehead to the base of the neck. **2.** hair braided tightly against the scalp. **Eg.** *"If it wuz'n cotters, it wah cane row. Dass all my sista use ta know ta do wit my hair when we wah growin' up."*

Cc

Canoe (kuh-noo) *Noun* – **1.** a primary means of transportation throughout the Cayman Islands during the 19th and early 20th centuries. **2.** a small elongated wooden boat which was used to transport several persons and their belongings to and from various origins. **Eg.** *"I hear dem Brackas from Creek used ta use canoe ta go check dey granparents in West End long time ago."*

Canteen (kyan-teen) *Noun* – **1.** the lunch room in any school or office facility. **2.** a dining hall. **3.** the school kitchen. **Eg.** *"Lunch time is da best time ta get good food from da canteen."*

Carnival (kar-nih-vul) *Noun* – **1.** a traveling amusement show, having sideshows, rides, etc. **2.** a popular attraction in Grand Cayman during the late 1980s and early 1990s. **Eg.** *"I wish da carnival would come back ta Cayman. I rememba dah time when I went on Galwatron (Galvatron) fortylebbenteen times n' I nehwa eeble chrow up aftawurds."*

Car Port (kar pohrt) *Noun* – **1.** garage for one or two cars consisting of a flat roof supported on poles. **2.** any facility which is attached to a house for the use of covering automobiles. **3.** the best place to keep tools and old junk. **Eg.** *"Ol' Fred gah all kinda fishin' lines n' old tools in he car port juss sittin' deh ketchin' duss!."*

Cartoon Box (kar-toon bawkz) *Noun* – **1.** any box which is made from thick cardboard. **2.** a cardboard or plastic box used typically for storage or shipping. **3.** any of various containers made from cardboard or coated paper. **Eg.** *"It kine ah intresstin' how Jackie Chan n' dem use cartoon box fah stunts instead ah ah real crash pad."*

Cassawa (kah-sah-wah) *Noun* – **1.** any of several tropical American plants belonging to the genus *Manihot*, of the spurge family, as *M. esculenta* (bitter cassava) and *M. dulcis* (sweet cassava), cultivated for their tuberous roots, which yield important food products. **2.** a nutritious starch from the roots, the source of tapioca. **3.** a favourite starch among Caymanians. **4.** the primary ingredient in Cassava Cake. **Eg.** *"Yam Cake is awright but nuttin' cyah beat my granny Cassawa Cake."*

Cc

Cassawa Cake (kah-sah-vah kayke) *Noun* – **1.** one of Cayman's famed 'heavy cakes', which is made from the Cassava root. **2.** a tasty cake which is thick, sweet and contains ingredients which are meant to last a long time. **Eg.** *"Dem people from Scranton mek Cassawa Cakes so good ya bite ya finga off."*

Catboat (k'yat bote) *Noun* – **1.** one of the most popular means of transportation for early Caymanian fishermen. **2.** a small double-ended sailboat used for turtling. **3.** a broad-beamed sailboat carrying a single sail on a mast stepped well forward and often fitted with a centerboard. **4.** a sailboat with a single mast set far forward. **5.** a small sailboat which measures approx. twelve to thirty feet in length and could cost anywhere from six to seventy pounds sterling. **6.** a boat which was always painted blue to blend with the water and trimmed in black or white. **Eg.** *"When Papa Jim had tell me 'bout dah time when he fall outta he catboat 15 miles out ta sea, I could'n believe when he say he wuz'n scared."*

Cat Tail (kyat tale) *Noun* – **1.** *Acalypha hispida*; the Chinille plant. **2.** a species of the Chinille plant which blooms almost every day of the year and produces long flowers that supposedly feel like the fabric 'chenille' and resemble a (red) cat's tail. **3.** a really beautiful plant which produces a reddish coloured flower that resembles a cat's tail. **Eg.** *"Mama, Miss Ivy waugh fine out if you kin ketch piece ah Cat Tail so ghee her ta put in her yaad."*

Cayman (kay-mahn) *Noun* – **1.** one of several tropical islands located 480 miles south of Florida. The Islands have had many names on maps and documents, including; *Las Tortugas* – the turtles (used by Columbus); *Las Yslas de los Latargos* – islands of the lizards; *Caymanas* – derived from the Carib word for crocodile, was first used on a chart around 1530. – Various spellings of the word Cayman on maps and documents include; *Caimanos; Keimanos; Caiman; Caimanes; Caymanns; Key of Manus. The Lesser Islands* (Sister Islands) were identified as: *Cayman Chicos; los Caymanes; Petit Camanis; Camanbrack; Cayman Breccia.* **2.** a British Overseas Territory which was discovered in 1503 when one of Christopher Columbus' ships became lost during a storm. **3.** any of various tropical American crocodilians of the genus... (cont'd >)

Cc

Cayman (continued) *Noun* – ...*Caiman* and related genera, resembling and closely related to the alligators. **4.** variant of *Caiman*. **5.** a semiaquatic reptile of Central and South America that resembles an alligator but has a more heavily armored belly [**syn:** *Caiman*]. **Eg.** *"Wheneva I go shoppin' in Miami; afta tree days, I get home sick n' waugh come back home."*

Caymanas (kay-mah-nuz) *Noun* – **1.** the Carib word for the marine crocodile, which was abundant in the Cayman Islands in 1670. **2.** the second recorded name for the Cayman Islands, whose first name (Las Tortugas) was given by Christopher Columbus in 1503, when he discovered the two Sister Islands. **Eg.** *"I doon' waugh hear nuttin' bout no Tortugas and no Caymanas. We name Cayman Islands now."*

Cayman Brac Bread (kay-mahn brack bred) *Noun* – **1.** a very tasty bread which comes from the Sister Island of Cayman Brac. **2.** a bread which is highly coveted by Grand Caymanians. **3.** real traditional homestyle bread. **Eg.** *"Boy I lowe ah Cayman Brac bread. Erry time I go deh, I gah bring back one or two juss fa me n' some fa my fam'leh."*

Cayman Foods (kay-mahn foodz) *Noun* – **1.** an old supermarket which was located on the same property as the current Lighthouse School. **2.** one of the first supermarkets to do business in the Cayman Islands. **3.** a popular parking lot to race radio controlled cars during the late 1980s and early 1990s. **Eg.** *"I kin rememba when dey had dah big rubba tree up by Cayman Foods cuz dah way my mama used ta park n' leave me n' my sistas in da car."*

Caymania (kay-mah-ny'ah) *Noun* – From Old People Times; **1.** the *SS Caymania*; a vessel which was originally bought to replace the *Cimboco* in 1946, which served as a cargo vessel between Jamaica, Tampa and the Cayman Islands. **2.** a 60 passenger yacht which was originally known as the 'Black Bear' and owned by the Singer Sewing Machine Company. **3.** one the most beautiful boats the Islands had ever seen at the time, which was a welcomed sight to Cayman residents. **Eg.** *"I really can't remember much 'bout da Caymania, but dey say it wah like watchin' ah angel floatin' on da sea."*

Cc

Caymanian (kay-mahn-yun) *Noun* – **1.** an individual who was born in one of the three Cayman Islands. **2.** one of several thousand people who became a Caymanian through parentage or grants of status for other reasons. **3.** one who has been naturalized as a citizen of the Cayman Islands. **4.** a proud individual who stereotypically loves sea food, island music, fishnin', goin' to the beach, and 'fassin' wit udda people. **Eg.** *"Boy, I use ta tink det when ya go stateside it be hard ta find ah Caymanian but I run up in one all da way in Alaska!"*

Caymanian Caymanian (kay-mahn-yun kay-mahn-yun) *Noun* – **1.** a special emphasis used to define a person who was born in the Cayman Islands and has a significant amount of family heritage. **2.** one who has been born and raised in the Cayman Islands, and having at least one parent who has two or more preceding generations of ancestry. **3.** a full Caymanian by birthright. **4.** one who is undisputably Caymanian. **Eg.** *"I know dah boy by face, but tell me someting? He Caymanian Caymanian or he juss raise up yah? Sometimes yih cyah tell."*

Caymanite (kay-mahn-nite) *Noun* – **1.** a rare semi-precious stone found only in the Cayman Islands. **2.** a composite of various precious metals and fossils. **3.** a sedimentary rock composed of narrow layers of various colours and usually found between thick deposits of white limestone. some of the layers are nearly as hard as quartz. **Eg.** *"When I get my house fix up I gah try get ah nice caymanite statue ta put in my livin' room."*

Caymanize (kay-mahn-eyze) *Verb* – **1.** to incorporate into the Cayman way of doing things. **2.** to make 'Caymanian'. **3.** to localize. **4.** adapt for use in Cayman. **Eg.** *"Sometimes if tings doon' wuk out da way yah want it ya juss gah try Caymanize it so people kin undastand."*

Caymanopoly (kay-mahn-op-a-leh) *Noun* – **1.** a Caymanized version of the popular board game 'Monopoly'. **2.** a board game which was first developed by the Junior Achievement program in the early 1990s. **3.** an excellent souvenir for tourists and locals alike. **Eg.** *"Erry year Junior Achievement used ta mek some serious dollas sellin' dem Caymanopoly games ta tourisses."*

Cc

Cayman Parrot (kay-mahn pah-rut) *Noun* – **1.** an indigineous, yet nearly extinct species of parrot which inhabits the Cayman Islands. **2.** one of only two thousand of the same species of parrot in existence in the Cayman Islands. **3.** a beautiful green and yellow bird, which bears a red-orange mask. **4.** the Cayman Islands' National Bird. **Eg.** *"I need ah nice pitcha ow ah Cayman Parrot so I kin puddit tup in my liwin' room when I bill my house."*

Cayman Ridge (kay-mahn ridj) *Noun* – **1.** a range of submarine mountains continuous with the *Sierra Misteriosa* range of Cuba and running west in the direction of British Honduras (Belize). **Eg.** *"doon' try go scuba divin' by yo'self ova da Cayman Ridge."*

Cayman Time (kay-mahn tyme) *Noun* – **1.** at least 10mins. to 1hr. past the reasonable time for any meeting or function to begin. **2.** expected delays. **3.** a common excuse for being late. **4.** an alibi for tardiness **Eg.** *"Any reggae show ya go to in Cayman dey always be startin' on Cayman time so I jess go layda den wah da flya say."*

Cayman Trench (kay-mahn trehn'ch) *Noun* – **1.** a submarine trench of the floor of the Caribbean Sea between the Cayman Islands and Jamaica. **2.** the area also known as the *Bartlett Trench* or *Bartlett Trough*. **3.** one of the deepest parts of the Caribbean sea, measuring just over 25,000 feet in depth **Eg.** *"I hear one time some Cubians had fall ova board ova da Cayman Trench tryin' reach Cayman."*

Cayman Wall (kay-man wohl) *Noun* – **1.** a steep submarine cliff which drops to 3,200 feet, (three miles) offshore. **2.** a popular dive destination for scuba divers, skin divers, and research submersibles. **3.** one of Cayman's main tourist attractions. **Eg.** *"Bobo, if you doon' stop messin' wit me, I gah cyar you out by da Cayman Wall n' pitch you ovaboard."*

Central (sen-trul) *Noun* – **1.** the Martin Drive area of George Town which is located behind Funky Tangs and Rohelio's Car Wash. **2.** the neighborhood behind Phillips Electrical. (also known as: **Down in da East**) **Eg.** *"People say Scranton n' Central people kin cook da bess heavy cakes n' local food."*

Cc

Charge (cha'aje) *Verb* – **1.** drunk and ready for more. **2.** slightly buzzed as a result of consuming alcoholic beverages. **3.** confident but reckless. **Eg.** *"Wheneva I charge, I be chattin' up all kine ah woman."*

Charge Up (cha'aje up) *Verb* – **1.** extremely drunk and rambunctious. **2.** disorderly. **3.** wildly boisterous. **4.** turbulently active and noisy. **5.** difficult to control or handle. **Eg.** *"Don't mess wit Renny when he charge up. He doon' business 'bout nuttin' n' anybody det say anyting ta him, gah get diss out."*

Chah (ch'ah) *Interjection* – **1.** a verbal release of inner tension. **2.** this is ridiculous. **3.** what-in-the-world? **Eg.** *"Chah man! You cyah see I sleepin' ah wah?"*

Chafe Up (chay'f upp) *Adverb* – **1.** painful from having the skin abraded. *Noun* – **3.** an affliction which is common among bicycle riders, due to constant rubbing against the seat, and also occurs in babies, due to moisture and friction inside the pampers. **Eg.** *"Aaron say afta he had finish wit dah bike-ah-ton lass week he wah so chafe up he hadda rub all kine ah lotion between he legs jess ta walk straight."*

Chat Up (chad up) *Verb* – **1.** to converse with someone of the opposite sex. **2.** to court. **3.** to talk flirtatiously with. **4.** to talk to in a friendly, open way. *Noun* – **1.** an informal conversation with underlying intensions. **Eg.** *"My boy Ricky only go by yoot club on Fridays so he kin chat up gyals n' look pretty."*

Chattin' Up (chat-in up) *Verb* – **1.** the act of courting via verbal flirtation. **2.** flirting in public through verbal means. **3.** conversing with a new acquaintance of the opposite sex. **Eg.** *"My cuz-in Arlond always used ta be chattin' up Katrina on da bus from school."*

Checkin' (chek in) *Verb* – **1.** the second stage in the four-part structure of a relationship, which involves: *1. talkin' 2. checkin' 3. dealin' 4. goin'.* **2.** courting. **3.** the dating era of an uncommitted relationship. **4.** a preliminary stage in a young relationship. **Eg.** *"Lacey say if I doon' hurry up n' decide wah I doin' she gah tell errybody we nah checkin' no more."*

Cc

Cheesy Foot (chee-zeh fuh't) *Noun* – **1.** an extremely smelly foot or pair of feet, due to sweat and dirt. **2.** stink feet. **Eg.** *"Aye! Get yoh ol' cheesy foot off me man! It smell like bun up Doritoes."*

Cheesy Socks (chee-zeh socks) *Noun* – **1.** any pair of socks which have been worn long enough to smell like sweat and dirt. **2.** toe jam central. **3.** stink socks. **Eg.** *"Felicia, ya brudda say muss come get yoh cheesy socks outta he bedroom fa he set um on fiyah."*

Cheesy Toes (chee-zeh toze) *Noun* – **1.** toe jam. **2.** any material that collects between the toes. **3.** the remains of sweat, dirt and fluids which settle between the toes. **4.** a strong odor which fills the room after removing ones shoes. **Eg.** *"If anyting kin be said about Franklin', I kin surely say he gah da rottenest cheesy toes I ehwah smell in my life."*

Cheh (cheh) *Adverb* – **1.** an common expression of disappointment or uncertainty **2.** a way of swearing without using profanity. (also pronounced: ***chah***) **Eg.** *"Cheh, how come Keisha nah come pick me up yet man?"*

Chello Mello (cheh-leh meh-low) *Noun* – **1.** a small, yellow, plum-like fruit which usually grows on a tall tree. **2.** a really sour plum (also called: ***chelly-melly***). **Eg.** *"Miss Sonia gah one sweet Chello Mello tree in her yard."*

Chicken Legs (chik-in) *Noun* – **1.** very skinny legs **2.** legs which are mostly undefined by musle or flesh. **3.** knobbly kneed legs. (see also: ***bird legs***) **Eg.** *"Sports Day da bess time ta teck ah camera ta school, so ya kin ketch all ah dem people wit chicken legs walkin' rong wit shorts n' tights."*

Chicken Pops (chih-kin popz) *Noun* – **1.** *Chicken Pox.* **2.** a disease, commonly of children, caused by the *varicella zoster* virus and characterized by mild headache and fever, malaise, and eruption of blisters on the skin and mucous membranes. **Eg.** *"Fe-Fe diddn' come ta work lass munt cuz she had chickin pops all up in her head n' ting."*

Chief (cheef) *Noun* – **1.** a common nickname for 'friend'. **2.** boss; sir; mister. **3.** reference to one who may be in authority. **Eg.** *"Aye chief, you kin len meh ah dolla ah wah?"*

Cc

Chillrin (chih'l-rin) *Noun, Pl.* – **1.** children. **2.** sons or daughters. **3.** young persons between birth and full growth; boys or girls. **4.** human offspring. **Eg.** *"Aye, unna chillrin come inside now. Rain soon come yih'nah."*

Chimmy (chih-meh) *Noun* – **1.** a small round pot used for collecting urine and fecal matter. **2.** an early toilet. **3.** a large metal bowl. **Eg.** *"Afta Iwan, I hadda mek ah chimmy outta ah ol' chair n' ah 5 gallon pail."*

Chimmy Days (chih-meh daze) *Noun* – **1.** Old People Times. **2.** An early part of the 20th Century when it was normal for people to use portable metal or ceramic utensils as toilets. **3.** An era of humble upbringings. **Eg.** *"My granny say durin' her chimmy days, people neva used ta be spiteful like t'day."*

Chinee (chy-nee) *Noun* – **1.** any person of Chinese origin or descent. **2.** a native or descendant of a native of China. **3.** of or pertaining to China, its inhabitants, or one of their language. **Eg.** *"Boosy say one Chinee man wah up in he store talkin' one ching-chong langwidge lass week'."*

Ching-Ching (ching-ching) *Noun* – **1.** the common Cayman black bird. **2.** a bird which scavenges on garbage and other other unwanted food. **3.** a real nuisance. **4.** one of the most common birds which when trapped inside a building, is virtually impossible to get out. **Eg.** *"One day one Ching-Ching took ah dump in my friend head."*

Chip-Chip (chipp-chipp) *Noun* – **1.** the Cayman Banana Bird. **2.** a small yellow bird with black wings which feeds primarily on banana, sweet sop, mango, guinep and other fruit trees. **Eg.** *"One chip-chip always eatin' my sweetsops."*

Choong Gum (chyoong'h gumm) *Noun* – **1.** chewing gum. **2.** a sweetened and flavored preparation for chewing, usually made of chicle. **Eg.** *"Sweetie, nex time when yah go CoMart's bring meh back some choong gum nah?"*

Chroo (ch'roo) *Adjective* – **1.** true. **2.** in accordance with the actual state or conditions; conforming to reality or fact; not false; a true story. **3.** sincere; not deceitful. **4.** legitimate or rightful. **Eg.** *"If it chroo wah you say, I gah string up Angie Lee if I ketch her with Rodney again."*

Cc

Chrow Way Baby (chrow way bay-beh) *Noun* – **1.** to remove an *embryo* or *fetus* prematurely, in order to end a pregnancy. **2.** to have an abortion so as not to conflict with one's future goals. **3.** to terminate a pregnancy. **Eg.** *"Dey say dah time when Windella had miss school fah tree weeks, she had went go chrow way baby."*

Chrute (ch'root) *Adjective* – **1.** the truth, or actual state of a matter. **2.** in accordance with the actual state or conditions; conforming to reality or fact; not false; the honest chrewt. **3.** conformity with fact or reality; verity. **4.** the legitimacy of known facts. **Eg.** *"If ya doon' believe wah I sayin' jess acks Rodney, n' he kin tell yah da chrute."*

Chub (ch'yubb) *Noun* – **1.** a single member in the family of Sea Chubs (*Kyphosidae*) which are considered *Perciformes* (the largest order of vertebrates). **2.** a large, yellowish fish, covered in dark, multi-coloured spotts. **Eg.** *"Puhpah, when we go fishnin' nex time, I waugh ketch ah Chub so I kin show Randy how stink dey look."*

Chubbs (chyubbz) *Noun* – **1.** an affectionate name for an overweight person. (see also: **bigga** or **biggs**) **2.** a friendly guy who is usually very quiet and reserved. **Eg.** *"Yow, Chubbs, wah goin' on? You waugh go see wah Marlon sayin' ah wah?"*

Church Clothes (chirch klohz) *Noun, Pl.* – **1.** formal clothing that is purchased with the specific intention of being worn only to church. **2.** an assortment of formal clothing and shoes. **Eg.** *"Even doh Mena is only 12, she look like ah big woman wheneva she got on her church clothes."*

Church Pants (chirch pahntz) *Noun, Pl.* – **1.** a pair of pants which were bought for and worn only to church. **2.** plain dress pants which may come in varying shades of brown, navy blue, gray or black. **Eg.** *"Daddy beat Burney cuz he had wear he church pants ta school n' ged um mess up wit marl."*

Church Shoes (chirch shuze) *Noun* – **1.** shoes which are specifically worn to church or other formal functions. **2.** boring, non-extravagant shoes. **3.** unfashionable and seemingly unattractive footwear. **Eg.** *"Wheneva Borven wear he church shoes ta school, errybody tease im ta death."*

Cc

Cimboco (sim-boh-koh) *Noun* – **1.** one of the first schooners built by Caymanian shipwright, Captain Rayal Brazley Bodden. **2.** a 120ft. vessel, built in a George Town shipyard and launched for the first time in 1927. **3.** a popular local restaurant which is currently located in the Marquee Plaza, and named after the popular schooner. **4.** the first locally-owned motorship, wich was named after the company that owned her, the *Cayman Islands Motor Boat Company* (whose President was Dr. Roy McTaggart). The Cimboco was sold to the Archibold Brothers of Columbia in 1947. **Eg.** *"I nehwa new dat Cimboco was ah boat. I always taught it wah juss da name ah ah restaurant."*

Cinema (sih-neh-mah) *Noun* – **1.** Reference to *Cinema I & II*; a large building containing two movie theatres, formerly located on West Bay road. **2.** one of the most popular meeting venues for teenagers throughout the 1980's and 90's. **Eg.** *"I used ta go Cinema erry Satday tell dey start dah ol' intermission fooshniss."*

Cistern (siss-turn) Noun – **1.** the primary household water source. **2.** a reservoir, tank, or container for storing or holding water or other liquid. **3.** a receptacle for water. **Eg.** *"Billy n' dem boys always used ta be playin' two-a-side football on dah cistern top."*

City Water (sitty waugh-tah) *Noun* – **1.** any water that comes from the public supply pipeline. **2.** liquid resources from either Water Authority or Cayman Water Company. **3.** the only public water system available. **Eg.** *"Juss cuz ouwa cistern keep goin' dry my daddy say we need ta hurry up n' get city water."*

Clean Out (kleen owt) *Adjective* – **1.** an old wives solution to any illness. **2.** of, pertaining to, or constituting a laxative; purgative. **3.** to enduce bowel movement by consuming a laxative or a traditional sursee concoction. **Eg.** *"Erry summa when we wah growin' up, my mama hadda ghee us ah good clean out b'fore school start back."*

Clearview (clare -vyew) *Noun* – **1.** one of the first tapeclubs on the island to feature pre-recorded beta and vhs tapes. **2.** a popular 1980s tapeclub located at Merren's Plaza. **Eg.** *"25 years ago, nobody nehwah know 'bout' no DVD. All dey had was Clearview n' Videomax."*

Cc

Clot (klawt) Verb – **1.** to strike or hit. **2.** to deliver a really devastating blow to a person's body. **3.** an attack on one's person. **Eg.** *"You shoulda see da way Rayburn had clot Frenzy in he head wit dah rake when dey wah fightin' down by Hurley's."*

Cochineal (koh-cheh-neel) *Noun* – **1.** one of the many species of medicinal plants (better known as 'bush med'sin), which has various uses. **2.** a form of cactus, of which the inside pulp was used (during Old People Times) as a shampoo and hair conditioner and also to treat wounds. **Eg.** *"Granny say she doon' care nuttin' bug no 'Head n' Shouldas' but it gah hawe do cuz dey doon' use cochineal ta wash ya hair no more."*

Coco Plum (kuh-kuh plum) *Noun* – **1.** a small yellow fruit with a white, meaty inside, which is thick, slightly slippery, and can be tartish in taste. **2.** a small fruit tree which grows primarily near the ocean, but can be found near other bodies of water including ponds. **Eg.** *"I wish I could get ah coco plum tree in my yaad but it nah gah grow cuz I doo'n live close ta da sea."*

Coke Bottle Glasses (koak bot-ul glah-siz) *Noun* – **1.** eyeglasses which resemble the bottom of a soda bottle. **2.** extremely thick eyeglasses. **3.** spectacles or reading glasses which are prescribed to persons with severely deteriorated eyesight. **Eg.** *"Randy say Colfurd coke bottle glasses so tick, he kin count all da stars up in heaven."*

Cold Chills (cole chih'lz) *Noun* – **1.** a sensation of coldness, often accompanied by shivering and pallor of the skin. **2.** an abnormal condition of the body, characterized by undue depression in temperature, lagging of the pulse, and disturbance of various body functions. **Eg.** *"Hot Tea wit Lime is da bess ting ta get rid ah Cold Chills any day."*

Cold Front (koal'd frunt) *Noun* – **1.** the transition zone where a cold air mass is replacing a warmer air mass. *cold fronts* generally move from northwest to southeast. **2.** a seemingly valid reason for Caymanians to break out full winter clothes and behave as if they are in Aspen. **Eg.** *"Wheneva ah cold front pass chrew Cayman I always feel like I walkin' round New York wit my bubble jacket n' tam."*

Cc

Coldy Nose (koal-eh noze) *Noun* – **1.** having clogged nostrils during illness; such as, with a common cold or flu. **2.** excessive fluid in the nostril region. **3.** runny nose. **4.** stuffy nose. **Eg.** *"If you doon' waugh see my coldy nose; look someway else den."*

Colliers (kawl-yerz) *Pronoun* – **1.** the East End community located between Gun Bay and Old Man Bay. **2.** the area of East End where Morritt's Tortuga Club is located. **3.** a great place to watch the sun come up in the morning. **Eg.** *"Dah time when Wilfred had get he leg break, yih could hear 'im screamin' all da way in Colliers."*

CoMart (coh-mah'rt) *Noun* – **1.** Will Coe Shop. **2.** an early mini mart which was located in the center of George Town, on Main Street, across from the Post Office. **3.** the best place to shop for a reasonable price during the late 1980s and early 1990s. **3.** a highly successful Caymanian-owned business for more than 30 years. **Eg.** *"I used ta buy all ah my t-shirts from CoMart cause dey wah cheap cheap."*

Comfitebble (kom-fi-teb-ul) *Adverb* – **1.** 'comfortable'. **2.** producing or affording physical comfort, support, or ease. **3.** being in a state of physical or mental comfort; contented and undisturbed; at ease. **4.** more than adequate or sufficient. **Eg.** *"Deez new shoes dat I juss buy from Roy's feel kinda comfitebble still."*

Computer Room (kum-pyoo-duh rume) *Noun* – **1.** any spare bedroom or home office where computers and other low-priced office equipment are kept. **2.** the room in the home which is used as a home office. **3.** a den, study or home library. **Eg.** *"Check me in da computer room when ya done. I gah be up in deh playin' solitaire."*

Conch Shell Blowin' (cunk sheh'l bloh-win) *Verb* – **1.** the art of sounding an alarm or signal from arriving fishermen to alert the area as to whether they were carrying fish to trade or sell. **2.** the technique used in sounding a traditional Caymanian horn of which (when blown) the sound travels a great distance to welcome buyers and sellers to the market. **Eg.** *"My gran-fadda use ta practice he conch shell blowin' erry weekend n' sometimes it use ta fool people inta tinkin' it wah da fishamen."*

Cc

Cook'nut (cook-nut) *Noun* – **1.** the coconut. **2.** the large, hard-shelled seed of the coconut tree lined with a white edible meat and containing a milky fluid. **Eg.** *"One day when my brudda wah walkin' rong da back ah da house, he hear one tump on da roof n' when he look, one cook'nut land right in he chest. I know dah mussa hurt!"*

Cook'nut Husk (cook-nut huss) *Noun* – **1.** the inner lining of the common coconut. **2.** the under-skin of the coconut shell, which is usually very dry and hairy. **Eg.** *"Da bess way tek off ah cook'nut husk is ta use ah pick axe."*

Cook'nut Meat (cook'nut meet) *Noun* – **1.** the edible white meat of a coconut; often shredded for use in cakes and curries. **2.** one of two favourite parts of a coconut. **3.** a Caymanian delicacy. **Eg.** *"I hear Craft Market sellin' cook'nut meat fa ah dolla ah bag."*

Cook'nut Wadda (cook'nut waugh-dah) *Noun* – **1.** coconut water. **2.** a clear to whitish fluid from within a fresh coconut. **3.** a refreshing liquid from the coconut. **Eg.** *"Coconut Wadda always taste best afta ya put it in da fridge fah at least two ouwas."*

Cook Rum (kook ruhm) *Noun* – From Old People Times; **1.** a large detached building (almost) as big as the main house and connected by a 'tramway' or wooden walk, where the fire hearth was kept. **2.** a traditional Caymanian kitchen, which was detatched from the main house, due to the heat of the cooking. **3.** the place where the 'caboose' (an early wooden-box oven filled with sand) was kept. **4.** a detatched building, built to protect the main house from fires, which would happen occasionally when the caboose would overheat. **5.** a 'Cooking Room'. **Eg.** *"Dah time when Uncle Carley cook rum ketch on fiyah all kine ah people wah bailin' wadda from he cistern ta try out it."*

Cool Drink (kool drink) *Noun* – **1.** cold soda or soft drink. **2.** any beverage which has been chilled to the point of satisfaction. **3.** a beverage that is not alcoholic or intoxicating and is usually carbonated; as root beer or ginger ale. **Eg.** *"Sissy, when ya go in da kitchen bring meh ah cool drink nah?"*

Cc

Cool Out (kool owt) *Verb* – **1.** to relax. **2.** forget about one's worries. **3.** an activity which brings about great joy and peace of mind. **4.** to make less tense, rigid, or firm. **5.** to find a spot in the shade, hang a hammock and rest. **6.** take a nap in the shade. **Eg.** *"Rum Point beach is one of the best places on the island to sit back, order some food and juss cool out."*

Co-op Hall (coh-opp) *Noun* – **1.** a large building which was formerly located west of the West Bay four-way stop. **2.** the area on which Heritage Square lies in West Bay; the current home of J&M Electronics. **3.** a former multi-purpose building which included the first Credit Union, a movie theatre, snack bar and multi-purpose hall. **Eg.** *"Granny say she used ta get down when dey used ta hawe dem quadrille parties at Co-op Hall."*

Cornas (kor-nahz) *Noun* – **1.** one's own private space. **2.** a place of solitude. **3.** oneself. **Eg.** *"Boy try so hold yoh cornas. You cyah see I tryin' play dis game?"*

Corn Fish (kawrn fish) *Pronoun* – **1.** a cooking recipe for fish, which is first salted and then hung out to dry thoroughly. **2.** a traditional Cayman meal which often resembles cooked codfish. **Eg.** *"I hate da smell ah corn fish but it taste good doh."*

Corn Flakes (korn flaykze) *Noun* – **1.** dandruff or dry scalp. **2.** large dry flakes which emerge from the scalp. **3.** an itchy fungus-like flake resulting from dandruff or dry scalp. **Eg.** *"Daddy say one guy name Doogeh used ta have so much corn flakes in he head, all ya hadda do wah add milk."*

Corn Turtle (korn tur-tul) *Adverb* – **1.** a process of marinating turtle meat, which involves salting prior to storage in several barrels. once marinated, the meat is taken out and stewed as needed. **2.** a treatment of turtle meat which looks like corned beef when cooked. **Eg.** *"If yah get some good corn turtle deez daze, ya bedda bite yah finga off eatin' it cuz yih nah gah see it again no time soon."*

Cotters (kaw-terz) *Pronoun* – **1.** a traditional hairstyle created by rolling one's hair into small clumps and fastening with bobby pins. **Eg.** *"Joy say anytime papa drop her school wit her hair in cotters, errybody tease 'er all day."*

Cc

Cow Itch (kuw itch) *Noun* – **1.** a vine carrying a series of furry pods which are prickly and irritant to the skin. **2.** an itchy pod-like plant. **3.** a plant which is notorious for blistering and irritating the skin. **Eg.** *"I hear dah time when dah MLA had get Cow Itch in he jacket, people say he had run from Fort Street ta Hospital in 1.5 minutes flat."*

Cow Killas (kuw kill-ahz) *Adjective* – **1.** really strong, tough looking shoes or boots. **2.** work boots. **3.** any large boot which is made of animal hide and contain a steel toe. **Eg.** *"Anytime it rain Timmy always used ta wear he cow killas ta school so he feet doon' get wet."*

Cowud (kuw-udd) *Adverb* – **1.** a cowardice. **2.** a person who lacks courage in facing danger, difficulty, opposition, pain, etc; a timid or easily intimidated person. **3.** lacking courage; very fearful. **4.** Expressive of fear or timidity. **Eg.** *"Boy Chet ah real ol' cowud y'see? I hear he run 'way when burglas break in he house n' dey tek erryting."*

Cow Well (kuw well) *Noun* – **1.** a large water facility used for watering cows which may be covered on uncovered. **2.** a large water trough for cows. **3.** an open pool from which cows are encouraged to drink. **Eg.** *"Daniel say one time he fall down in some horse dung n' he hadda rinse off in ah cow well."*

Crabbin' (krah-bin) *Verb* – **1.** the act of hunting for land crabs during crab season. **2.** a traditional Caymanian past time which involves a flash light, a croca sack, several large buckets and a stick. (see also: **crab hunt**) **3.** a local tradition, whereby, a group of people arrange to meet in the late evening and board a pick-up truck. From there, they will make several stops, at random, and attempt to catch around ten to fifteen crabs per stop. The last stop is usually a beach where they boil the live crabs in large pots or five gallon oil drums filled with salt water. **Eg.** *"Doon' go crabbin' with Sheila; erry time she see ah crab, she jump up n' drop da flashlight n' den da crab get 'way."*

Crab Head (krabb hed) *Adverb* – **1.** someone who is either stubborn or difficult. **2.** a useless person. **3.** an insult targeted at a person who is being difficult. **Eg.** *"Cha! You ol' crab head ting. You hadda go mess wit my new blouse when it nah yours, eh?"*

Cc

Crab Hunt (krab hunt) *Noun* – **1.** a traditional game of tracking, following and capturing the Cayman land crab. **2.** a pastime which results in the capture and securement of crabs. **Eg.** *"If you see daddy get he stick n' he croca sack n' he flash light, ya know he goin' on ah crab hunt t'night."*

Crab Season (krab see-z'n) *Noun* – **1.** the designated period to hunt for local land crabs, which generally begins in May and ends in August of each year. **2.** the best time to catch a crab for dinner. **3.** the time when crabs come out of the bush, run across the road and risk being crushed by an oncoming vehicle. **Eg.** *"I hate when it crab season ya'see? Dem lil' tings be runnin' all ova da road n' one time I nearly run up in one wall juss tryin' ta awoid um."*

Crack (krah'kk) *Adjective* – **1.** crazy; stupid; insane. **2.** fool. **3.** dumb as doornails. **Eg.** *"Marshall crack yih'see? All he kin find ta talk 'bout is night fishnin' n' chasin' big woman."*

Cream (kreem) *Noun* – **1.** any milk product. **2.** the fatty part of milk, which rises to the surface when the liquid is allowed to stand unless homogenized. **3.** the best part of anything. **Eg.** *"I doon' care wah nobody say, I gah hawe at least tree spoons ah cream wit my Milo."*

Cripsy (krip-seh) *Adverb* – **1.** crispy; brittle. **2.** partially stale or dry, resulting in a crisp, crunchy feel. **3.** firm but easily broken or crumbled. **4.** having small ripples. **Eg.** *"Boy, I lowe ah Ruffles. Dem tings is cripsy man!"*

Croca Sack (cro-kah sak) *Noun* – **1.** a large potato sack. **2.** a large sack used for catching land crabs during crab season. **3.** a bag which is nearly impenetrable and has multiple uses. **Eg.** *"Ta get ready fah crab huntin', all ya gah do is mek sure ya gah ah flashlight, ah stick, ah croca sack, n' buckets."*

Crotons (kroh-t'nz) *Noun, Pl.* – **1.** a reddish purple plant which can be found in hedges and sandyards throughout the Islands. **2.** a beautiful plant which grows best in an open area and requires minimum pruning. **3.** a tall plant with plastic-looking leaves. **Eg.** *"I like how crotons look, but sometimes dey harba spidas n' ting n' dah da part I cyah tek."*

Cc

Cruff (kruff) *Noun* – **1.** a really scruffy and ill-mannered person. **2.** a bad element. **3.** a badly carried person. **4.** a hard head. **5.** uncultured and insensitive. **Eg.** *"If I eva have ah pool party again I gah hawe make sure I gah nuff nuff security. Lass time one cruff wah up in my yaad eatin' out all da food n' tryin' feel up people woman. I hadda run im."*

Crusty Foot (krus-teh foot) *Noun* – **1.** dry, parched, malnourished feet. **2.** really scaley feet. **3.** a nasty-looking skin disorder which targets the sole of the foot and most of its toes. **Eg.** *"Jerry always gah lotion up he feet when he wear sandals cuz he doon' waugh nobody see he ol' crusty foot."*

Cry Cry Baby (kry kry bay-beh) *Adverb* – **1.** a very emotional person. **2.** one who cries excessively for no apparent reason. **3.** a softy. **4.** a pansy. **5.** to cry without warning. **Eg.** *"Ya waugh see ah real cry cry baby? Juss take da control away from Justin when he playin' PlayStation."*

Crystal Valley (kriss-tull vah-leh) *Noun* – **1.** a housing development in West Bay which is surrounded by Mount Pleasant, Birch Tree Hill, Parkway Crescent and Papagallo Road. **2.** a popular West Bay suburb. **Eg.** *"My sista had try buy piece ah land in Crystal Valley but most ah it wah all sell out she say."*

Cubians (kyu-bee-yunz) *Noun, Pl.* – **1.** Cubans. **2.** people of Cuban descent or origin. **3.** Spanish-speaking natives of the Caribbean island of Cuba. **Eg.** *"I hear dem Cubians lowe ah Merengue Town y'see?"*

Cumpneh (kump-neh) *Noun* – **1.** 'company'; a number of individuals assembled or associated together; group of people. **2.** one's usual companions. **3.** one's place of employment. **Eg.** *"Sweetie, I doon' like da kinda cumpneh you be keepin' deez days."*

Cun (kun) *Adverb* – **1.** can. **2.** to be able to; have the ability, power, or skill to. **3.** to know how to. **4.** to have the possibility. **Eg.** *"I know you tink you cun fight but ah reckon I kin run some licks in ya too."*

Cc

Cunk (cunk) *Verb* – From the Eastern Districts of Grand Cayman (Bodden Town, North Side, East End) **1.** to check over (the separate units or groups of a collection) one by one to determine the total number; add up; enumerate: He cunk up all da money erry day afta da store close. **2.** to reckon numerically. **3.** to include in a reckoning; take into account. **4.** to strike. **Eg.** *"Try so cunk up all dem fish so we kin mek some money, nah?"* or; *"If you doon' leewe me 'lone I gah cunk you in yo head wit dis rula."*

Cupple (kuh-p'l) *Adverb* – **1.** more than one of the same thing, but less than ten. **2.** several. **3.** a few. **4.** a manageable amount. **Eg.** *"When ya go by Fosta's mek sure bring me cupple mangoes nah?"*

Curry (cuh-reh) *Verb* – **1.** to cover. **2.** to be or serve as a covering for; extend over; rest on the surface of. **3.** to place something over or upon, as for protection, concealment or warmth. **Eg.** *"Look yah man? I taught I tole dem children muss curry up da food wit file paypah so flies doo'n ketch it."*

Cush Cush (koosh koosh) *Noun* – **1.** a popular perfume during the Mid-20th Century, which was originally imported from Cuba. **2.** the standard perfume amonst Caymanian women during the 1950s and 60s. **3.** a popular medium-odor perfume. **Eg.** *"Boy, if Kirk Freeports kin bring back some cush cush, I know some women would buy some juss ta keep as ah souvenir."*

Cuss Out (kuh'ce owt) *Verb* – **1.** to swear at or promote violence to another; verbally. **2.** to use profanity; curse; swear. **3.** to argue by tone of voice alone; minus the loud volume and profanity that is generally associated with an argument. **Eg.** *"I know if I go home widdout my homework bein' done I gah get cuss out n' I nah gah be able ta sleep ova yoh house dis weekend."*

Cut Loose (kutt loo'ce) *Verb* – **1.** to release. **2.** to give way, or give up; to deliver. **3.** to throw; let go. **Eg.** *"I memba one time when Papa Jim wah drunk, my daddy went go check im n' he cut loose one punch at im yih'see? I betcha he nah fass wit ah drunk man again afta dat"* or *"Dah time when Troy had cut loose one poomp in church, Pastor Leroy hadda bless it wit holy water before people would go back inside."*

Cc

Cutty Bush (kuh-deh bush) *Pronoun* – **1.** a former name for the area immediately behind the George Town Public Library. **2.** the former home of the Cayman Islands Boxing Association. **Eg.** *"Papa Jim say dem soljahs used ta be tick like ants rong Cutty Bush when da war wah goin' on."*

Cuzzy (cuz-eh) *Noun* – **1.** friend. **2.** brethren. **3.** cousin. **4.** a way of referring to someone who is a friend or a new acquaintance. **5.** reference to someone when their name does not come to mind. **Eg.** *"Yeah cuzzy, I gah check yah back 'bout goin' Miami diss weekend."*

Cyah (k'yah) *Auxiliary Verb* – **1.** can't; cannot; can not. **2.** an expression of incapacity, inability or withholding of permission. **3.** unable to; should not; will not. **Eg.** *"It doon' madda ta me if you cyah go Miami diss weekend cuz I nah gah eeben rememba you when I up in Dolphin Mall."*

Cyahkihlaydah (kyah-kih-lay-dah) *Noun* – **1.** a 'calculator'. **2.** a small electronic or mechanical device that performs calculations, requiring manual action for each individual opertion. **2.** the instrument most commonly used in summing up one's personal finances. **Eg.** *"Burnsy say Chesleh had get ketch usin' ah cyahkihlaydah in Ms. McLaughlin' mahts tess n' she nearly fling im out da class."*

Cyar (kyarr) *Verb* – **1.** to carry. **2.** to take or support from one place to another; convey; transport:, **3.** to serve as a conduit for. **4.** to act as a bearer or conductor. **Eg.** *"Errybody kin rememba when dey use ta go supamahkit wit dey mama n' when she find all da junk dey had fill up da cart wit, she tell um muss cyar dem tings right back."*

Most people use a *cyahkihlaydah* to manage their finances

Cc

Da (da) *Definite article* – **1.** Caymanian pronounciation of the word 'the'. **2.** used, esp. before a noun with a specifying or particularizing effect, as opposed to the indefinite or generalizing force of the indefinite article 'a' or 'an'. **Eg.** *"Da bess ting you kin do wit yoh life rite now is ta get outta my face."*

Daah (d'aahh) *Pronoun* – **1.** Caymanian pronunciation of the word 'that'. **2.** used to indicate a person, thing, idea, state, event, time, remark, etc. **Eg.** *"If I ketch you fassin' wit daah boy one more time it gah be me n' you."*

Daddy (dah-deh) *Noun* – **1.** father. **2.** one who father's a child. **3.** the male figure in a traditional family. **Eg.** *"My daddy say if I doo'n get good grades, he gah sehn me boardin' school."*

D'da-daah (duh-da-daahh) *Interjection* – **1.** whatever. **2.** something like this, or like that. **3.** this, that, and the next thing. **Eg.** *"Swee-deh, all ya gah do is turn diss ova n' d'da-daah n' it gah jess open up like nuttin'."*

D'udda Day (dih-udda day) *Adjective* – **1.** the other day. **2.** of late occurrence, appearance, or origin; lately happening, done, made, etc. **3.** years ago. **4.** a non-specific reference to the past. **Eg.** *"Gee, I cyah believe it wah juss d'udda day we wah goin' chrew Ivan n' now errybody forget it like it wah nuttin' yih'nah?"*

Dan (dahn) *Noun* – **1.** one who deserves great respect and admiration. **2.** worthy of praise and applaud. **3.** a highly commendable individual. **Eg.** *"Frankie da dan still yih'nah. Nobody had know how ta fix da remote n' he jess figga it out."*

Dandruss (dan-d'russ) *Noun* – **1.** 'Dandruff. **2.** a seborrheic scurf that forms on the scalp and comes off in small scales. **3.** a condition in which light-coloured scales of dead skin are shed by the scalp. **Eg.** *"Any time yih gah dandruss juss go in da sea ta clear it up."*

Dd

Dan Man (dahn mahn) *Noun* – **1.** a man who could possibly walk on water if given the opportunity. **2.** a gifted individual who is loved and respected by many. **3.** a person of superior intellect and ability. **Eg.** *"When Carson had win dah Gen'ral Knowledge Quiz, errybody had say he wah da Dan Man."*

Dappa (dah-pah) *Adverb* – **1.** immaculately dressed. **2.** neat; trim; smart. **3.** an individual who is gifted in the art of dress. **4.** very stylish. **Eg.** *"Michael use ta be so dappa people say he use ta dress up ta go ta da bathroom."*

Darkers (dar-kuz) *Noun* – **1.** really dark sunglasses. **2.** shades. **3.** eyeglasses with colored or tinted lenses that protect the eyes from the glare of sunlight. **Eg.** *"Always mek sure ta wear ya darkers when ya goin' out in bright sunlight."*

Dass (dah'ce) *Pronoun* – **1.** that's. **2.** a contraction of that is or that has. **3.** short for that had, that would, that will, that is. **Eg.** *"Dass da bess piece ah cassawa cake I ewa had in my life."*

Dat (dah't) *Pronoun* – **1.** that. **2.** used to indicate a person, thing, idea, state, event, time, remark, etc..., as pointed out or present, mentioned before, supposed to be understood, or by way of emphasis. **Eg.** *"Look ah dat eh? Dah man nah clean my car good n' talkin' bug he ready fa he money."*

Dead House (dade how'ce) *Noun* – From Old People Times; **1.** a mortuary. **2.** a funeral home where dead bodies are kept before burial or cremation. **3.** a preliminary resting place for the deceased. **Eg.** *"One time when Sicily had went go check on her husband in da hospital, dey accidentally tell 'er he wah up in da dead house. When she fine out it wuz'n chrew, she nearly faint 'way."*

Dealin' (dee-lin) *Adverb* – **1.** the third stage in the four-part structure of a relationship, which involves: *1. talkin' 2. checkin' 3. dealin' 4. goin'.* **2.** preliminary commitment to a relationship in which full monogamy is considered but not yet outlined and agreed upon. **3.** a partially-committed stage in a young relationship. **Eg.** *"Erin tell Tod she n' him nah dealin' no more cuz he love too much woman."*

Dd

Deal wit da Case (deel wid da kayce) *Verb* – **1.** to handle one's business. **2.** to defend one's reputation, family, or property by violence or verbal retaliation. **3.** to get rowdy or aggressive with another person. **4.** to beat someone up while having good reason to do so. **Eg.** *"If Birdy doo'n stop messin' wit my sista I gah jess hawe deal wit da case still."*

Dear (dere) *Adverb* – **1.** expensive or unaffordable. **2.** a price which exceeds the ideal range of an individual. **3.** over-priced. **Eg.** *"When I wah small we used ta shop at By-Rite's cuz my mama say Merren shop wah too dear."*

Dee-Dee (dee-dee) *Noun* – **1.** waste matter discharged from the intestines through the anus; excrement. **2.** stool. **3.** number two. **4.** solid excretory product evacuated from the bowels [syn: fecal matter]. (also known as: **ca-ca**) **Eg.** *"Shawanna wah mad dah time when she had step in dee-dee wit her new shoes."*

Deh (deh) *Adverb* – **1.** there. **2.** in or at that place; opposed to 'here'. **3.** reference to either a specific or figurative location that is not in close proximity. **Eg.** *"Oh, so ya like popsicles? I hear ya deh."*

Delworth's (del-wurtz) *Noun* – **1.** a popular gas station and mini mart located on the corner of Eastern Avenue and across from the Watler's Road (Dog City) area. **2.** a common hotspot for after hours snacking and loitering. **3.** the gas station across from Dixie Cemetary. **Eg.** *"I rememba when Delworth's used ta hawe da bess corn beef sangwiches in George Town."*

Dem (dehm) *Pronoun* – **1.** the objective case of 'they', used as a direct or indirect object. **2.** reference to a group of people or objects. **Eg.** *"Dem man deh always seem to be gettin' in trouble y'see."*

Dem Boys (dehm boyz) *Pronoun, Pl.* – **1.** those guys. **2.** my good friends. **3.** the fellas. **Eg.** *"Mee-mee, tell ya mama I gah be home late tonight. I goin' check dem boys cuz it Harry birtday n' we juss goin' cool out n' play some dominoes."*

Dem Man (dehm mahn) *Pronoun* – **1.** those guys. **2.** some men. **3.** male friends; aquintances. **Eg.** *"Greggy n' dem man always gah be up in dah bar room erry Friday boy."*

Dd

Dem Old People (dem ole pee-pull) *Pronoun* – **1.** older persons or individuals who came before us. **2.** our ancestors. **3.** grandparents. **4.** all individuals over the age of 75. **5.** senior citizens. **Eg.** *"Dem old people say 'trouble doon' blow shell'. Dah why we diddn' know Ivan wah comin'."*

Deown (deaown) *Noun* – From Cayman Brac; **1.** the word 'down' - pronounced with a Cayman Brac accent. **2.** the opposite of up. **3.** the lower portion of anything. **Eg.** *"I cyah undastand why dem Wess Bayas always be sayin' dey goin' up ta George Town n' deown Wess Bay. Dey doo'n hawe ah compass ah wah?"*

Dereckleh (dih-reck-leh) *Adverb* – **1.** later. **2.** the not-so-distant future. **3.** a future time to come. (also pronounced: '**ereckleh**', '**areckleh**', or '**tereckleh**' in some areas) **Eg.** *"If yah cyah doo it now juss check meh dereckleh n' I probly be ready fah yah den."*

Dew Plum (d'yoo plumb) *Noun* – **1.** a small yellowish fruit with brown spots which is sweet, yet also tartish in taste. **Eg.** *"Troy lowe ah good Dew Plum wit salt, boy."*

Dey (daye) *Pronoun, Pl.* – **1.** they. **2.** nominative plural of HE, SHE, and IT. **3.** people in general. **Eg.** *"Mummy, I call Chris n' J.C. ta come eat lunch but dey say dey nah hongry."*

Dickons (dih-kunz) *Noun* – **1.** Caymanian translation of the word 'dickens'. **2.** a word used in exclamations of confusion, excitement, or disbelief. **Eg.** *"Wah da dickon's wrong wit you? You cyah hear I say stop mekkin' nize cuz yoh granfadda up'na bed sleepin'?"*

Didd'n Did (did'in did) *Verb* – **1.** did not do. **2.** neglected to perform a particular activity. **3.** an alibi. **Eg.** *"When da judge acks Ol' Fred if he had teef chickins outta Pastor Roy yaad, he say "no yah honour, I didd'n did it."*

Diffrunts (dih-fruntz) *Adverb* – **1.** difference; the state or relation of being different; dissimilarity. **2.** a significant change in or effect on a situation. **3.** a distinguishing characteristic; distinctive quality, feature, etc. **Eg.** *"Alright! I doon' see wah diffrunts it make if he waugh play wit yoh Transforma since ya doon' waugh him ta play wit da G.I. Joes."*

Dd

Dilly Dallyin' (dih-leh dah-leh-yinkunz) *Verb* – **1.** wasting time and energy especially by stopping often. **2.** idling. **3.** loitering foolishly. **Eg.** *"Look yah man! Hurry up n' stop dilly dallyin' or else we gah be late fah da movies."*

Dimmy John (dih-meh jon) *Noun* – **1.** a large iron pot used for cooking outdoors as well as inside. **2.** a pot used for brewing soups, cooking beef and turtle and boiling crabs. **Eg.** *"Yah cyah go wrong wid ah good Dimmy John on da stove."*

Dippa (dih-pah) *Noun* – **1.** a small to medium-size bucket used to collect water from a well or cistern. **2.** a cup-like container with a long handle used for dipping liquids. **Eg.** *"One time Harry had drop da dippa in da cistern, so none ah us couldin' bade fah tree days."*

Diss (dih'ce) *Pronoun* – **1.** this; (used to indicate a person, thing, idea, state, event, time, remark, etc., as present, near, just mentioned or pointed out, supposed to be understood, or by way of emphasis). **2.** being nearer or more immediate. **Eg.** *"Eric, come so see if diss pants kin still fit ya nah?"*

Diss Out (dih'ce owt) *Adverb* – **1.** to disrespect. **2.** to display complete disregard for respect. **3.** to shame another. **Eg.** *"Nexx time hurricane come yah, I know he gah get ah big diss out, cuz Shekira goin' stateside."*

Dixie (dickz-eh) *Noun* – **1.** the area surrounding the stoplight at the junction of North Church Street and Eastern Avenue. **2.** a community of houses and businesses which include Delworth's Esso, Watler's Road, and Kentucky Fried Chicken. **Eg.** *"One time I walk from Wess Bay ta Dixie in 30 minutes."*

Dixie Cemetary (dickz-eh) *Noun* – **1.** a renown cemetary in George Town located adjacent to Delworth's Esso. **Eg.** *"My granny bin buried dong in Dixie Cemetary b'fore I born."*

Docta (dawk-tuh) *Noun* – **1.** the *Doctor Fish*. **2.** any fish of the genus *Acanthurus*; the surgeon fish; so called from a sharp lance-like spine on each side of the tail. (also called: **Barber Fish**).

Dd

Docta (dawk-tuh) *Noun (continued)* **3.** a species similar to the *Trigger fish*, and having a solid, dark blue to black coloured hide. **Eg.** *"Nex time I go fishnin', I waugh ketch ah nice Docta n' get im mounted ta put on my wall in da den."*

Docta Shirt (dok-tah shurt) *Noun* – **1.** a semi-casual shirt which features four or more pockets on the front; two on the top and two on the bottom. **3.** also known as a 'bush jacket'. **Eg.** *"Mista Milla always used ta keep a stick ah chalk in he docta shirt when he wah teachin' mahts."*

Dog City (dawg sitty) *Noun* – **1.** the Watler's Road area, first nicknamed for it's abundance of canines. **2.** the neighborhood behind Bay Town Plaza on North Church Street. **3.** a housing community located directly to the northeast of Delworth's Esso. **Eg.** *"My friend dat live dong in Dog City say she wouldn' live noway else."*

Dog City'ans (dawg siddy-yunz) *Noun, Pl.* – **1.** any gathering of people from the Watler's Road area. **2.** person's from the neighborhood of Dog City. **3.** most people who live near Delworth's Esso and shop at Kirk Supermarket. **Eg.** *"I know dem Dog City'ans muss be sick ah eatin' Kentucky chicken all da time."*

Dogg-eh (dawg-eh) *Slang* – **1.** a good friend or acquaintance. **2.** brethren or breddren. **3.** my boy. **4.** friend. **Eg.** *"Yeah dogg-eh, I see wah ya sayin' 'bout dem rims but I doon' really like um still."*

Doll Baby (dawl bay-beh) *Noun* – From West Bay **1.** any toy doll, including a *Barbie* doll. **2.** a small figure representing a baby or other human being, esp. for use as a child's toy. **Eg.** *"Mina say Melissa always use ta mess wit her doll baby when she in da bahtchroom pretendin' ta bade."*

Dominoes (daw-mih-noze) *Noun, Pl.* – **1.** one of the most popular pastimes amongst Caymanian men (of any age). **2.** a series of flat, thumbsized, rectangular blocks of which the faces of which are divided into two parts, with each either blank or bearing from one to six pips or dots. 28 such pieces form a complete set. **3.** any of various games played by matching the ends of pieces and laying them down in lines and angular patterns. **Eg.** *"You get da table, I gah get da dominoes n' meet ya unda da almond tree."*

Dd

Dong (dawng) *Adverb* – **1.** down. **2.** from higher to lower; in descending direction or order; toward, into, or in a lower position. **3.** to or in a sitting or lying position. **Eg.** *"Tell me sump'm? Why come Wess Bayas always say dey goin' up ta town and down ta Wess Bay even doh Wess Bay is da northernmost part ah Grand Cayman?"*

Donkey (dong-keh) *Noun* – **1.** a real idiot. **2.** dummy. **3.** fool. **4.** a person with little or no sense whatsoever. **Eg.** *"If I wah born ah Policeman I would arress erry donkey who try cut me off when it my turn ta cross at ah fourway stop."*

Donkey Ages (dawng-key yarez) *Noun* – **1.** forever and ever. **2.** light years. **Eg.** *"I wonda how Priscilla bin doin' ballet fa donkey ages and still nah no good at it."*

Donkey Man (dawng-keh mahn) *Noun* – **1.** the sole operator of the engine on early ships, such as freighters, schooners and yachts. **2.** the man responsible for the 'donkey engines'. **Eg.** *"I hear people say da donkey man wah da lass man ta get out when da Balboa sink but some say he went dong wid it."*

Donkey Years (dawng-key yarez) *Noun* – **1.** a very long time. **2.** years and years and years. **3.** decades ago. **Eg.** *"I hear Pastor Ebanks bin runnin' dah church fa donkey years now."*

Doo-Doo (du-du) *Noun* – **1.** waste matter discharged from the intestines through the anus; excrement. **2.** stool. **3.** number two (see also: **Dee-Dee**). **4.** solid excretory product evacuated from the bowels [syn: **fecal matter**]. **Eg.** *"Baby's always seem to doo-doo up demselves at da worst possible moment."*

Doon' (doo'n) *Verb* – **1.** contraction of *do not.* **2.** be careful. *Noun* – **3.** a statement of what should not be done. **Eg.** *"Pee-Wee! Doon' go in my room when I nah deh man! I gah private stuff in deh yih'nah?"*

Doon' Mess (doo'n meh'ce) *Adverb* – **1.** a contraction of the phrase *'Don't mess with me...*" **2.** be careful. **3.** be cautious; move or speak carefully. **4.** "don't even try it" **Eg.** *"Aye, doon' mess! I kin kick ya up n' down diss street n' you cyah touch me cuz I'm ah woman yih'nah?"*

Dd

Doonut (doo-nutt) *Noun* – **1.** a 360-degree skidmark left after burning tires in a parking lot or marl pit. **2.** a favorite pastime for young men who have just acquired their driver's license. **Eg.** *"My sista doon' lemme her car no more cuz she hear I wah doin' doonuts wid it up at Breaker's Speedway."*

Dory (doh-rih) *Noun* – **1.** a boat with a narrow, flat bottom, high bow, and flaring sides, pulled with eight oars and steered with a rudder. **2.** a small, narrow, flatbottom fishing boat with high sides and a sharp prow. **3.** an early form of marine transportation. **4.** a boat used for carrying logwood from the beach to boats or bringing imports ashore, and for transporting thatch from Long Bay (east of present Frank Sound crossroads). **Eg.** *"Dah car so long it look like one ol' dory my puhpah use ta have."*

Down in the East (down in da east) *Noun* – **1.** the area of George Town which encompasses everything on the southside of Shedden Road; from MacDonald's Restaurant to Eastern Avenue. **2.** the area encompassing all parts between Linwood Street, Tigris Street and Martin Drive. **3.** a combination of the Central and Scranton communities. **4.** a good place to get some of the best cooked food on the island. **Eg.** *"I know some ah dem boys from Down in the East cuz I grew up wid um."*

Down Pee (down-pee) *Noun* – **1.** comrade. **2.** one's brother-in-arms. **3.** trusted friend. **4.** breddren or brethren. **5.** a person of great meaning. **6.** a like-minded individual who shares the same interests. **Eg.** *"I rate Orvin as my real down pee mainly because he always come check me to see wah goin' on."*

Draws (drawz) *Noun* – **1.** one's underwear; briefs or panties **2.** any undergarment. **3.** bloomers. **Eg.** *"I hate drivin' pass people house n' seein' dey draws outside on da clothesline yih'see"* or; *"Mummy, dis mornin' Lionel tell Randel he mama wear croca sack draws n' Randel tek one big rock n' pelt im right in he head yih'nah."*

Drape (draype) *Verb* – **1.** to string someone up and attack them to the point of fatigue. **2.** to hold someone in a compromising position. **3.** to hold up. **Eg.** *"I hear one ol' man had get drape up by two lil' boys lass week."*

Dd

Drive-In (dryve in) *Noun* – **1.** the Ever Glow outdoor movie facility. **2.** one of the most popular hotspots on Grand Cayman during the late 1970s and early 1980s. **3.** a motion picture theatre, refreshment stand, etc. designed to accommodate patrons in their automobiles. **Eg.** *"Watchin' kung fu moowiz at Drive-In when we wah small wah da bess ting det eva happen ta me."*

Druggy (druh-geh) *Noun* – **1.** one who takes or is addicted to drugs. **2.** any individual who is known to consume marijuana, cocaine, heroin, or any other narcotic on a regular basis. **3.** a drug addict. **4.** one who loves drugs more than life itself. **Eg.** *"Mahma, one druggy juss walk chrew ouwah yard and teef Daddy boxers off da clothesline."*

Drug Head (drug hade) *Noun* – **1.** a junkie; an addict, esp. one addicted to cocaine or heroin, etc. **2.** a person with an insatiable craving for drugs. **3.** a narcotics addict. **4.** one who is ardently a follower of everything related to illegal drugs. **Eg.** *"I hate when I see how James turn into one ol' drug head, when he had so much potential when we wah in highschool."*

Dry as Chip (drye iz chipp) *Slang* – **1.** very dry. **2.** 'bone dry'. **3.** without a trace of moisture; as dry as a weathered bone. **Eg.** *"I cyah believe nuttin' wah Randy say, cuz wheneva I tell im ta go bade, he come back out da baffroom dry as chip n' expeck people ta beliewe he juss bade."*

Dry it Up (drye it uhpp) *Slang* – From West Bay; **1.** encouragement to stop; especially when one has been crying or moaning for an extensive period of time. **2.** a mother or grandmother's favourite phrase to use after delivering a beating or scolding to an unruly child. **Eg.** *"Come now Quinton, I nah beat ya dah hard so dry it up or else yih gah get anudda lashin' wit diss belt."*

Dry Land Tourist (drye lan tore-iss) *Noun* – **1.** a nickname for local people who walk around the island behaving like tourists, but have never left the island. **Eg.** *"When Rudy went off he had start walkin' round George Town like he wah one ol' Dry Land Tourist."*

Dd

Duck Pond (duk pawnd) *Noun* – **1.** a secluded area off of the coast of the North Sound, where shipwrights would pull schooners up to dry dock and tilt them to either side to scrub their bottoms and remove all moss and barnacles. **Eg.** *"Mama say one time dey hadda pull up Granfadda boat up by Duck Pond cuz it had ketch up in one fishin' net n' da motor wuz'n workin'."*

Duppy (duh-peh) *Imaginary Noun* – **1.** a ghost, shadow or spirit of a dead person. **2.** a disembodied spirit imagined, usually as a vague, shadowy or evanescent form, as wandering among or haunting living persons. **3.** a reason to be afraid while walking at night. **Eg.** *"I hate walkin' chrew town when it dark cuz I 'fraid duppy gah ketch me."*

Duppy Cap (duh-peh kyap) *Noun* – **1.** a large mushroom-like plant which comes up from the earth after heavy rain. **2.** an inedible plant favouring a mushroom. **3.** a whitish coloured shrub. **Eg.** *"Boy doon' touch dah duppy cap. I hear dey pyzinuss, yih'nah."*

Duppy Nose (duh-peh noze) *Noun* – **1.** a reddish, sponge like shrub which tends to favor a person's nose. **2.** a nasty-looking plant filled with dew and dirt, which comes up in the early morning. **Eg.** *"Wheneva I used ta see ah duppy nose in da mornin' it used ta turn my stomach."*

Duppy Tree (duh-peh tree) *Noun* – **1.** the remains of a dead, hollowed *Ironwood Tree* from the logging period of the 1700s. **2.** a tree which has been said to contain the spirits of dead slaves. **3.** a haunted tree. **4.** a tree with a curse on it. **Eg.** *"Some people say dah duppy tree up by Bowsin' Bay cemetery wah chop dong by duppies in da graveyard."*

Duss Out (duss owt) *Verb* – **1.** to leave in a great haste. **2.** to stir up dust by kicking, scraping or rotating car tires at a high velocity. **3.** gone with the wind. **Eg.** *"If yah waugh see people duss out jess acks fah help wit cleanin' up afta ah big party."*

Duss Up (duss up) *Verb* – **1.** to cause a great dusty commotion. **2.** to become covered in dust or dirt. **3.** to soil one's clothing with dust. **Eg.** *"Wheneva I tell Randy ta rake da ol' yaad all he do is duss up da place."*

Dd

Dusta (dus-tah) *Noun* – **1.** a woman's lightweight sleeping garment. **2.** a thin, robe-like garment which covers a woman's bed clothes; including pajamas and lingerie. **Eg.** *"Granny always used ta hawe on her dusta from 6:00 in da evenin' even doh she diddn' go bed 'til 8:00."*

Dusty Place (duss-tih playce) *Noun* – **1.** a former name for the area between Batabano Road and Mount Pleasant in West Bay. **Eg.** *"My cousin' always used ta be runnin' 'bout Dusty Place y'see."*

Dyappah (die-yap-ah) *Noun* – **1.** diaper. **2.** a piece of cloth or other absorbent material folded and worn as underpants by a baby not yet toilet-trained. **3.** a linen or cotton fabric with a woven pattern of small, constantly repeated figures, as diamonds. **Eg.** *"I hate changin' my lil' sista diyappah. She always hawe dee-dee all owa da place n' she be pee-pee'in' while ya tryin' change 'er."*

Dyke Road (dyke rode) *Noun* – **1.** one in a series of roads which were carved into the swamps throughout the Islands to create a passage for the *'fogger'* - a truck armed with chemicals for controlling mosquitos. **2.** a side road made of white marl (usually through a swamp) which has not been authorized for public use. **Eg.** *"I feel sorry fa anybody who get ketch down in dem dike roads wit no flash light."*

Dyke Roads were created to accommodate mosquito research and population control.

Dd

Ear Hole (air hoal) *Noun* – **1.** the entrance to one's ear. **2.** a passage between the inner ear and outer ear. **3.** part of the instrument used for receiving sound, which is processed by the brain. **Eg.** *"Lissin' yah man. If ya cyah hear wah I sayin', clean yah ear hole next time n' stop acksin' so much questions."*

East (eace) *Adverb* – **1.** the eastern districts, including; Bodden Town, Breakers, East End and North Side. **2.** a cardinal point of the compass, 90-degrees to the right of north. **3.** the longitude of the area from which the sun rises. **Eg.** *"Anytime I go East I always feel like I in ah diffrunt country cuz it so peaceful."*

East End (eece-tend) *Noun* – **1.** the second largest district on Grand Cayman with an area of approximately 20.9 square miles and a population of 1,064 people (1989 census). **2.** the area of which has been rumored to belong to William Foster in 1741 during a land grant of 100 plus acres. Foster supposedly lived in this area with his servants and slaves for a time, but migrated later to Bodden Town and then Cayman Brac (1833). **3.** the easternmost district on Grand Cayman. **4.** the place where East Enders live. **5.** a good place for spear fishin', surfin' and reef divin'. **Eg.** *"Dem East End boys always lowe brag about how good dey kin' fishin' betta dan Wess Bayas."*

Eat Out (eet owtt) *Verb* – **1.** to devour every morsel in sight. **2.** to swallow or eat up hungrily, voraciously, or ravenously. **3.** to consume destructively, recklessly, or wantonly. **Eg.** *"If I eva ketch whoeva eat out my Funyuns it gah be pure licks fah da person."*

Edieyut (eed'yutt) *Noun* – **1.** an idiot. **2.** anyone who lacks common knowledge or common sense. **3.** a fool. **Eg.** *"Lissin' ta me? You tink I ah edieyut ah wah? I know it nah no such ting as fortylebbenteen, but it song like ah big numba so I like it"* or; *Margaret!? I tell you ta keep da birtday party small n' you gone n' invite fortylebbenteen people ta come mash up my house?*

Ee

Eech (ee'ch) *Adjective* – **1.** to itch. **2.** to have or feel a peculiar tingling or uneasy irritation of the skin that causes a desire to scratch the part affected. **Eg.** *"Sometimes I gah sleep wit no sheet cuz it be eechin' me man."*

Eeble (ee-bull) *Adjective* – **1.** a combination of the words *even* and *able*, meaning; just. **2.** having the ability to perform. **3.** capable without obstruction or hesitation. **Eg.** *"You couldn' eeble hurt ah fly if you tried."*

Eed'yut (ee-d'yutt) *Noun* – **1.** a complete and total idiot. **2.** an utterly foolish or senseless person. **3.** a person so mentally deficient as to be incapable of ordinary reasoning. **4.** an uneducated or ignorant person. **Eg.** *"You's ah real eed'yut fa lennin' Pursley yoh bicycle again."*

Eeease (eeee'zzz) *Interjection* – **1.** cool. **2.** excellent; first rate. **3.** a general response to a favourable statement. **4.** acceptable; satisfactory. **Eg.** *"Bobby: Cuz, check out diss new Playstation game my friend bring me from Japan nah? O'neil: Eeeaase... it look criss still. Lemme play first nah?"*

Een (een) *Preposition* – Primarily from East End; **1.** in. **2.** on the inside; within. **3.** used to indicate inclusion within something abstract or immaterial. **Eg.** *"Harry it come een like Josie Lee cyah cook fish or sump'm cuz she always be bunnin' up erryting I bring home when I go fishnin'."*

Either or Either (ee-thur er eye-thur) *Adjective* – **1.** either way. **2.** anyway. **3.** however. **4.** whatever. **5.** don't care. **6.** a way of showing indecisiveness or lack of concern or commitment. **Eg.** *"Either or either way I still know you gah go behind my back n' doo foolishniss."*

Elizabethan (ee-liz-uh-bee-tun) *Noun* – **1.** Elizabethan Square. **2.** one of the most active business complexes in George Town. **3.** the current location of the Monetary Authority Building, Cayman Travel Services and FedEx. **Eg.** *"Me n' my gyalfriend use ta hawe lunch around da fountain at Elizabethan erry day."*

Ereckleh (eh-reck-leh) *Adverb* – **1.** later. **2.** the not-so-distant future. **3.** a future time to come. (also pronounced: 'areckleh', 'dereckleh', or 'tereckleh' in some areas) **Eg.** *"check meh ereckleh, n' I gah see wah we kin doo."*

Ee

Errybody (err-eh baw-deh) *Pronoun* – **1.** everybody. **2.** every person. **3.** everyone. **4.** all persons involved. **5.** the whole crew. **Eg.** *"It kinda funny how ya cyah invite errybody ta ya weddin but dey still come ta ya funeral."*

Erryting (err-eh ting) *Pronoun* – **1.** every thing. **2.** every aspect or particular of an aggregate or total; all. **3.** something extremely important: *it means erryting to me.* **Eg.** *"When playin' marbles we use ta call erryting on da next man taw n' he could'n say nuttin'."*

Erryway (err-eh way) *Pronoun* – **1.** every where. **2.** in every place or part; in all places. **3.** all over. **4.** vast coverage. **Eg.** *"Erryway ya go it seem like yih kin' buy phone cards or cigarettes easier dun yih kin buy food."*

Ever Glow (ev-ah glo) *Pronoun* – **1.** the trade name of a former drive-in movie theatre located in Pease Bay during the 1970s and 80s. **2.** one of the most popular hotspots during the late 1970s and early 1980s. **3.** an outdoor motion picture theatre and refreshment stand designed to accommodate patrons in their automobiles. **Eg.** *"I always use'ta love watchin' dem ol' black n' white kung fu movies at Ever Glow drive-in."*

The word 'erreckleh' cannot be found on any standard timepiece.

Ee

Facety (fay'ce-teh) *Adjective* – **1.** full of audacity. **2.** bold. **3.** not hesitating to break the rules of propriety; forward; impudent. **4.** enterprising. **5.** assuming; rude; sassy; immodest. **6.** smart-alecky. **Eg.** *"Dat facety gyal gah soon get ah sahpapah if she doon' hush up."*

Fah (fuh) *Preposition* – **1.** for. **2.** with the object or purpose of. **3.** intended to belong to, or be used in connection with. **4.** suiting the purpose or needs of. **Eg.** *"I hate when dem ol' people acks 'who you fah?' n' dey neva know who ya mama n' daddy is."*

Fah True (fuh troo) *Adverb* – **1.** true; not merely ostensible, nominal, or apparent. **2.** absolutely true. **3.** not a lie. **4.** an actual thing; having objective existence; not imaginary. **Eg.** *"When I say Marlon had fling he bicycle ova Miss Ann fence ta go pick plums. Dah wah fah true yih'nah?"*

Farm Soldier (fahrm sol-jah) *Noun* – **1.** a position held by Caymanian O'chester "Pad'sin" Patterson during World War II. **2.** the words which were emblazoned on the back of Ochester Patterson's army jacket, which he wore with pride, and defended jealously. **Eg.** *"I like how Luigi re-make dem Farm Soldier t-shirts yih'see. Now dass some real Caymanian stuff man."*

Fass (fahce) *Verb* – **1.** fast. **2.** moving or able to move, operate, function, or take effect quickly; quick; swift; rapid. *Adverb* – **3.** mischievous and bothersome. **4.** troublesome. **Eg.** *"Randy juss lowe ta fass wit da gyals on da bus, but one time Leanne fix he bizness fa him."*

Fass-eh (fah'ce-ih) *Pronoun* – **1.** one who interferes with the property or affairs of others. **2.** a mischiefmaker. **3.** a browser. **4.** a busybody. **Eg.** *"You ol' fass-eh. Why u hadda go trubble my 'Days of Our Lives?"*

Fassniss (fah'ce-niss) *Adjective* – **1.** mischievousness. **2.** child-like playfulness. **Eg.** *"I dunno why you hadda mess wit my car wit yah fassniss n' now it nah workin'."*

Ff

Fass Hand (fahce han) *Adverb* – **1.** having the propensity to handle the property of others without permission. **2.** compelled to steal. **3.** thieving. **4.** unable to resist the temptation to mis-handle or misplace the property of others. **5.** having 'sticky fingers'. **Eg.** *"Dah ol' fass hand ting ah Corbert always gah be messin' wit my stuff."*

Feel Up (feele-upp) *Verb* – **1.** to touch or fondle inappropriately. **2.** to handle an object in an unbecoming manner. **3.** to examine extensively by touching. **Eg.** *"It hard to get wah ya waugh sometimes, cuz even when ya go supamahkit all da fruits be all feel up"* or *"Miss Parchment ghee Jude detention cuz he had try feel up Maria when she wuz'n lookin'."*

Fensic (fehn-zik) *Noun* – From Old People Times; **1.** a pain killer. **2.** a small white-coloured tablet, containing medication with the ability to ease pain from headaches, soreness, etc. **3.** a very popular pain reliever amongst older people. **Eg.** *"I hear dey say Fensic kin cure anyting yih'nah? Even Cyansa, Diarrhea, n' Food Pyzin."*

Feva Grass (fee-vuh grah'ce) *Noun* – From Old People Times; **1.** an old wives remedy for most types of fever. **2.** a very ordinary-looking type of tea grass, which can often be confused with *'ginuea grass'* (a non-edible grass), measuring approx. three feet tall. **3.** a green grass found in most overgrown areas which has herbal qualities and is used to treat colds and fever. **4.** a 'bush med'sin'; drunk as a tea. **Eg.** *"Papa Jim always say dat even if yah nah gah no money ta buy med'sin yih kin always go pick some feva grass."*

Fiancheh (fee-yahn-chehh) *Noun* – **1.** one's fiance'. **2.** a man or woman who is engaged to be married; a man to whom a woman is engaged. **3.** one's future husband or wife. **Eg.** *"I dunno why Gilbert be runnin' rong tellin' people dat Charlotte he fiancheh when errybody know he still be foolin' rong wit Paulette."*

Fine Teet Comb (fyne teet koomb) *Noun* – **1.** a figurative notion toward a thorough investigation.. **2.** a very small comb. **3.** an imaginary pair of magnifying glasses. **Eg.** *"Boy you bess try so go chrew yoh room wit ah fine teet comb n' find my MC Hammer cd or you gah buy it right back."*

Ff

Fingas (fee'ng-ahz) *Noun, Pl.* – **1.** a nickname for Caymanian dumplings. **2.** the five digits of the hand. **Eg.** *"I love when babies hold onto my hand wit dey lil' fingas."*

Fingle (fee'ng-guhl) *Verb* – **1.** to fondle; mishandle; grope. **Fingle-in'** (fee'ng-guhl-in) **1.** touching or stroking the property of another without permission. **Eg.** *"Sasha! Stop finglin' up my dress nah. You gah get all kinda smudges on it n' I nah even wear it yet."*

File Paypah (fyle pay-puh) *Noun* – **1.** foil paper; a thin, metal wrapping made of foil, for the purpose of protecting food from bacteria, insects, dust and mould. **2.** an essential cooking item. **3.** the cheap alternative to installing 'grills' on one's teeth (most attractive amongst 'B.E.T. babies'). **Eg.** *"Anytime I see my neffew puttin' file paypah on he teet I jess gah shake my head cuz I know it wouldn' be me walkin' rong wit all ah dah metal in my mout."*

Fire Box (fye-ah bawkz) *Noun* – From Old People Times; **1.** a small wooden box filled with sand and candle-wood, which was burned to produce light at night. **2.** an early alternative to lamps and lanterns. **3.** a traditional Cayman light source. **Eg.** *"Dey say one time it wah easy ta get stuff ta put in ya fire box but yah cyah hardly do dat no more."*

Fishes (fih-shiz) *Noun, Pl.* – **1.** more than one fish. **2.** any of numerous cold-blooded vertebrate animals that live in water. **3.** one of the types of food of which Jesus fed to the multitude. **Eg.** *"Two little fishes and five loaves of bread."*

Fishnin' (fish-nin) *Verb* – **1.** fishing. **2.** the act of catching fish. **3.** to fish for food on water using a boat, or on land, via ironshore. **4.** the technique, occupation, or diversion of catching fish. **Eg.** *"My unka Harold cun fishnin' betta dun mos' people in Wess Bay."*

Fish Pot (fish pawt) *Noun* – **1.** a 'fish trap', which is made from sticks and chicken wire, and placed in shallow waters to collect fish, lobsters, and conch. **2.** a large box, whose frame can be made from lightweight timber, and outlined in chicken wire; used for capturing fish near to shore or in shallow waters. **3.** a great way to catch fish without using bait. **Eg.** *"Sometimes ya gah curry up yah fish pot or else somebody gah steal it when ya nah deh."*

Ff

Fish Tea (fih-she tee) *Noun* – **1.** a traditional Caymanian soup made primarily from small fish such as grunts, squabs (parrot fish), butterfish, doctor fish, etc. mixed with breadkind, salt, pepper, onions and other seasonings. **2.** a standard menu item at any Caribbean restaurant on Grand Cayman. **Eg.** *"Geezumpiece! Boy diss wah ya call some good fish tea!"*

Fix Wheel Bicycle (fickz weel by-sick'l) *Noun* – **1.** a constricted alteration of one's bicycle crank shaft to increase speed. **2.** a bicycle that is really difficult to stop. **3.** a really fast bike. **Eg.** *"One time when we wah jumpin' in da sea up by Smit Barcadere somebody teef Eldon fix wheel bicycle."*

Fiyah Antses (f'eye-yah ahntz-iz) *Noun, Pl.* – **1.** large stinging ants. **2.** an army of large black or red ants which are notorious for painful bites. **3.** a species of the red ant. **4.** biting ants. **Eg.** *"Anytime ya go rake da yaad, yih cyah help but get bite up by fiyah antses."*

Flawesome (flaugh-sum) *Slang* – **1.** flawlessly awesome. **2.** a combination of the words *"flawless"* and *"awesome"*. **3.** something that is extremely excellent. **4.** an expression to use when there is no other word to describe something great. **Eg.** *"I used to be flawesome at doin' flips offa da iron shore when I wah small."*

Fling (fleengh) *Verb* – **1.** to throw, cast, or hurl with force or violence. **2.** to move an object from one space to another by throwing. **3.** to transport. **Eg.** *"Mama, kin u come fling me ta da movies, please?"*

Flit (fliht) *Noun* – From Old People Times; **1.** the brand name for an insecticide with the primary active ingredient being *permethrin*, which was most often used to control adult mosquitos. **2.** an insect spray which is delivered through a hand-pumped device called a 'flit gun'. **Eg.** *"I need my flit gun so I kin kill off all ah deez miskittas."*

Flitters (flih-duz) *Noun, Pl.* – **1.** traditional Caymaian buns, having a yellowish-brown colour and made of flour, salt, butter, baking powder, and having a solid crust on the outside and a soft, sweet inside. **2.** one of the most popular side dishes for any meal, especially fried fish.

Ff

Flitters (cont'd) **3.** a small yellow bun. (also pronounced: fritters) **Eg.** *"Gee-doh! Yoh Daddy kin mek frittas good yih'see? Axe im if I kin cyar some ah deez home nah?"*

Flood Out (fludd owt) *Noun* – **1.** to overcome with water or other substance. **2.** overflowing with water. *Adverb* – **3.** the state of most houses following Hurricane Ivan. **Eg.** *"In 1988, I went Miami fa ah week n' when I come back Gilbert had my house all flood out."*

Flowa Nose (fluh-wah nohz) *Noun* – **1.** an odd-shaped pair of nostrils that are usually flared and twisted or irregular. **2.** a funny looking nose. **Eg.** *"Oh my Gosh, Hilary, looka Lucy-Ann boyfriend. Way he goin' wit dah flowa nose, man?"*

Flusteritis (fluss-tuh-rye-dis) *Noun* – **1.** an affliction which preys on the weak-willed and those who lack the capacity to maintain composure during intense situations. **2.** a tendency to become overly flustered while under pressure. **3.** a severe breakdown of all mental and moral values during times of frustration. **Eg.** *"You gah flusteritis again ah wah? Errytime somebody gettin' on yoh nerves you gah walk rong wit yo face all screw up like somebody stole yoh guineps."*

Flusstrated (fluh'ce-tray-did) *Adjective* – **1.** flustered and frustrated. **2.** disappointed; thwarted. **3.** thrown into a state of agitated confusion. **Eg.** *"Maannn! Lee me alone nah? You juss gets me so flusstrated sometimes I juss waugh grab ya n' shake ya ta pieces."*

Folla Fashion (foh-lah fash-un) *Adjective* – **1.** inclined to follow others; a follower. **2.** a human sheep. **3.** one who lacks individuality or originality. **4.** void of originalality. **Eg.** *"Ya too folla fashion man. Erryting I do, you ga do it too."*

Fool as Fly (fool iz flye) *Adverb* – **1.** unable to comprehend any information. *Noun* – **4.** a nincompoop; birdbrain; blockhead; halfwit; numskull; simpleton; dumbbell. **Eg.** *"Anybody who be speedin' in da rain muss be fool as fly."*

Fooleh (foo-leh) *Noun* – **1.** a silly or stupid person; one who lacks judgement or sense. **2.** someone who loves to tease others. **3.** a dummy. **4.** an idiot. **Eg.** *"You ol' fooleh, you cyah hear I doon' like eggs wit pancakes ah wah?"*

Ff

Fool-Fool (fool-fool) *Noun* – **1.** crazy. **2.** a nutcase. **3.** a complete idiot. **4.** a rampaging maniac. **5.** a mentally deranged person; demented; insane. **Eg.** *"Do not mess wit Brenard when he eatin' he dumplins'. He fool-fool yih'nah."*

Fooshniss (foo-sh-niss) *Noun* – **1.** foolishness. **2.** resulting from or showing a lack of sense; ill-considered; unwise. **3.** lacking forethought or caution. **4.** trifling, insignificant, or paltry. **Eg.** *"I hadda walk outta dah movie lass night, cuz it wah nuttin' but fooshniss man."*

Football (foot-bawl) *Noun* – **1.** the world's most popular sport. **2.** the Cayman Islands' national sport. **3.** any of various games played with a ball in which two teams try to kick the ball across a field and into each other's goal. **4.** a round, inflated object made of canvas; used in the sport of football. **Eg.** *"Anytime I hear people callin' football 'soccer', it mek meh dizzy cuz I doon' know who made up dah name."*

Foots (footz) *Noun, Pl.* – **1.** plural of the word 'foot'. **2.** two or more feet. **3.** the area of the human anatomy which supports the vertical positioning of the body. **4.** a reknown sculptor who lives on the island of Cayman Brac. **Eg.** *"Aie man! Deez fiyah antses is bitin' up all ah my foots."*

Fop (fawp) *Noun* – **1.** a person who is excessively vain and concerned about his/her dress, appearance, and manners. **2.** a person who is preoccupied with and often vain and about clothes, manners and material objects. **3.** a dandy. **Eg.** *"If I eva met ah real fop, Richard is one ah wum."*

Foppish (fawp-ish) *Adjective* – **1.** resembling or befitting a fop; excessively refined and fastidious in taste and manner. **2.** overly cultured and attracted to finer things. **3.** dandified. **4.** affecting extreme elegance in dress and manner. **Eg.** *"Carol Ann kin be really foppish sometimes when she get rong dem rich people."*

Formin' (faw'r-min) *Verb* – **1.** pretending. **2.** acting. **3.** demonstrating; giving a false appearance. **Eg.** *"Anytime my mama used ta ketch me formin' like I wah sleepin' she used ta slap me in my head."*

Ff

For'nahs (fawr'nuzz) *Noun, Pl.* – **1.** foreigners; a collective group of people who came to the island from a foreign place. **2.** outsiders. **3.** groups of visiting guests from the outside. **Eg.** *"Some people say we learn erryting we know from for'nahs. But I tink we's jess is capable ah learnin' on owa own."*

Forrid (faw-rid) *Noun* – **1.** the human forehead. **2.** the part of the face above the eyebrows; brow. **3.** the fore or front part of anything. **Eg.** *"Lucas get tease in class all da time cuz he gah one piece ah forrid on im y'see?"*

Fortylebbenteen (for-deh-leb-in-tene) *Adjective* – **1.** any high number that is seemingly impossible to count. **2.** a lot. **3.** an unbelievable amount. **Eg.** *"I hear say dey gah 'bout fortylebbenteen chickens up by Franklin Farm."*

Foster's Bag (faw'ce-tuhz baigh) *Noun* – **1.** any common plastic shopping bag, which can be reused several times. **2.** any shopping bag, regardless of which supermarket it came from. **3.** a used shopping bag from Foster's Food Fair. **4.** a bag that can be used to line wastebaskets, or, when doubled, be used as a sack for carrying mangoes, guineps, and other fruits. **Eg.** *"Tarik, bring me one Foster's bag so I kin use it ta wrap up my head afta I cream it."*

Freeniss (free-niss) *Adjective* – **1.** free; without charge. **2.** not belonging to anyone. **3.** open to ownership. **4.** any object or special rights which have been given to an individual 'free-of-charge'. **Eg.** *"Boy Big Low hook me up wit some freeniss dah time when he win $500 playin' numbas."*

Frenny-Frenny (freh-neh freh-neh) *Adjective* – **1.** overly committed to being one's friend. **2.** a stifling show of affection. **3.** a perceived friendship with adverse intentions. **Eg.** *"I don't like how dem women up in da bank always be so frenny-frenny cuz all dey waugh do is talk yah bizniss when yih nah lookin'."*

Fren Up (frehn upp) *Verb* – **1.** to befriend another for personal gain or attention. **2.** to pretend to be friends with another person. **3.** to plot against an enemy deceptively by befriending them first. **Eg.** *"I hate da way you always come try fren up people when yah waugh someting, but udda times yah doon' know nobody."*

Ff

Fries (fryze) *Noun, Pl.* – **1.** a school of small fish which closely resemble *Sprats*, although they are much smaller in size and tend to resemble a small *Barracuda*. **2.** a small silver-ish blue fish having a long slender body. **3.** a really small fish that is great for bait, but not generally eaten. **Eg.** *"Daddy, looka all ah dem fries goin' pass deh. You tink ah Groupa or someting chasin' um?"*

Fritters (frih-duz) *Noun, Pl.* – **1.** traditional Caymanian buns, having a yellowish-brown colour, and made of flour, salt, butter, baking powder, and having a solid crust on the outside and a soft, sweet inside. **2.** one of the most popular side dishes for any meal, especially fried fish. **3.** a small yellow bun. (also called: **Flitters**) **Eg.** *"Way Bobby gone? Tell im bring back some ah dem flitters he teef from out da kitchen or else he gah hawe deal wit me."*

From Mornin' (fruhm mawr'nin') *Adverb* – **1.** since the beginning. **2.** since childhood. **3.** forever. **Eg.** *"I dunno wah I gah do widdout deez shoes cuz I had um from mornin' n' I lowe um ta det."*

From Time (fruhm tyme) *Adverb* – **1.** a long time. **2.** since childhood. **3.** years and years and years. **Eg.** *"Billy, come man, you know me from time, n' you cyah lemme ah lil' five dolla ta get some food man?"*

Frowsy (frow-zeh) *Adverb* – **1.** having a musty or otherwise unpleasant smell. **2.** stink. **3.** full of bad odor. **4.** sweaty; smelly. **Eg.** *"Gee-doh, you cyah hear get offa my lap ah wah? You smell frowsy yih'nah."*

Full Up (full upp) *Verb, trans.* – **1.** filled; stuffed; packed. **2.** to lack availability within a place or thing. **3.** to fill with people or objects or substance. **4.** to exceed capacity. **Eg.** *"Anytime I go Fosta's on Satdeh mornin' it always be full-up wit people, so I jess go get my hair done n' come back."*

Furd (fird) *Adverb* – **1.** far. **2.** at or to a great distance; a long way off; at or to a remote point. **3.** far far away. **4.** too far to be measured. **Eg.** *"I had ta get a car because five miles is too furd for me ta walk ta work erry mornin'!"*

Ff

Gah (g'ah) *Verb* – **1.** to have. **2.** going to. **3.** have to. **4.** to cause to, as by command or invitation. **5.** to show or exhibit in action or words. **Eg.** *"If you doon' do it, I gah have ta do it."*

Galavant (gal-a-vahnt) *Verb* – **1.** to roam about in search of pleasure or amusement. **2.** to walk around endlessly for no apparent reason. **3.** to prance around town sporting new clothes, hoping that others will see. **Eg.** *"If ya see Paul-O galavantin' all day, he mad up 'bout sump'm."*

Galleon (gyal-yun) *Noun* – **1.** Galleon Beach. **2.** the former Galleon Beach Hotel. **3.** one of the first luxury hotels on Grand Cayman. **4.** the area between the Ritz-Carlton Hotel and the Governor's House. **Eg.** *"My mama use ta work down by Galleon Beach Hotel in da 60's."*

Ganja (gyan-jaah) *Noun* – **1.** the *marijuana* plant and any of its products. **2.** *marijuana*, esp. in the form of a potent preparation used chiefly for smoking. **3.** an illegal substance. **Eg.** *"I hear dem hitta's be smokin' ganja dong in da bush way nobody cyah fine um."*

Ganja Head (gyan-jaah hedd) *Noun* – **1.** an individual who eats, sleeps, dreams, talks, walks, and is fully consumed by marijuana. **2.** the marijuana equivalent of a crackhead. **Eg.** *"Curtis used ta be ah ganja head one time but he tun Christian now."*

Gapseed (gyap-seed) *Noun* – **1.** the passage of information. **2.** chatter; hearsay; news. *Verb* – **3.** to engage in idle talk or rumor, esp. about the personal or private affairs of others. **4.** rumor mongering. **Eg.** *"Erry election time all kinda gapseed be spreadin' bout dem MLA's."*

Gauldin' (gawl-din) *Noun* – **1.** a tall, skinny person with bird-like legs. **2.** any of numerous long-legged, long-necked, usually long-billed birds of the family *Ardeidae*. **Eg.** *"Fredrick look like one ol' long neck gauldin' y'see?"*

Gg

Guava (g'waugh-wah) *Noun* – **1.** a small yellowish fruit, filled with seeds and a pasty inside. **2.** a fruit, used for making jam, jelly, etc. **3.** a large lump on one's head after physical contact with a blunt object. **Eg.** *"My tweedums, lil' Joseph juss fall down n' get ah lil' guava on he head."*

Gauwa Dosey (gaw-ah doh-seh) *Noun* – **1.** a thick, solid, jelly-like jam which has origins in Cuba, but has become known as *'sweet meat'* throughout the Cayman Islands. **2.** a thick jam-like treat, similar to a sweet heavy cake, made entirely from guava. **3.** a traditional Caymanian delicacy, which is sliced into even portions, and served on a slice of bread (just like hard cheese). **Eg.** *"Gimme ah good slice ah gauwa dosey any day n' I'll love you fa life."*

Gee (jee) *Interjection* – **1.** wow. **2.** an exclamation of extreme surprise. **3.** holy mackerel. **4.** oh my gosh! **5.** short for *'geezumpiece'*. **Eg.** *"Gee! You see how furd he kin jump man?"*

Gee-Doh (jee-doh) *Interjection* – **1.** an exclamation of wonder, pleasure, or the like. **2.** to gain an enthusiastic response from a thrilling occurence. **Eg.** *"Gee-Doh, I diddn' know Skinny Minny had buy ah new car."*

Geezum (jee-z'um) *Interjection* – **1.** an expression of excitement and disbelief. **2.** oh goodness. **3.** really? **4.** I can't believe it. **5.** oh-my-gosh. **6.** one's first reaction to a major accident or natural disaster. (used interchangeably with: **Geezumpiece**) **Eg.** *"Geezumpiece! I didd'n tink Iwan woulda mash up da place like diss!"*

George Town (jorge town) *Noun* – **1.** the capital district of the Cayman Islands. **2.** one of the world's leading financial centers. **3.** the second capital district of the Cayman Islands (Bodden Town was first). **Eg.** *"My mail keep gettin' sent ta Guyana and Washington sometimes, cuz dey also have ah George Town."*

George Town Barcadere (jawr'j taown bar-kuh-dehr) *Noun* – **1.** a former name for the embankment at the very end of North Sound Road which opens up to the North Sound. **2.** a boat dock and marina near the CUC power plant. **Eg.** *"I hear Curry used ta go swimmin' by George Town Barcadere till people tell im it wah full ah jellyfish."*

Gg

Ghee (g'ee) *Verb* – **1.** to give. **2.** to present voluntarily and without expecting compensation; bestow. **3.** to hand to someone. **4.** to furnish, provide, or proffer. **Eg.** *"When I finish wit dis movie I gah ghee it ta you, but you bedda cyar it bak Blockbusta when ya finish."*

Giddy-Giddy (gih-deh gih-deh) *Adverb* – **1.** extremely giddy. **2.** affected with vertigo; dizzy. **3.** attended with or causing dizziness. *Noun* – **4.** lightheaded, vertiginous. **Eg.** *"Sometimes when I sleep too much I feel kinda giddy-giddy when I stand up so I juss lay back down n' sleep again."*

Giddy Head (gih-deh hed) *Adjective* – **1.** indecisive and incompetent. **2.** unable to make up one's mind or make constructive decisions. **3.** free-spirited. **Eg.** *"Why you don't try stop foolin' rong wit dem giddy head gyals n' fine ah half-decent woman ta settle down wit?"*

Gig (gihg) *Noun* – **1.** a small wooden toy, often inversely conical, with a point on which it is made to spin. **2.** a store-bought or handmade 'top'. **3.** a favourite pastime among Caymanian boys up until the late 1980's. **Eg.** *"Ian kin spin gig good boy. I see im split Ed gig in two lass week."*

Gillambo (gih-lum-boh) *Noun* – **1.** a species of *Parrotfish*. **2.** brightly-coloured fish which feed on the reefs and excrete particles of sand. **3.** a great source of protein. **Eg.** *"My friend say one time when he wah spearfishin', one Barra eat he Gillambo before he could reel it in, yih'nah?"*

Gine (gyne) *Verb* – **1.** going. **2.** to put into motion. **3.** to head towards a particular direction. **Eg.** *"Boy bobo, I doon' know wah you doin', but I gine home right now n' run my head up in da pillow n' ketch two z's still."*

Ginnall (jin-ul) *Noun* – **1.** an extremely talented con artist. **2.** a person adept at swindling by means of confidence games; swindler. **3.** a liar; thief; cheat; fraud; scam artist; smooth talker. **Eg.** *"You's ah real ginnall doh yih'nah. I nah buyin' nuttin' from you no more."*

Girls Home (gurlz hoom) *Noun* – **1.** a foster home for young girls. **2.** a residential program for young women who are victims of neglect or abuse. **Eg.** *"Me n' Keisha use ta have all kine-ah fun up in Girls Home, boy."*

Gg

Goat Yard (gote yaard) *Noun* – **1.** a neighborhood in the District of West Bay which encompasses the Water Course Road/Boatswain Bay Road junction. **2.** the area of Boatswain Bay Road which begins at the lighthouse and ends near the Turtle Farm. **3.** a neighborhood in West Bay near the sea. **Eg.** *"Robert say Police ketch im ridin' chrew Goat Yard wit no light on he bicycle n' nuttin' nah happin'."*

Go Deh (goh-deh) *Slang* – **1.** exactly right; precisely. **2.** right on. **3.** to express one's agreement with the decision or action of another. **4.** a form of verbal support. **Eg.** *"Yeah, go deh. I knew you could do it!"*

Goggle Eye (gaw-gul eye) *Noun* – **1.** a person with enormous eyes. **2.** a greedy person. **3.** a very nosey person. **4.** a small saltwater fish also known as a *frisky gog* or *bigeye scad*. **Eg.** *"Look ah dah ol' goggle eye ting droolin' ohwah erryting he see nah?"*

Goin' (goh-yin) *Verb* – **1.** the final stage in the four-part structure of a relationship, which involves: *1. talkin' 2. checkin' 3. dealin' 4. goin'.* **2.** commited to a serious relationship. **3.** embarking on a long-term relationship. **4.** having a boyfriend or gyalfriend. **Eg.** *"If you don't stop chattin' up Christina me n' you nah goin' no more."*

Goin' Off (goh-yin awf) *Adverb* – **1.** going crazy. **2.** losing one's sanity. **3.** getting really angry. **4.** losing control. **5.** becoming entempered. **Eg.** *"David be goin' off sometimes at work cuz dem customers be gettin' on he nerves."*

Goin' Out Clothes (goh-in owt kloh'ze) *Noun* – **1.** one's dress clothes. **2.** good clothes. **3.** the best clothes in one's closet. **4.** smart casual or semi-formal attire. **Eg.** *"Richard, you diddn' have ta wear ya goin' out clothes ta come ova my house fa ah babbecue."*

[The] Goldfield (gole-feel) *Noun* – **1.** one of the early turtling schooners, built by the James Arch Shipyard in 1929, and launched amidst much celebration nine months later. **2.** a schooner, weighing 99 tons and measuring 105 feet long, which was the sixth ship to be launched into the waters of Hog Sty Bay during 1930. **Eg.** *"I rememba when dey had say da Goldfield had come back ta Cayman afta bein' all ova da world fa 85 years."*

Gg

Gone Clear (gawn kleer) *Adverb* – **1.** free and clear. **2.** in the clear. **3.** successful. **Eg.** *"Yeah, ya gone clear now doh! I know you had really waugh dah job and ya get it too, dass good man!"*

Good Hair (gud hare) *Noun* – **1.** often considered a superior quality of hair. **2.** having hair that is easier to comb and more attractive than others. **3.** straight hair. **Eg.** *"You cyah say nuttin! You jess get da good hair n' I gah da bad hair. Dah why I gah cream it erry munt."*

Goodnight! (gud-nyte) *Interjection* – **1.** an exclamatory expression of excitement or amazement. **2.** watch out. **3.** a warning of something to come. **Eg.** *"Goodnight! I know he mussa tear up he pants when he fall off dah bicycle."*

Good Treatment (gud treet'ment) *Noun* – **1.** pampering. **2.** charity. **3.** excessive indulgence. **4.** external satisfaction. **Eg.** *"Paula like good treatment y'see? Anytime ya miss 'er juss go down by da spa n' I betcha anyting she gettin' ah massage."*

Government House (guv-ah-ment how'ce) *Noun* – **1.** the official residence of the Governor of the Cayman Islands. **2.** the original administrative offices built for former Commissioner Hirst, from his own plans, at Elgin Avenue, by Edmund Parson, JP and Thomas Coe. in 1972, fire gutted the original Government House, resulting in a tragic loss of Government documents and historical data. **Eg.** *"Dey needa moo Government House cuz da Guv'na should be in ah bigga place since he representin' da Queen."*

Gowament (gow-ah-mehnt) *Noun* – **1.** the government. **2.** the form or system of rule by which a country is governed. **3.** the Cabinet, all Elected Members, departments, statutory authorities, etc... **Eg.** *"I hear one man det used ta wuk fa gowament in India gettin' paid $1 ah day fa he pension. I glad we nah gah deal wit daah."*

Grafitti's (gruh-fee-deez) *Noun* – **1.** a popular nightclub for teenagers in 1990 and 1991. **2.** the best place to wear parachute pants on a Friday night in 1990. **3.** a very successful fundraiser for the Rotary Club in the early 1990s. **Eg.** *"I wish you coulda see me when I used ta be up in Graffitis doin' 'runnin man' all night."*

Gg

Granny (grah-neh) *Noun* – **1.** a grandmother. **2.** an elderly woman. **3.** a fussy individual who has very little or no teeth. **4.** a woman, whose children have children of their own. **Eg.** *"Granny used ta mix up all kinda bush med'sin ta correck my liss tongue, but it diddn' work."*

Granny Behind the Door (grah-neh b'hine da dore) *Noun* – **1.** a really chewy, muscular beef, taken from the base of a cow's neck. **2.** a type of meat that takes forever and a day to chew. **3.** the 'gobstopper' of all beef. **Eg.** *"If I eva have ta eat 'Granny behind the door' again I gah chrow it up. Lass time I nearly get lock jaw from all ah dah chewin'!"*

Granny Dress (grah-neh dreh'ce) *Noun* – **1.** a large ugly dress. **2.** any ill-fitting dress which is either old or unfashionable. **Eg.** *"Mummy, how you expeck me ta wear dah ol' granny dress ta my prom?"*

Granfadda (gran-fah-dah) *Noun* – **1.** the father of one's father or mother. **2.** a forefather. **3.** an old man who smells like vwick's sahwe (vick's rub), chews tobacco, and wears nothing but khaki pants and marina's. **Eg.** *"My granfadda wuz ah really popula man fah some reason. I tink it muss be cuz he wah up in gowament."*

Granfadda Pants (gran-fah-dah pahnt'z) *Noun* – **1.** any tight, unfashionable pants, having no pleats, stitching, or bagginess whatsoever. **2.** really ugly pants. **Eg.** *"Erry time Andrew mama fa'get ta wash he always come school wit deez granfadda pants."*

Grass Piece (grah'ce pee'ce) *Noun* – **1.** an extensive, level or somewhat undulating, mostly treeless tract of land on which cows and horses are free to graze. **2.** piece of bush land for feedin' cows. **3.** a cow pasture. **Eg.** *"Wheneva ya walk chrew Mista Powell grasspiece yau bet'nah be wearin' red cuz dah bull gah run ya ova wit dem horns."*

Gravalishous (grah-vuh-lih-shuss) *Adjective* – **1.** greedy. **2.** excessively or inordinately desirous of wealth, profit, etc. **3.** avaricious. **4.** roots keenly desirous; eager. **5.** conniving; deceitful. **Eg.** *"I keep hearin' det ya gah be careful who ya hang 'rong wit deez days cuz ya gah some gravalishous people who only wauh wah yah gah."*

Gg

Graveyard Fruit (gray'vh yahrd froot) *Noun* – **1.** a local reference to the *Noni* fruit; a greenish-yellow fruit which is prickly on the outside and filled with seeds on the inside (similar to a sour sop), which is commonly found in graveyards throughout the Islands. **2.** *Morinda citrifolia, Noni;* a shrub or small tree in the family *Rubiaceae.* **Eg.** *"Some people tell me mussn' eat dem tings wah dey call graveyard fruit, but I hear it good fa yah still."*

Green (gree'n) *Adjective* – **1.** gullible and inexperienced. **2.** simple; unsophisticated; easily fooled. **3.** having no common sense. **4.** lacking the experience or intellect to comprehend the simplest of things. **Eg.** *"Boy you green doh yih'nah. You don' see he all wah is yoh money?"*

Green Mango (gree'n maiyn'g-goh) *Noun* – **1.** any unripe mango(es). **2.** a Caymanian delicacy. **3.** a favourite snack amongst teenagers. **Eg.** *"Man, I cyah wait till mango season so I kin get my hands on some good green mango wit sauce."*

Ground Provisions (graown pruh-vizgh-unz) *Noun, Pl.* – **1.** any vegetables or other produce which has been grown or cultivated in the earth. **2.** roots and other vegetables grown underground such as: yam, cassava, lettuce and cabbage. **3.** the source of most *'bread kind'* used in traditional Caymanian meals. **Eg.** *"I dunno wah I would do if I diddn' have no ground provisions ta go wit my Fry Snappa."*

Guard House (gard how'ce) *Noun* – **1.** an area in Bodden Town which is located on the left of the first incline as one enters the district. **2.** one of Bodden Town's early lines of defence against invading pirates and Spanish marauders. **3.** a popular picture-taking area for tourists to the Bodden Town district. **Eg.** *"I used ta liwe close by Guard House but afta Iwan I hadda moo dong ta Nortwurd since Bodden Tong had get all mash up."*

Guinep (gih-nip) *Noun* – **1.** *Melicoccus Bijugatus;* a round tropical fruit bearing a large seed and a sweet juicy translucent pulp; encased in a leathery shell. **2.** one of Cayman's favourite seasonal fruits. **3.** a fruit which varies in taste due to the quality of the soil in which the tree is planted. **Eg.** *"All ya gah do is bring one bag ah guineps ta work n' people gah love ya fah life."*

Gg

Gun Bay (guhn bay) *Noun* – **1.** a community in the district of *East End*. **2.** the area between the town of *East End* and the area known as *Colliers*. **Eg.** *"No, fool-eh, I nah from East End, I from Gun Bay."*

Gun Muzzle Pants (guhn muh-zul pahntz) *Noun* – **1.** a fashion trend in which a man's pants are tapered from the hip, straight down to the ankle. **2.** straight leg pants. **3.** a popular way of altering one's pants in the late 1980s and early 1990s. **Eg.** *"I wish I could still wear dem gun muzzle pants I use ta have long time ago."*

Gun Square (gun sk'ware) *Noun* – **1.** a point of defence in the District of Bodden Town in the early days of settlement; identified by two of the original cannons pointing in the ground. **2.** a battery which was very important to Bodden Town as it overlooked the district's principal channels of the day. **3.** a popular picture-taking area for tourists visiting the Bodden Town district. **Eg.** *"I hear dey ketch one man walkin' rong drunk up by Gun Square. Dey say he wah only wearin' he brief n' nuttin' else."*

Gyahbbage (gyah-bidge) *Noun* – **1.** garbage. **2.** a collection of solid or liquid waste. **3.** discarded animal or vegetable matter, as from a kitchen; refuse. **4.** any matter that is no longer wanted or needed; trash. **Eg.** *"Moo frum rong yah wit dah piece ah gyahbbage man."*

Gyahbbage Pan (gyah-bidge pahn) *Noun* – **1.** a trash receptacle. **2.** a wastebasket. **3.** a dumpster. **Eg.** *"Phew! dah ol' gyabbage pan you gah rong da back ah yoh house smell stink!"*

Gyal (g'yull) *Noun* – **1.** any person belonging to the female gender. **2.** a woman or girl. **3.** a female child, from birth to full growth. **4.** a young, immature woman; a young unmarried female. **5.** the opposite of boy. **Eg.** *"Aye you gyal, you waugh come wit me ta Kimmin' Brike fa da weekend ah wah?"*

Gye'n (gye'nh) *Adjective* – **1.** going. **2.** leaving or departing. **3.** the process of moving from one position to the other. (see also: **gine**) **Eg.** *"Morris, I hear say you gye'n Miami diss weekend."*

Gg

Had Went (hahd went) *Verb* – **1.** past tense of the word 'go'. **2.** went. **3.** to have gone before. **Eg.** *"Dah time when me n' Wilfurd had went Miami Carnival, we come back wit nuff gyal phone numbas."*

Hahwe (ha'hwe) *Verb* – **1.** *have*; to possess; own; hold for use; contain. **2.** to hold, get, receive, or take. **3.** to experience. **Eg.** *"I doon' know why, but somehow you juss always hawe ta touch my stuff."*

Hape-neh (hayp-nih) *Noun* – From Old People Times; **1.** half pence; half penny (.5 cents). **2.** the British decimal half penny (1/2 p). **3.** the decimal half penny, worth 1.2 pre-decimal pence. **4.** a small coin, minted in bronze; the smallest decimal coin by both size and value, weighing 1.78 grams and measuring 17.14 millimetres in diameter. **Eg.** *"Deez days yi cyah buy nuttin' wit ten hape-neh's, even if ya wanted ta."*

Harden (hard-inn) *Adverb* – **1.** hard of hearing. **2.** having reduced or deficient hearing ability. **3.** unwilling or unable to learn. **4.** stubborn and ignorant. **5.** fixed or set in purpose or opinion. **Eg.** *"Boy you harden yih'see! Erry time I tell you ta leawe my iPod alone, you keep fassin' wid it like it yours."*

Hardheadedness (hard-hed-id-niss) *Adverb* – **1.** stubbornness. **2.** pigheadedness. **3.** blatant disregard for the law, discipline, or rules of any kind. **Eg.** *"Erryting wah goin' good til Steven come in wit he hardheadedness and switch da channel. Dah how come I nah get ta see how Miss Cayman dress look at Miss World."*

Harlem (ha'ah-lem) *Noun* – **1.** the area of George Town which is located on Mcfield Lane. **2.** the road between Mary Street and School House Road. **3.** a bypass to the Annex Playing Field. **Eg.** *"Man, anytime I needa borra some dollas I kin jess go check Andre down by Harlem, still."*

Hh

Haven (hay-vin) *Noun* – **1.** the first feature length film to be written and directed by Frank E. Flowers Jr. **2.** the first movie filmed entirely in the Cayman Islands. **3.** an independent film featuring nuff nuff Caymanians as extras. **Eg.** *"Frank-eh really did ah good job on Haven, still."*

Hawaiian Sling (hah-why-yun sleengh) *Noun* – **1.** a long, hand-made speargun crafted from PVC pipe, thick rubber bands and string. **2.** a speargun that operates like a slingshot. **Eg.** *"One time, Chris wah walkin' wit one Hawaiian Sling n' accidentleh shoot it chrew he foot."*

Hawk Up (hawk ap) *Verb* – **1.** to make an effort to raise phlegm from the throat. **2.** to bring up cold. **3.** a noisy effort to clear the throat. **Eg.** *"One time when I wah wukkin' supamahkit, Troy had hawk up cold n' spit it on da ceilin."*

Head Top (hed tawp) *Noun* – **1.** the top of one's skull. **2.** the very top of the head. **3.** the hardest bone in the human body. **Eg.** *"Randa got paint all up in her head top when she walk pass dah building way wah unda construction."*

Hear Wah (hare wuh) *Interjection* – **1.** now hear this. **2.** pay attention. **3.** listen closely. **4.** this is the last time I'm going to say this. **5.** heads up. **Eg.** *"Awright, hear wah? I gah jess go check some food while you fix up da place lil' bit n' when I come back we kin start da dominoes."*

Heavy Foot (heh-vih foot) *Noun* – **1.** the inability to control one's foot or feet, properly. **2.** having an affinity for speed. **Eg.** *"Daddy always be screamin' at Dara, cuz she gah one heavy foot n' he tell her she nah gah pass her driver's licence if she doon' slow down."*

Hedgehog (hay'dj hawg) *Noun* – **1.** a *'Balloonfish'* or *'Globefish'* (*Diodon holocanthus*); a species of *'Pufferfish'*, having very long spines on its head and body, while appearing to have dusky bands of colour over its body. **2.** a fish which has the ability to suck in large amounts of water until it is the size of a football. **3.** a bug-eyed fish with crusty lips, large spikes and a flat head. **Eg.** *"Daddy, kin people eat Hedgehog?; or dey juss da kine a fish yah ketch and fling back in da sea?"*

Hh

Hell (hehl) *Noun* – **1.** an area of the district of West Bay which features a unique, complex pattern of pinnacles and miniature ridges intricately sculpted into jagged, sharp-edged masses which are quite hard but at the same time brittle. The formation is said to be about 2 million years old and its gray/blackened colour is due to the weather and algae activity. **2.** the area of West Bay which earned its name after a time when Commissioner Cardinall and a friend were out shooting. After the friend missed a bird, he uttered the words "Oh Hell", which, among other things, led the commissioner to name the place 'Hell'. **3.** an area of the district of West Bay which was formerly known as 'fountain'. **4.** the area comprising of the Hell Gas Station, the Hell Post Office, and the nightclub *Inferno*. **Eg.** *"I dunno how come errybody be teckin' one whole pile ah pitchas ah Hell fah."*

Henry Theatre (hen-reh tee-aye-dah) *Noun* – From Old People Times; **1.** a popular movie theater in the District West Bay, which was located at the corner of Reverend Blackman Road and West Church Street. **2.** a movie theater which sat on the same property as the current Banks Plaza, where the West Bay Licensing office is currently located. **3.** a great place to watch a movie and enjoy various treats during the 1970s and 80s. **Eg.** *"My mama say she kin rememba when people used ta dress up ta da tee and go watch black n' white movies at Henry Theatre."*

He Tree (hee tree) *Noun* – **1.** any species of fruit bearing tree which is infertile or barren. **2.** a 'male tree'. **3.** a fruit tree which is unable to bear viable fruit, although some tend to blossom and produce fruit which are empty or inedible inside. **Eg.** *"I hate when guinep season come. Da only tree close ta my house is ah He Tree n' I nah gah no way ta go lookin' fa ah next one."*

Hiccatee (hih-k-ah-tee) *Noun* – **1.** (also called: *Higgity*) a fresh water *terrapin*. **2.** one of Cayman's rare freshwater turtles, which dwells primarly in ponds and swamps throughout the Islands. **3.** an ugly little snapping turtle. **4.** a species of reptile of the order *Testudines*, of which most of its body is shielded by a special bony or cartilagenous shell developed from its ribs. **Eg.** *"Daddy watch out! You gah run ova dah lil' baby hiccatee! "*

Hh

Hicker (hih-kurr) *Noun* – **1.** any young boy or girl who is a student of George Hicks High School. **2.** a member of the George Hicks High School student body. **Eg.** *"I used ta hate when we would go movies and see all ah dem Hickers runnin' 'bout mekkin' nize."*

Hickly Pickly (hik-leh pik-leh) *Adverb* – **1.** in a state of disorder or disarray. **2.** chaotic. **3.** messy and disorganized. **4.** unbelievably messy. (also: **hicklety-pickle**) **Eg.** *"Sandra! How you expect Jodie Ann to come sleep ova when you gah yoh room so hickly pickly?"*

High Up (hye upp) *Adjective* – **1.** in a euphoric state as a result of inducing alcohol, drugs, etc. **2.** high on drugs. **Eg.** *"Boy, you shoulda see how you had look diss mornin' when you wake up. You wah all high up so I hadda leave ya right deh so ya could ress up lil' bit."*

High Tide (hye tyde) *Adjective* – **1.** shrunken or shortened; as in pants which are unable to reach one's shoes. **2.** old-fashioned clothing. **Eg.** *"I wouldn' be caught dead or alive wit dem ol' high tide pants on."*

Hitta (hih-duh) *Noun* – **1.** a junkie or drug addict. **2.** one who is addicted to narcotics. **3.** a cokehead. (see also: **druggy** or **drughead**) **Eg.** *"You had look like ah hitta dah time when you came school all drug up wit cold medicine."*

Hoggish (hawg-ish) *Adverb* – **1.** coarsely self-indulgent or gluttonous. **2.** selfish. **3.** befitting a hog. **4.** unable to control one's temptation to eat excessively. **Eg.** *"Burman n' Nicole got a divorce cuz erry time they went out he went on too hoggish."*

Hog Plum (hawg pluhm) *Noun* – **1.** *Spondias mombin*; a species of flowering plant in the family *Anacardiaceae*, originating from and distributed throughout the neotropics, including Central America, South America, and the West Indies. **2.** a fruit which has leathery skin and a thin layer of pulp. The pulp is either eaten fresh or made into juice, concentrate, jellies and sherbets. (also called: *Yellow Mombin, Spanish Plum, Gully Plum, Ashanti Plum, True Yellow Mombin, Golden Apple,* or *Java Plum*) **Eg.** *"Bobo, hook meh up wit one ah dem hog plums nah? I nah eat nuttin' all day."*

Hh

Hog Sty Bay (hawg stye bay) *Noun* – **1.** a large bay, (leading into the George Town area) which was originally titled *"Ye Hoggstyes"* in the 1700s, for its modest trade in yams, limes, fowls and hoggs. **2.** the primary location for the annual Schooner Regatta during the early 20th Century. **3.** the body of water in which cruise ships are parked during tourist visits. **Eg.** *"Anytime ya see Hog Sty Bay full ah cruise ships, yih know dem tourist shops gah mek nuff money, n' tourisses gah be walkin' up in down blockin' traffic."*

Holla (haw-lah) *Verb* – **1.** to scream or shout loudly. **2.** a very loud utterance. **3.** to call out to someone from a great distance. **Eg.** *"If somebody axe you fah ah dolla, tell um muss go down in da Sound n' holla."*

Hondas (hawn-duhz) *Adverb* – **1.** hundreds. **2.** the sum of many parts. **3.** a really large number. **4.** nuff nuff. **5.** many many. **Eg.** *"My papa say when he gah ah good can ah flit he kin kill miskittas by da hondas."*

Hongry (hawng-greh) *Adverb* – **1.** hungry. **2.** having a desire, craving, or need for food: feeling hunger. **3.** strongly or eagerly desirous. **4.** marked by a scarcity of food. **Eg.** *"Boy try so go feed dah ol' hongry belly dog."*

Horse Laugh (hawr'se lahf) *Noun* – **1.** an uncontrollable outburst of laughter. **2.** rough and noisy, jolly or rowdy, clamorous, unrestrained laughter. **Eg.** *"Dah time when Samuel had run ta he car in da rain n' slip down in one big puddle ah mud, errybody let out one horse laugh, yih'see."*

Hot Sun (hot sun) *Noun* – **1.** heat which emanates from the sky, causing dryness, skin irritation, allergic reactions, etc. **2.** concentrated heat from the sun. **3.** bright/hot day. **4.** the bathwater of construction workers. **Eg.** *"It's ah good ting I went school fa accountin' cuz I nah inta goin' out in dah hot sun 'bout poundin' nails."*

Hummuck (huh-muk) *Noun* – **1.** a hammock. **2.** a hanging bed or couch made of canvas, netted cord, or the like, with cords attached to supports at each end. **3.** the best thing to have on the beach hanging between two Willow trees. **Eg.** *"Look, get yoh backside outta my hummuck so I kin lay down n' get some ress."*

Hh

Hundareenian (hun-dah-reen-ih-yun) *Noun* – **1.** any person of Honduran origin or descent. **2.** a native or descendant of a native of Honduras. **3.** of or pertaining to Honduras or its inhabitants. **Eg.** *"I gah one Hundareenian friend det be teachin' me all kine ah Spanish n' I kin barely speak English good."*

Hurley's (her-lihz) *Noun* – **1.** Hurley's Supermarket. **2.** a chain of local supermarkets. **Eg.** *"Me n' Jerome used ta meet up by Hurley's wit ouwa bicycles n' go ridin' chrew South Sound."*

Hurtfullest (hert-fuhl-iss) *Adjective* – **1.** the most painful. **2.** full of pain, anguish,; frustration, grief or annoyance. **3.** heartwrenching, disgusting. **Eg.** *"I dunno why Arlette always gah mess wit people man but dah hurtfullest part is dat she already gah one."*

Hydramatic (hy-dra-mah-dik) *Pronoun* – From Old People Times; **1.** an early 'automatic' transmission automobile. **2.** an automatic transmission developed by General Motors's Oldsmobile division. Introduced for the 1940 model year, the Hydramatic was the first fully automatic mass-produced transmission developed for passenger automobile use. **Eg.** *"If yah ewah hear dem ol' people talk 'bout hydramatic, dah na nuttin special; dey jess talkin' bout ah automatic car."*

A really good joke always ends with a Horse Laugh.

Hh

-idge (idjh) *Suffix/Slang* – **1.** an extension or suffix, which can be added to most words for emphasis. **2.** a creative way of making new words. The suffix 'idge' can be added to many words in very creative ways to develop original slang. For example:

Work-idge:	one's job or workplace or work in general.
Stink-idge:	a really foul odor or an ugly object
Mar-idge:	an extension of the name Mario
Car-idge:	one's automobile
Sleep-idge:	having to sleep, or needing to sleep.
Drunk-idge:	hung over; drunk
Nyam-idge:	to eat; consume food or drink
Pipe-idge:	a PVC pipe
Rump-idge:	one's buttocks
Funk-idge:	the scent which eminates from one's shoe

...or any such combination of words and phrases using the suffix '–idge'. **Eg.** *"Yeow!! Wah kine ah stink-idge Leroy goin' on wid up in dah bahtchroom man?"*

Ile (eyele) *Noun* – **1.** oil. **2.** any of a large class of substances typically unctuous, viscous, combustible, liquid at ordinary temperatures, and soluble in ether or alcohol but not in water. **Eg.** *"Richard gah clean off da car port erry Satday cuz he daddy truck leakin' ile."*

In Joinin' (in joy-nin) *Adverb* – **1.** cursive handwriting. **2.** to write in flowing strokes with the letters joined together. **3.** a cursive letter or character. **Eg.** *"In penmanship class Miss Joy say I gah good script but I needa practice my in joinin'."*

Ii

In-Manly (in-man-leh) *Adjective* – **1.** ill-mannered. **2.** impolite; discourteous; rude. **3.** lacking or indicating a lack of good manners. **Eg.** *"Try so don't bring Kenrick no way wit us. He be goin' on too inmanly, man."*

Iron Shore (eye-urn showre) *Noun* – **1.** the common name for *microkarst*, the eroded, ancient reef structure that forms the shoreline in many areas of the Cayman Islands. **2.** a variety of formations with a common, blackened, jagged appearance. **3.** a shoreline which is comprised primarily of large, spikey, dark rocks made of weathered *dolomite*. **Eg.** *"Goin' fishnin' out on dah iron shore is ah real Cayman tradition."*

Ironwood (eye-yun wood) *Noun* – **1.** (*Chionanthus Caymansis*); a large hardwood tree endemic to the Cayman Islands. **2.** a hard, heavy, strong, and termite-resistant tree. **3.** a tree which was used in old people times to create foundation posts for houses and fence posts for yards and grasspieces. **Eg.** *"Daddy, you tink if dey mek ah boat outta Ironwood it would be bullet proof?"*

It's (ih'tz) *Contraction* – **1.** contraction of *there is*. **2.** it is. **3.** there's. **Eg.** *"You cyah hear when I say it's no more corn meal leff ah wah?"*

Ivan (eye-vun) *Noun* – **1.** Hurricane Ivan. **2.** a category four hurricane which devastated the Cayman Islands for 36 hours in September 2004. **3.** the Great Hurricane of 2004. **4.** one of the worst hurricanes to ever hit the Cayman Islands. **Eg.** *"Since Ivan, all now I nah get my house back t'gedda yet."*

Ivanized (eye-vun-eye-z'd) *Adverb* – **1.** permanently affected or afflicted in some way as a result of Hurricane Ivan. **2.** destroyed by Hurricane Ivan. **3.** flood damaged. **Eg.** *"Even doh gow'ment say 10,000 cars had get Ivanized, it still plenty cars on da road t'day."*

I'yurn (eye-vun-eye-z'd) *Adverb* – **1.** iron. **2.** something hard, strong, rigid, unyielding, or the like. **3.** a really strong metal object. **4.** an instrument used for hot pressing clothes. **Eg.** *"Boy yoh clothes mash up. You nah gah no i'yurn at home ah wah?" or "Jed say when he punch Turby in he stomach, it feel like it wah made ouka i'yurn."*

Ii

Jamaykian (juh-may-kee-yun) *Noun* – **1.** any person of Jamaican origin or descent. **2.** a native or descendant of a native of Jamaica. **3.** of or pertaining to Jamaica, or its inhabitants. **Eg.** *"All I kin tell yah is, you gah hawe go check one Jamaykian man name Mr. Brown if ya waugh yoh car fix up good."*

Jam Down (jahm down) *Noun* – **1.** the Caribbean island of Jamaica. **2.** an island in the West Indies, 4413 sq. miles south of Cuba. **3.** the closest neighboring country to the Cayman Islands. (also called: **Jam**) **Eg.** *"I goin' Jam Down fah da weekend ta look some new reggae music."*

Japanee (jah-pah-nee) *Noun* – **1.** any person of Japanese origin or descent. **2.** a native or descendant of a native of Japan. **3.** of or pertaining to Japan or its inhabitants. **Eg.** *"One a deez days, I waugh marry ah pretty Japanee gyal and settle down."*

Jeans Pants (jeenz pahntz) *Noun* – **1.** pants made of jean, denim, or another durable fabric. **2.** pants of various fabrics, styled or constructed like blue jeans. **3.** common everyday pants which are generally durable and comfortable. **Eg.** *"I always gah rememba ta wear my jeans pants ta work on Friday, cuz sometimes I forget n' errybody tell me I be too dress up."*

Jess Cool (jeh'ce kule) – *Slang* – **1.** please relax. **2.** stop right there. **3.** get ahold of yourself. **4.** calm down. **5.** help me out. (see also: **juss cool**) **Eg.** *"Yow, jess cool y'self or else my daddy gah come send you home."*

Jew Plum (jew plum) *Noun* – **1.** a type of 'Tahitian apple' which closely resembles a large guinep, while having a crunchy, tartish meat on the inside. **3.** a favourite Caymanian fruit, whose name is often confused with the 'June Plum'. **Eg.** *"Granfadda, if diss fruit name Jew Plum dah mean I gah be ah Jew ta eat it?"*

Jj

John-Joe (jon-joh) *Noun* – **1.** common household mould. **2.** a fungus that produces a superficial growth on various kinds of damp or decaying organic matter. **3.** the green stuff on stale bread and meat. **Eg.** *"Boy, you cyah see dah bread full ah John Joe ah wah? Doon' eat dat."*

Johnny Cake (jaw-neh kaykh) *Noun* – **1.** a large pancake-like bun, similar to a *Fritter*, made from baking soda, butter, salt, flour, etc. and baked in a frying pan. **2.** a frying-pan-sized fritter, which features a heavy crust on the outside, while being soft on the inside. A Johnny Cake is thick and chewy, and allows for 5-6 servings when cut into equal portions. **Eg.** *"Mama, you kin mek meh ah Johnny Cake wit Swanky fa lunch please? I doo waugh nuttin else."*

Jose's (hoo-sayz) *Noun* – **1.** *Jose's Escape*: a prominent Texaco service station. **2.** a popular gas station located on the corner of Crewe Road and Halfway Pond. **3.** one of the first full-service gas stations in the Cayman Islands. **Eg.** *"I betcha anyting I kin walk from Windsor Park ta Jose's in 20 minutes."*

Juck (juk) *Verb* – **1.** to jerk. **2.** to grab and pull with excessive force. **3.** to draw or haul toward oneself or itself, in a particular direction, or into a particular position. **4.** tug. **Eg.** *"Dah time when I went Graffiti's widdout acksin' my mama, she had come juck me out n' errybody wah laffin' at me."*

Juggy (juh-geh) *Noun* – **1.** the largest piece in a sack of playing marbles. **2.** the big marble. **3.** the best marble to use for clearing the ring. **4.** the most vulnerable marble when being called on by an opponent. **Eg.** *"If you see da size ah my juggy yih nah gah waugh play marbles wit me again."*

Jump-Up Church (juhm'p upp chirtch) *Noun* – **1.** any high-spirited church which involves dancing choirs, tambourines, a live-band and/or an interactive audience. **2.** a lively church. **3.** a non-traditional church. **Eg.** *"One time when Joyce-Ann had acks me ta go church on Sunday, I went wid 'er but I diddn' know it wah gah be ah jump-up church, so I nehva went back."*

Jj

June Plum (joon plum) *Noun* – **1.** a type of *'Tahitian Apple'*, closely related to the *'Hog Plum'*, *'Jew Plum'* or *'Golden Apple'* which comes from an equatorial or tropical tree. **2.** a small green fruit which may be eaten raw, although the flesh is crunchy and a little sour. **3.** a favourite Caymanian fruit whose spikey seed can be replanted easily to bear more trees. **Eg.** *"I rememba when dey had ah nice June Plum tree on Goring Avenue b'fore dey bill dah parkin' lot fa Royal Bank."*

Juss Cool (juss kool) *Slang* – **1.** please relax. **2.** stop right there. **3.** get ahold of yourself. **4.** calm down. **5.** help me out. (also pronounced: *jess kool*) **Eg.** *"Yow! Juss cool nah? All I waugh is ah dolla ta ketch da bus."*

Just Minute (juss mih-nitt) *Adverb* – **1.** almost to the minute. **2.** anytime within the last five minutes. **3.** just now. **Eg.** *"How ya mean you bin waitin' long fa me? I just minute came chrew da door n' you wuz'n yah."*

Juug (juug) *Verb* – **1.** to prick. **2.** to puncture with a needle, thorn, or the like. **3.** to jab the body with a pointed object. *Noun* – **4.** a sharp pain caused by or as if by being pricked. **Eg.** *"If you juug me again wit dah pencil I gah tell Teacha McField."*

June Plums

Jj

Kangaroos (kaing-gah-ruze) *Noun* – **1.** a brand of running shoes which were popular throughout the 1970s and 80s. **2.** the only shoe that had to be inconveniently removed in order to retrieve one's money from built-in zippered pouches on the side, in the tongue and on the back. **Eg.** *"I had all kine-ah kangaroos but my mama ghee um 'way."*

Keds (kedz) *Noun* – **1.** any type of sneaker, regardless of colour, shape or brand. **2.** the first brand of shoes to feature a rubber sole. **3.** the world's first sneaker manufacturer. **Eg.** *"Afta work, all I do is fling down my stuff, put on my track suit n' my keds n' jess go runnin'."*

Keel Out (keele owt) *Verb* – **1.** to stretch out and relax due to fatigue. **2.** laying in a peculiar position. **3.** fully relaxed. **Eg.** *"My cat always be keel out on da settee in da sittin' room."*

Ketch (ketch) *Verb* – **1.** to catch. **2.** to seize or capture, esp. after pursuit. **3.** to lay hold on. **4.** to check or restrain suddenly. **5.** to attend. **6.** to contract an illness. **Eg.** *"If ya doon' get outta dah rain yih gah ketch ringworm."*

Ketchin' (keh-chin) *Noun* – **1.** a popular game for children whereby two teams draw straws (by counting feet) to decide who will become (A:) the chasers, and who will become (B:) the chasees. The B team is based in a central location (its 'home') with members spread across a large field, while members of the A team roam around hoping to tag a member of the B team before they can make it home. The A team has the power to 'freeze' a member of the B team by touch (tagging). B team members can free their frozen teammates by touching them, which allows them to re-enter the game. If the A team manages to 'freeze' (tag) all members of the B team, the game is over. **2.** a great way for children get exercise and learn about teamwork simultaneously.(also known as *"Freeze Tag"*) **Eg.** *"Erry Mondeh mornin' before school start we juss hadda get ah game ah ketchin' ta start da day off."*

Kk

Ketchin' News (ketch-in nuze) *Verb* – **1.** getting up to speed on current events through gossip or spying. **2.** sharing the secrets of unsuspecting people. **3.** listening to bad things about good people. **Eg.** *"If ya see Pat n' Alice sittin' down close t'gedda, all dey doin' is ketchin' news."*

Kick Up (kik-up) *Verb* – **1.** to beat up. **2.** to strike violently or forcefully and repeatedly. **3.** to cause painful injury. **4.** to throw a tantrum. **Eg.** *"If you had walk home wit Julio yestaday he wouldn'a get kick up by dem lil' cruffs."*

Killin' Sleep (kih-lin sleep) *Verb* – **1.** hibernating. **2.** having the best sleep of one's life. **3.** sleeping hard; without regard. **Eg.** *"Anytime you miss Tisha, she be up 'n dah bed killin' sleep, boy."*

Kill Off (kihl awf) *Verb* – **1.** to consume or deplete one's resources to the point of extinction. **2.** to overabuse. **3.** to eat, drink, steal, scavenge, scrounge, etc., so as to exceed the reasonable amount of impact. **Eg.** *"Man, one time me n' Shaykeh had kill off two Foster's bags full ah mangoes n' guineps n' we could barely moo aftawurds, yih'nah."*

Kill Out (kihl outt) *Verb* – **1.** to reduce to utter ruin or nonexistence; destroy utterly. **2.** to make extinct. **3.** to annul; make void. **4.** to encroach on the lives of others without regard. **Eg.** *"Fredrick, now you know it nah necessary ta kill out errybody wit yoh stink cologne juss cuz you goin' out wit Petrina t'night."*

Kimmin' (kih-min) *Noun* – From Cayman Brac; **1.** 'Cayman'. **2.** the way *Brackers* pronounce the word *Cayman*. **Eg.** *"I hate when anybody acks me if people from Kimmin' Braick eat soldier crabs fa breakfast."*

Kin (kin) *Auxilliary Verb* – **1.** can. **2.** able to. **3.** having the ability, power, or skill to. **4.** to have the means, qualifications or possibility. **Eg.** *"If he kin do it, I kin do it."*

Kinense Milk (kin-ents milk) *Noun* – **1.** condensed milk. **2.** whole milk reduced by process of evaporation to a thick consistency, with sugar added. **3.** a very thick milk which requires several parts water prior to use. **Eg.** *"Tonight, I gah bayde, comb my hair, and make me ah nice kinense milk sangwich b'fore I go ta bed."*

Kk

Kink Neck (keenk nek) *Noun* – **1.** acute soreness in the neck, resulting from a bad sleeping position. **2.** a cramp in the neck. **3.** the result of sleeping on too many pillows or laying in an awkward position for a long time. **Eg.** *"I hadda go check one Kyraprackta dis mornin' cuz I had one bad ole' kink neck lass night n' I couldn' get no sleep."*

Kirk Plaza (kurk plah-zah) *Noun* – **1.** the largest supermarket in central George Town during the 1970s, 80s and 90s. **2.** a large, open parking lot which was formerly used as the hub for many taxis and tour buses when the original supermarket was demolished. **3.** the best place to catch a bus to East End or West Bay in 1990. **Eg.** *"When I used ta liwe Prospect I hadda ketch da 5:15 bus by Kirk Plaza ta get home 5:30."*

Kissin' Up (kih-sin uhpp) *Noun* – **1.** kissing and carressing; necking. **2.** making out. **3.** a popular activity in the early stages of a serious relationship. **Eg.** *"Man, dah time when Miss Julie Ann had find Lesa n' Brenton up in dah Grade 5 closet kissin' up, she turn red like ah lopsta."*

Kiss Up (kih'ce uhpp) *Verb* – **1.** to brown nose. **2.** to curry favor or behave obsequiously. **3.** to seek favors from a person. **4.** to follow behind someone who has something of value. **5.** to pretend to be interested in one's company. **Eg.** *"I doon' like da way Charlotte had kiss up ta Mista Wight juss so she could get ah bigga cubicle."*

Kite (kyte) *Noun* – **1.** a traditional Caymanian kite, made of brown paper, dried coconut sticks and twine. **2.** a light frame covered with some thin material, to be flown in the wind at the end of a long string. **Eg.** *"Erry summa all ya could see wah dem pretty kite runnin' chrew Mr. Tommy grasspiece."*

Knee Cup (nee kup) *Noun* – **1.** the knee cap. **2.** the flexible part of the leg between the *femur* and the *shin*. **3.** the knee bone. (also called: **Knee Pan**) **Eg.** *"Dah time when Chunky knee cup had come outta place, I nearly faint 'way when I see it"* or; *"Sweety, if any man put he hand on you, juss close yoh eyes and kick im right in he knee pan."*

Kk

Knife & Fork (nyfe 'n fawrk) *Noun* – **1.** the name of a road in West Bay, approx. several hundred feet past the West Bay Fire Station. **2.** the former name of the road which is currently called 'Earnest Jackson Drive'. **Eg.** *"I dunno who liwe dong in Knife n' Fork, but if dey house ketch fiyah, dey nah ga hawe worry 'bout fiyah truck getting' deh late."*

Knock Knee (nok nee) *Noun* – **1.** *Genu Valgum:* a condition where the knees angle in and touch one another when the legs are straightened. **2.** an inward curvature of the legs, causing the knees to rub together when walking. **3.** the opposite of bow legs. **Eg.** *"Boy, if you had see Poosey runnin' down Sports Complex wit her knock knee, you woulda had ah good laugh."*

Knotty Head (naw-deh hed) *Noun* – **1.** having a head full of tangled hair. **2.** rugged locks of hair. **3.** an idiot. **Eg.** *"Look ah dah ol' knotty head ting ah Carwell 'eh? I tell im muss mix da cement n' he gone look 'bout paintin'."*

Kriss (kriss) *Adverb* – **1.** having the appearance of outstanding quality or superior merit; remarkably good. **2.** extraordinary. **3.** of the highest or finest quality. **4.** exceptional. **Eg.** *"Dem new Jordan's look kriss! Mama, you kin buy um fa me fa my birtday?"*

Krissen (kriss-in) *Verb* – **1.** to make use of for the first time. **2.** to name and dedicate. **3.** to engage in ceremony for a special occasion; however trivial. **Eg.** *"Dis year, when street dance come, I gah hawe krissen my new shoes, still."*

Kunk Out (kunk owt) *Verb* – **1.** to stop working. **2.** to fall into a deep sleep. **3.** to lose consciousness; faint. **4.** to stop operating or functioning. **Eg.** *"One time my car had kunk out on me on Queen's Highway, n' I hadda walk 5 miles ta get gas."*

Kyle (kyle) *Verb* – **1.** to coil. **2.** to wind in continuous, regularly spaced rings one above the other: *always mek sure ya kyle up da hose afta ya use it.* **3.** to wind on a flat surface into rings one around the other. **Eg.** *"Lemme see how fass you kin kyle up dah electrical cord nah?"*

Kk

Lady Hair (lay-deh hare) *Noun* – **1.** *Malpigihia cubensis*; a local fern featuring fine hairs that react to human skin like fiberglass. **2.** an innocuous-looking plant which offers a surprise to unwary hikers as the undersides of the leaves have stinging irritating hairs. **3.** a plant which causes misery for anyone who comes in contact with it. **Eg.** *"Mista Burns-eh say he hadda chop out all da lady hair bush in he grasspiece so he grandchildren could play in it."*

Lass (lahce) *Adjective* – **1.** last. **2.** occurring or coming after all others, as in time, order, or place. **3.** being the only one remaining. **4.** the end or conclusion. **Eg.** *"If it's da lass ting I do, I gah clean out dah garage dis weekend."*

Lass Lick (lahce lik) *Noun* – **1.** a popular children's game, where the object is to become the last one to tag the other. **2.** a common cause for children to be beaten with a tamarind switch because they won't get in the car to leave a friend's house. **Eg.** *"Lass week, me n' Turney wah playin' lass lick so much dat I could barely walk the next day."*

Las Tortugas (lahce tawr-too-gus) *Noun* – **1.** the first name given to the Cayman Islands by the famous explorer Christopher Columbus, due to the turtle population on the beach when he arrived. **2.** a word which simply means "the turtles". **Eg.** *"I nehwa even rememba we wah name Las Tortugas until dey had dah Quincentennial ting up by Lion's Centre."*

Late (layte) *Adjective* – **1.** slow to understand. **2.** behind in time. **3.** delayed in reaction. **Eg.** *"Mama, you so late. You didd'n know Mike Tyson had bite piece ah Holyfield ear off?"*

Lazyritis (lay-zeh-rye-dis) *Noun* – **1.** a stroke of sleepiness or fatigue, usually after a large heavy meal. *Verb* – **1.** an uncontrollable need to sleep after eating. *Adverb* – **1.** compelled to sleep. **2.** a zombie-like state due to overeating. **Eg.** *"Anytime lazyritis start sett'n in, ya gah eyeda tek ah nap or go bade quick time ta get rid ah it"*

Ll

Lead Bonkey (led boung-keh) *Noun* – **1.** an extremely lazy person. **2.** one who is unable to move due to laziness. **3.** overcome by laziness or fatigue. **Eg.** *"One time when I wah wukkin' dong in Dog City, Shaundell had call me lead bonkey cuz I didd'n waugh do no work."*

Leady (lay-deh) *Noun* – **1.** a playing marble made of metal. **2.** the metal bearing in an empty can of spray paint, which can be cleaned and used as a marble. **3.** the best marble to use in most cases. **Eg.** *"If you see da way my leady mash up he taw, you would'n beliewe it."*

Leafy (lee-feh) *Noun* – **1.** a 'common marble' which features a pattern on the inside that closely resembles a leaf. **2.** a leafy looking marble. **3.** any marbles of little value due to commonality. **Eg.** *"Hear wah; I ghee you tree ah deez ol' leafy's fah one ah yoh black magics."*

Leff (leh'f) *Verb* – **1.** leave. **2.** to go out of or away from, as a place. **3.** to depart from permanently. **4.** to let remain or have remaining behind after going, disappearing, etc. **Eg.** *"Aye man, leff me 'lone nah? I tryin' sleep."*

Leffin' (leh-fin) *Verb* – **1.** leaving. **2.** moving. **3.** migrating to another place. **Eg.** *"Boy, when Patrick had tell me he wah leffin' outta yah, I diddn' beliewe it till I see he plane ticket."*

Leguene (leh-gih-nee) *Noun* – **1.** the area behind the Truman Bodden Sports Complex. **2.** a neighborhood located behind the University College of the Cayman Islands. **Eg.** *"My daddy had build nuff nuff houses up in Leguene when he had he own construction company."*

Lemme (leh-mih) *Adverb* – **1.** let me. **2.** to allow or permit. **3.** to allow to pass, go or come. **4.** to cause to; make. **5.** to lend. **Eg.** *"Yow brudda man, lemme ah dolla nah?"*

Licenin' (ly-sin-in) *Noun* – **1.** formal permission from a governmental or other constituted authority to do something, as to carry on some business or profession. **2.** permission to do or not to do something. **3.** a document, plate, or tag that is issued as proof of official or legal permission. **Eg.** *"I hear Bugu had get 6 months in Nortward fah nah licenin' he car fah tree years, n' drivin' it same way. He mussa tink Police wuz'n gah ketch im."*

Ff

Lick (lih'k) *Verb* – **1.** to succeed in striking. **2.** to deal a blow or stroke to. **3.** to hit. **4.** to come against with an impact or collision, as a flying fragment, falling body, slap from the hand, or the like. **Eg.** *"Moo from me or else I gah lick you in yoh ol' big lip."*

Lick Up (lih'k upp) *Verb* – **1.** to collide. **2.** to strike one another or one against the other with a forceful impact; come into violent contact; crash. **Eg.** *"Carson! Stop playin' wit dah skateboard in dis house or else one ah deez days yih gah lick up in dah wall n' knock ya teet out."*

Light (lyte) *Adverb* – **1.** lightheaded. **2.** gullible or unintelligent. **3.** slow to understand. **4.** unable to comprehend the simplest thing. **5.** having little or no common sense. **Eg.** *"You light boy. You tink I would really set yoh head on fiyah?"*

Like Off (lyke awff) *Adverb* – **1.** to become intrigued with a person, place or thing. **2.** to arouse the curiosity or interest of by unusual, new, or otherwise fascinating or compelling qualities. **Eg.** *"Sandra say dah time when she had like off dah new iPhone 12, she woulda work erry day fa ten years just ta buy it."*

Lil' Caymanian' (lill kay-mahn'yun) *Noun* – **1.** any person who was either born on Little Cayman or who resides there permanently. **2.** any person from the sister island of Little Cayman. **Eg.** *"Ta be honest I nah meet ah Lil' Caymanian in my life."*

Lion Tongue (ly-un tung) *Noun* – **1.** a thick, greenish coloured shrub, covered in light coloured spots and having a leather-like texture. **2.** a thick leaf, which can used in lieu of a belt during discipline. **Eg.** *"If you eva hear bug somebody gettin' beat wit piece ah Lion Tongue, ya know dey buhind muss be red."*

Livin' wit Man (lih-vin witt mah'n) *Adverb* – **1.** a situation whereby a young woman has moved out of her parents house to reside with a male. **2.** sharing a home with a man. **3.** shacking up. **4.** an eighteen year-old woman's alternative to living with strict parents. **Eg.** *"Ya see wah happin' ta Janis fah livin' wit man? She hadda go live wit her granny cuz her boyfriend run up all kinda bills n' den leff 'er."*

Ll

Liss Tongue (liss tung) *Noun* – **1.** a lisp. **2.** a speech defect consisting in pronouncing s and z like or nearly like the 'th' sounds of *thin* and *this*, respectively. **3.** to pronounce or speak with a lisp. **Eg.** *"Mummy, Andrew gah liss tongue n' when he talk, spit be flyin' all up in my mout."*

Log Woods (laowg woodz) *Noun* – **1.** a neighborhood in the district of West Bay located between Hell and Watercourse Road. **2.** an area of West Bay which has been known for its abundance of logwood trees. **Eg.** *"I cyah tell da lass time I went dong in Logwoods, but I nah plannin' go deh no time soon nidda."*

Look Yah (luuk yuh) *Interjection* – **1.** look here. **2.** take a look at this. **3.** have a look. **4.** pay special attention. **5.** see here. **Eg.** *"Boy look yah, you cyah hear stop messin' wit my buggin' CD's ah wah?"*

Long Out (lawng owt) *Verb* – **1.** to stretch. **2.** to draw out or extend. **3.** to extend, spread, or place (something) so as to reach from one point to another. **4.** to hold out; reach forth. **Eg.** *"Babies seem ta always long out dey mout before dey start cryin'!"*

Long Wit (lawng witt) *Conjunction* – From Old People Times; **1.** a phrase which is used to identify the relationship of two or more persons. **2.** engaged or married to. **3.** going out with. **Eg.** *"Elmie, tell me something. If Arliss supposed ta be long wit Lucian, how come I see 'er wit Cap'n Curly lass week?"*

Lopsta (lawp-stah) *Noun* – **1.** a lobster. **2.** any of various large, edible, marine, usually dull-green, stalk-eyed decapod crustaceans of the family *Homaridae*, esp. of the genus *Homarus*, having large, asymmetrical pincers on the first pair of legs, one used for crushing and the other for cutting and tearing; the shell turns bright red when cooked. **Eg.** *"Me n' my friend always gah go fa lunch at Lopsta Pot at least once ah week."*

Loud Mout (lowd mowt) *Noun* – **1.** having a big mouth. **2.** a large voice. **3.** having the inability to control one's voice. **4.** a voice which is carried a great distance. **5.** a deep voice. **Eg.** *"You ol' loud mout ting! If I had waugh errybody know my business I woulda print it in da newspaper."*

LI

Lowud (laow-udd) *Adverb* – **1.** the leeward. **2.** the lee side; the point or quarter toward which the wind blows. **3.** the side of something that is sheltered from the wind. **Eg.** *"Dey say dat it's best ta hang yah clothes ta da lowud so dey kin ketch breeze but nah enough dat duss kin blow on um."*

Low Walley (low wah-leh) *Noun* – **1.** the area known as Lower Valley. **2.** a sub-district located between Savannah and Bodden Town, which encompasses Savannah Meadows, Beach Bay and Northward. **3. Eg.** *"I used ta go look fa my friend up in Low Walley but it had get too furd so I stop goin'."*

Luv-in' (luv-inn) *Noun* – **1.** affection. **2.** fond attachment, devotion, or love. **3.** a tender feeling toward another. **Eg.** *"Baby, how come you always gah run off on me and I don't get no luv-in' man?"*

Luv Off (luv awf) *Adverb* – **1.** to become infatuated with someone or something. **2.** to develop a crush on someone. **3.** to have belief that one is in love. **Eg.** *"Breddren! Memba wah I tell you. I luv off dem new Jordans dat jess come out."*

Lyrics (lih-rickz) *Noun, Pl.* – **1.** beautiful words. **2.** having a natural ability to improvise verbally as to convince, or pacify. **3.** the ability to speak convincingly. **4.** a sweet mouth. **Eg.** *"Man, by da time I had finish runnin' da lyrics on dah gyal, her head wah spinnin'."*

Lyurd (lye-urd) *Noun* – **1.** liar; a person who tells untruths. **2.** one who tells lies. **3.** a storyteller. **4.** one who knowingly miscarries information. **5.** a person who loves to talk a lot and will make up anything just to impress others. (also: **Lyud**) **Eg.** *"Troy one ol' lyurd ya see? He always be goin' on bout how he mango tree full ta da brim, so I went ova he house yestaday n' he nah eable had ah mango tree."*

Ll

___

Mad Up (mah'd upp) *Verb* – **1.** in an overwhelming state of frustration. **2.** disappointed; thwarted. **3.** unhappy; unsatisfied. **Eg.** *"I doon know wah you sittin' down deh all mad up fah cuz you nah goin' movies wit dem pile ah hooligans I see you runnin' rong wit."*

Maedac (may-dack) *Noun* – **1.** *Maedac House.* **2.** a popular gas station and mini mart located off of Crewe Road, next to the Lion's Centre. **3.** the best place to clean your car yourself (except for home). **4.** a popular hang out spot for car lovers. **Eg.** *"If you miss Minny, he gah be up by Maedac cleanin' he car."*

Mahmah (mah-mah) *Noun* – **1.** one's mother. **2.** the mother of one's children. **3.** the female figure in a traditional family consisting of a *husband, wife* and *children.* **4.** a grandmother who is close to her grandchildren. **Eg.** *"Mahmah Linette, kin me n' Howard go play kite in Misteh Seppy grasspiece?"*

Maiden Plum (may-din pluhm) *Noun* – **1.** *Comocladia Dentata;* Cayman's equivalent to *Poison Ivy.* **2.** a tall, skinny plant, with grapevine-looking leaves, which bears the ability to infect a person with an uncomfortable rash, boils and sores; usually from a great distance; or through prolonged contact with its leaves or milk. **Eg.** *"Don't you go up in dah maiden plum bush 'bout lookin' mangoes. All you gah do is come back all sore up."*

Maiyngah's (maiyng-ahz) *Noun, Pl.* – **1.** several mangoes. **2.** a collection of favorite Caymanian fruits. **3.** fruits which are best eaten in 'sauce' when green, or while swimming in the sea when ripe. **Eg.** *"Granfadda used ta cyar me ta pick maingah's up'na-bush long time ago."*

Man Business (mahn biz-niss) *Noun* – **1.** private matters which relate to men only. **2.** any topic(s) which may only be of interest to men. **3.** classified male-only conversation. **Eg.** *"Sweetie, ya know we love ya but I gah talk man business wit Cranston right now."*

Mm

Makin' Midnight (may-kin mid-nite) *Verb* – **1.** catching up on lost sleep. **2.** hibernating. **3.** indulging in much needed rest. **4.** giving sleep a new name. **Eg.** *"Aye, you gah ah camera? I waugh tek ah pitcha ah Tisha up in dah bed makin' midnight."*

Manchineel Tree (mahn-chi-neel ch'ree) *Noun* – **1.** (*Hippomane mancinella*) a member of the *Euphorbia* family which includes the ornamental *Poinsettia*. **2.** a dangerous plant, due to its milky sap, which is a strong skin irritant; one should never stand under a manchineel to shelter from rain as the oil contains the irritant. **4.** a tree bearing small, green apple-looking fruits which are poisonous to humans, but eaten by the Cayman Blue Iguana. **Eg.** *"Sonny, I know it rainin' but doon' stand unda da Manchineel tree or else it ga strip ya skin off."*

Mango (maiyng-goh) *Noun* – **1.** large oval tropical fruit having smooth skin, juicy aromatic pulp, and a large hairy seed. **2.** the oblong sweet fruit of a tropical tree, *Mangifera indica*, of the cashew family, eaten ripe, or preserved or pickled. **3.** the tree itself. **Eg.** *"Cuzzy, set meh up wit one mango nah? I nah had nuttin' fa lunch."*

There are several types of Mangoes available throughout the Cayman Islands, although only the following two are considered native:
    Long – (Scruffy, Suga, Flat Seed)
    Round – (a bright yellow mango with
    stringy meat)
Several imported species include:
    Number 11 – (long, w/ a pointed seed)
    Turpentine – (favours an oversized round
    mango with a really strong, pleasant smell)
    Purple Bird – (really purple skin, with
    yellow inside)
    Black – (dark green; skin stays the same
    whether ripe or green)

Mango Bush (maiyng-goh) *Noun* – **1.** a large thick brush; usually in a secluded area, where there is an abundance of Mango trees. **2.** a mango jungle. **3.** the area next to a grass piece, where there are many mango trees. **Eg.** *"I tell you 'bug goin' up in dah mango bush all da time. I know dah Maiden Plum muss feel good now."*

Mm

Mango Stick (maiyng-goh stik) *Noun* – **1.** a long stick used for picking fruit from a mango tree. **2.** a long stick that is much shorter and slender than a breadfruit stick, but much larger than an ackee stick. **3.** a mango picking stick. **4.** a homemade fruit picker. **Eg.** *"Lilly, go so bring me my mango stick nah? I waugh pick some fah Mista Arlee wife so I kin cyar dem ta church t'night so ghee her."*

Man Licks (mahn-likz) *Noun, Pl.* – **1.** strikes or blows which are delivered by a woman with the force and commitment of a man. **2.** to hit as hard as a man. **3.** hard hitting. **Eg.** *"Wheneva Tara used ta get in fights wit her sista, all yih could hear is one whole pile ah man licks ih'nah."*

Mannish (mah-nish) *Adjective* – **1.** being typical or suggestive of a man rather than a woman. **2.** resembling a man, as in size or manner. **3.** characteristic of, or natural to a man. **Eg.** *"Some people say Claudette look kinda mannish but I tink she still gah some girly girly ways."*

Manowar (mahn-a-wawr) *Noun* – **1.** a large bird which spends most of its time soaring above large bodies of water, in search of fish and other game. The body is mostly black, with a long beak, strong, stiff wings and a forked tail. **2.** the large black birds often seen circling over the beachside fish market near North Church Street. **Eg.** *"Anytime ya go out fishin' in a boat, it good ta look up cuz if yah see manowars circlin' dah mean fish close ta da surface."*

Man Shoes (mahn shooze) *Noun* – **1.** a young boy's interpretation of very elegant dress shoes which resemble those that a man would wear to work or church. **2.** hard shoes. **3.** a boy's dress shoes. **Eg.** *"Lass week Satday, Mama mek me an Kirwin put on uwah man shoes so we cun go walkin' out in tong."*

Marina (mah-ree-nah) *Noun* – **1.** a man's white, sleeveless undershirt. **2.** a tight-fitting tank top. **3.** a close-fitting, low-cut top having shoulder straps and often made of lightweight, knitted fabric. **4.** the equivalent of a 'wifebeater'. **Eg.** *"If ya see me go outside in my marina, dem miskittas gah have me all bite up by da time I come back in."*

Mm

Marl Road (mah'rl rode) *Noun* – **1.** the word on the street. **2.** hearsay. **3.** what people are saying. **4.** the latest news or gossip. **5.** a road made of marl. **Eg.** *"I just goin' by marl road still. People say Shekira used ta check Rodney, but she get ketch kissin' Larden ova by Marcella house. Wahhename nearly kick Larden ta pieces n' he run home ta he mama."*

Mash Up (masche upp) *Adverb* – **1.** haggard; having a gaunt, wasted, or exhausted appearance, as from prolonged suffering, exertion, or anxiety; worn. **2.** the state of one's appearance due to lack of sleep or rest. **3.** wasted. **Eg.** *"Bobo, you bedda try so go back ta bed cuz you look all mash up man."*

May Cow (mey kow) *Noun* – **1.** a folklore created by early farmers on the island of Cayman Brac to keep children away from the mango trees. **2.** a ghost story similar to the *Rolling Calf*, and derived from lower Caribbean bedtime stories. **3.** an old wives fable featuring a mythical cow-like creature with fiery red eyes, stripes on its body, and a large chain around its neck. **4.** a ghost story created to scare children to sleep. **5.** a form of 'duppy' (spirit), which is also referred to as *Willgo, Old Willie Go, Rolling Calf* and *Roaring Calf*. **Eg.** *"Loyce Ann say when she wah small, if you had tell her May Cow wah comin', she wah in dah bed n' out like ah light before you could cunk ta tree."*

May Pole (mey pole) *Noun* – From Old People Times; **1.** a traditional Caymanian 'ribbon dance', which involves a tall pole (like a flag pole), from which several ribbons are stretched out and held by dancers. The dancers move to traditional folk music, while weaving in and out of each other; this is especially attractive and entertaining to onlookers. **2.** a tradional dance, similar to the quadrille, but using ribbons and a pole. **3.** a social dance which originated in England as part of the May Day celebrations. **Eg.** *"Erry Agricultcha Fair yih kin see da East End Quadrille Troop dancin' May Pole."*

Meany (mee-neh) *Noun* – **1.** one who has the tendency to disappoint. **2.** a mean person. **3.** one who does not give in to the requests of others. **4.** a scrooge. **5.** a cheapskate. **Eg.** *"Mummy, Darwin' is ah ol' meany. He doon' waugh me play wit he G.I. Joes."*

Mm

Meat Head (meet hed) *Noun* – **1.** extra skin on the back of the head which forms into rolls when the head is tilted backwards, as in looking up. **2.** fatty, loose skin on the back of the head. **Eg.** *"Ahh, haaah! You gah meat head, doh!"*

Meat Kind (meet kine) *Noun* – **1.** any type of meat that is the focal point of a traditional Caymanian meal. **2.** roast beef, Cayman-Style Beef, curry chicken, pork, spare ribs, etc. **3.** an order of cooked meat that is accompanied by several sides, including rice, macaroni, cole slaw, and mash potatoes. **Eg.** *"You nah gah have no meat kind wit yoh dinna, Mr. Frank?"*

Meckin' Down (mehk-in dawng) *Verb* – **1.** approaching. **2.** of the relative near future. **3.** the event of one object coming closer to another. **4.** the temporal property of becoming nearer in time. **5.** the act of drawing spatially closer to something. **Eg.** *"Boy, try so hurry n' nail up dah plywood on dem windows. You cyah see bad wedda meckin' down now ah wah?"*

Meenayse (mee-naze) *Noun* – **1.** mayonnaise; a thick dressing of egg yolks, vinegar or lemon juice, oil, and seasonings, used for salads, sandwiches, vegetable dishes, etc. **2.** mayonnaise (1807), said to have been named in allusion to *Mahon*, seaport capital of island of *Minorca*, captured by France 1756; the sauce introduced in commemoration of the victory. But the dates make this seem doubtful. Shortened form *mayo* first attested c.1930. **Eg.** *"Hi, kin I hawe some meenayse on my sangwich please?"*

Merengue Town (mih-ring-eh tawng) *Noun* – **1.** the neighborhood located along Boilers Road. **2.** a popular nightclub located on Boilers Road. **3.** the area between Walkers Road and South Church Street. **Eg.** *"If yah waugh look ah nice Spanish woman, jess go dong by Merengue Town any Wednesday night."*

'Mericans (mear-ih-kunz) *Noun* – **1.** Americans. **2.** any group of tourists which may have originated in the United States or Canada. **3.** tourists. **Eg.** *"Anytime ya see dem 'Mericans walkin' bout da street when cruise ship in, it make yah kine ah jealous cuz dey kin walk 'rong wit nuttin' but baydin' suit n' we gah dress up erry way we go."*

Mm

Mess Around (meh'ce ah-rownd) *Interjection* – **1.** an exclamation of surprise, wonder, pleasure, or the like. **2.** excitement, interest, great pleasure, or the like. **Eg.** *"Wauugghhh! Mess Around! I always know ya woulda get in ta college but I diddn' tink ya woulda get ah scholarship too."*

Messmaker of the World (mehce may-kuh uv da wurl) *Noun* – **1.** a title given to one who is talented at making a mess of everything. **2.** the supreme messmaker. **3.** a very clumsy person who tends to drop and spill everything. **4.** a super clutz. **5.** a butterfingered buffoon. **Eg.** *"Anhh-huh! Mr. Messmaker of the World. Dah wah ya get fah fassin' wit my blenda. I gah mek ya clean up all ah diss condense milk an' waddamelon mess right now."*

Michette (mih-shet, mah-chet or mah-sheet) *Noun* – **1.** a common household machete. **2.** a large heavy knife used esp. in Caribbean countries in cutting sugar cane and clearing underbrush and as a weapon. **3.** the weapon of choice for most fights during the 1990s. **Eg.** *"One time Carlos had tell me 'bout how he wah diggin' ah hole wit he michette ta plant yams n' he slice he foot open on da blade."*

Milo (my-low) *Noun* – **1.** a popular brand of hot chocolate, which has been the standard for several decades. **2.** the breakfast of champions. **3.** a hot drink. **3.** an alternative to a cup of tea. **Eg.** *"My Granny used ta mek da bess Milo in all ah Wess Bay."*

M'lowe (mih'luwe) *Noun* – From West Bay; **1.** my love. **2.** my sweetheart. **3.** my friend. **Eg.** *"M'lowe, you cyah get me some wadda t'drink ah wah?"*

Mindin' Baby (myne-in bay-beh) *Verb* – **1.** attending to a young baby. **2.** taking care of one's child. **3.** watching over a crib or bed while a baby sleeps. **4.** staying home to take care of one's child. **5.** responding to one's duty as a mother. **Eg.** *"Wah in dah world you know about mindin' baby?"*

Mines (mynez) *Pronoun, Pl.* – **1.** belonging to oneself. **2.** the nominative singular pronoun used by a speaker in referring to himself or herself. **3.** used to indicate the one or ones belonging to *me*. **Eg.** *"I kinda like da way yoh dog look, but mines look betta, still."*

Mm

Miskittas (miss-kid-uz) *Noun, Pl. –* **1.** mosquitos. **2.** any of numerous dipterous insects of the family *Culicidae*, the females of which suck the blood of animals and humans, some species transmitting certain diseases, as *malaria* and *yellow fever*. **3.** really annoying insects. **4.** large biting insects which come out in abundance after a rain. (also called: **Gallon Nippers**) **Eg.** *"I ready fah dem miskittas t'night. I gah my smoke pan, my miskitta stick, my fly swat, fly paper, n' da 'fogga commin' chrew 'rong sebb'm-a-clock."*

Miskitta Plane (miss-kih-duh pleen) *Noun –* **1.** a small black and yellow cropduster type of plane which sprays the entire Island to kill mosquitoes. **2.** the mosquito spray plane. **3.** a small plane owned by the Mosquito Research Unit. **Eg.** *"Anytime ya see dah miskitta plane comin', mek sure ya close ya eyes or else dey gah get burn wit da stink spray."*

Miskitta Stick (miss-kih-dah stik) *Noun –* **1.** a special brand of green, outdoor mosquito repellant coils, designed to keep mosquitoes away from humans. **2.** a mosquito repellent, of which the active ingredient is *d-trans allethrin*, and having the ability to produce a smoldering chemical vapour (to ward off mosquitos) when lit. **3.** a revolutionary replacement to the Cayman smoke pan. **Eg.** *"Afta Ivan, I hadda go out n' buy bout ten box ah miskitta sticks cuz my yaad wah full ah wadda n' we neva had no powa."*

Mission (mih-shun) *Noun –* **1.** an intimate encounter during the after hours. **2.** late night courting. **3.** to visit one's boyfriend or girlfriend late at night, so as to not disturb his or her family. **4.** a long journey to a friend's house in the middle of the night. **Eg.** *"One time, I see Alrick walk from Wess, all da way Sawannah juss ta go check Hilary. Now dah wah ah serious mission."*

Miss Ma'am (mih'ss ma'ahm) *Noun –* **1.** a young lady who may have the tendency of behaving like an older woman. **2.** a very mature female child. **3.** a mature teenage girl. **4.** a girl who may either be dressed like an older woman or conduct herself in such a manner. **Eg.** *"Yes, miss ma'am. You tink cuz you gettin' ready fah college now you kin run abug all time ah night wit God knows who, doin' who knows what?"*

Mm

Mista Arthur's (miss-tuh ar-tuz) *Noun* – **1.** one of the longest standing all-purpose stores on Grand Cayman. **2.** a 7-11 mini mart located on the waterfront near Burger King. **3.** a great place to get an Island Taste Patty, a newspaper and Pepsi for breakfast. **Eg.** *"Boy, I dunno how Mr. Arthur's shop lass so long in Cayman wit all da competition we gah deez daze."*

Mista Man (mihs-tah mahn) *Noun* – **1.** a young boy or teenager who has the tendency to behave as if he were an adult. **2.** a boy who does not know his place. **3.** a phrase used to identify a young boy who is in trouble. **Eg.** *"Yeah Mista Man. So you feel you ah big shot now cuz you win all kinda track n' feel trophies lass munt? Well, I gah show you who still boss; ya grounded till dah end ah da munt!"*

Misteh (miss-teh) *Noun* – From Old People Times; **1.** mister. **2.** a conventional title of respect for a man, prefixed to the name and to certain official designations. **3.** the proper way to address an older man, regardless of affiliation. **Eg.** *"Misteh Frank always seem ta stop 'bout diss muchness from da garage wall. One ah deez dayz he gah hit it."*

Mix-Up Business (mikz-up biz-niss) *Noun* – **1.** confusion. **2.** a misinterpretation; misconception; misjudgement. **3.** an unfortunate predicament. **Eg.** *"My uncle had went jail one time fa some kinda mix-up business n' he say he nah goin' back."*

Miya Zwell (my-ah-z'well) *Adverb* – **1.** a consolidation of the phrase "may as well". **2.** to disregard conventional methods. **3.** to go ahead; regardless of the outcome. **Eg.** *"I know it gah be hard still, but we miya zwell break up now, cuz we nah gettin' along, n' I doo' waugh have nuttin' more ta do wit you."*

Mizzarebble (mih-zah-reh-bull) *Adverb* – **1.** a mispronunciation of the word 'miserable'. **2.** wretchedly unhappy, uneasy, or uncomfortable. **3.** deserving or inciting pity. **Eg.** *"Boy sometimes deez miskittas kin mek ya feel mizzarebble y'see? Especially when it hot n' da fan nah coolin' good".* or; *"Boy my granfadda mizzarebble yih-see? All he do all day is stay home n' cuss 'bout politicians, da light bill, flies on he plate, n' how he pension soon run out."*

Mm

MLA (em elle aye) *Noun* – **1.** an elected Member of the Legislative Assembly. **2.** one of over a dozen elected members of the Assembly which represents the Islands' six voting districts. **3.** a Cayman politician. **4.** a current member of government. **Eg.** *"Kurwell say anytime he hawe any trubble wit people messin' wit he cows, he jess go check ah MLA n' dey try dey bess ta sort it out fah im."*

Mobbies (maw-biz) *Noun, Pl.* – **1.** small non-threatening brown flies which circulate around stale foods; especially fruits. **2.** small fruit flies – usually found circulating around a bag of ripening mangoes. **3.** mango flies **4.** brown flies. **Eg.** *"Look ah dem ol' mobbies, eh? Ya cyah leave food out fa too long or else dey gah come rong it."*

Mom (mawm) *Noun* – **1.** the title of a woman who is the mother of children that are either rich, well-cultured, or have spent some time living in the United States or Canada. **2.** a contemporary word used among Caymanian children to identify the mother. **3.** the title of choice among contemporary Caymanian women, due to it's elitist appeal over the word 'mahmah'. **4.** a word that is more attractive than 'mummy'. **Eg.** *"When we go Canada fah summa, my mom is gonna take me ta see killer whales."*

Money Man (muh-neh mahn) *Noun* – **1.** a male individual who is known to carry a significant amount of cash on his person at all times. **2.** a rich person. **3.** a prime target for beggars. **Eg.** *"Aye, money man; lemme ah dollah nah? I jess waugh buy one small dinna from Welly's."*

Monkey Brown (mung-keh brow'n) *Adjective* – **1.** a derogatory term used to describe a person who shares a similar complexion to that of a monkey or chimpanzee. **2.** a dark, chocolate-brown skinned person. **3.** a nickname for a dark brown person. **4.** a chocolate brown colour. **Eg.** *"You shoulda see dah lil' clot Sandra ghee Yolanda fah callin' her mama 'monkey brown'."*

Monkey Town (mung-keh tawng) *Noun* – **1.** a nickname for the area between Central and Scranton where houses are conjested and trees are abundant. Hence the name 'Monkey Town'. **2.** a source of excellent cooked food and many talented football players and business people. **Eg.** *"Some ah Cayman best footballas come from Monkey Town."*

Mm

Moo (moo) *Verb* – **1.** move. **2.** to pass from one place or position to another. **3.** to force someone out of the way. **4.** to take action; proceed. **Eg.** *"Boy, try so moo frum me wit dah fooshniss."*

Mop Head (mawp hed) *Noun* – **1.** the state of one's hair, which may closely resemble a mop. **2.** thick, stringy hair, which may be wet or dry but literally uncombable. **3.** really thick hair; knotted dreadlocks. **Eg.** *"Boy, look ah dah mop head you gah deh. You cyah try so go cut dat ah wah?"*

More Bedda (moh're beh-dah) *Adverb* – **1.** of superior quality or excellence. **2.** morally superior; more virtuous. **3.** larger; greater. **Eg.** *"Gran-fadda, you kin buy me a new bicycle fa Christmas? I see one det more bedda dun wah I gah now n' it look kriss too."*

Morrows (maw-rose) *Adverb* – **1.** tomorrow or the next day. **2.** a future period in time. **3.** some future time. **4.** see you later. **Eg.** *"Bobo, I gah check yah in da morrows, still."*

Morta 'n Pissle (mawr-dah n' pissul) *Noun* – From Old People Times; **1.** *Mortar and Pestle*; a traditional cooking instrument – the *Mortar*, was made from the bark of a tree, measuring approx. three feet tall, and having the center carved out in a deep, dish-like shape. the *Pestle*, was made of solid wood, and shaped like a chubby baseball bat. Various grain, coffee, and vegetables were placed inside the *Mortar* for grinding using the *Pistle* to pound (mash) them into powders or sauces. **Eg.** *"I hear dey gah lil' small souvenir Morta 'n Pissle up by Pedro Castle deez days, so tourisses kin see way we come from."*

Mout (mowt) *Noun* – **1.** one's mouth. **2.** the opening through which an animal or human takes in food. **3.** the oral cavity considered as the source of vocul utterance. **4.** the area of the human body which includes the lips, jaw, tongue, and teeth. **Eg.** *"Hush ya mout! You cyah hear wah I say ah wah?"*

Mout Champion (mowt cham-pee-yun) *Noun* – **1.** a braggart. **2.** one who exhibits self-importance; big talk. **3.** a very boastful and talkative person. **Eg.** *"Doon' lissin' ta wah Marvin say sometimes. He ah ol' mout champion n' ya cyah truss im."*

Mm

Muchness (mutch-niss) *Adverb* – **1.** a measure of distance between two objects or places. **2.** quantity, or degree. **3.** an approximate measurement. **3.** just about. **4.** relative closeness. **Eg.** *"Wah Jermaine kickin' up all kine ah fuss fah? All I tek is 'bout diss muchness ah he lemonade."*

Mucky Face (muh-kih fayce) *Adjective* – **1.** a face filled with dirt or grime, mixed with water, sweat or another liquid. **2.** a nasty looking face. **3.** a face full of mucus. **4.** the result of crying with too much make-up on. **Eg.** *"Look ah her mucky face man? You eva see something look like dah before?"*

Mudda Country (muh-dah kun-treh) *Noun* – **1.** the 'Mother Country; a kingdom in NW Europe, consisting of Great Britain and Northern Ireland. **2.** the country from which some of the first settlers of the Cayman Islands originally came. **3.** the country which has claimed ownership over the Cayman Islands. **Eg.** *"Dis year, I doin' sump'm different fa summa. Me n' my wife gyne England ta see wah da mudda country look like once n' fa all."*

Muhbee (muh-bee) *Helping Verb* – From East End; **1.** must be. **2.** obliged or bound by an imperative requirement. **3.** compelled to either fulfill some need or to achieve an aim. **Eg.** *"Boy, you muhbee stchupid if you tink I gah lend ya my new fishin' line ta go out on dah iron shore."*

Mummah (muh-maah) *Noun* – **1.** one's mother. **2.** a grandmother. **3.** an older mother. **4.** a grandmother who is close to her grandchildren. **Eg.** *"Juss acks yah mummah n' she kin tell ya how we used ta play when we wah small."*

Mummy (muh-meh) *Noun* – **1.** mother. **2.** a contemporary word used among Caymanian children to identify the mother. **3.** the title of choice among contemporary Caymanian women, due to it's elitist appeal over the word mahmah. **Eg.** *"My mummy say she gah buy me ah Xbox fah Krissmuss diss year."*

Muss (muh'ce) *Auxilliary Verb* – **1.** must. **2.** to be under the necessity to; need to. **3.** to be compelled in order to fulfill some need or achieve an aim. **4.** to feel urged to;

Mm

Muss (muh'ce) *Auxilliary Verb - (continued)* ...ought to. (also interjected as: **Mussa**) **Eg.** *"Nah-naah! I nah drivin' all ah way Wess Bay jess ta get BBQ chicken from Liberty's."*

Mussle Up (muss-el up) *Adverb* – **1.** very muscular. **2.** of or pertaining to muscle or the muscles. **3.** having very well-developed muscles; brawny. **4.** resembling a bodybuilder. **Eg.** *"Man, you shoulda see how Lennox wah all mussle up dah time when he wah trainin' fah dah bodybuildin' championships."*

My Boy (mye boye) *Personal Pronoun* (2nd or 3rd. person singular, masculine) – **1.** reference to one's close friend, or acquaintaince. **2.** a common phrase used to identify a particular person without giving a name. **3.** one's friend. **Eg.** *"Tell meh sump'm my boy, you gah eat dah piece ah cassava cake or I kin have it?"*

My Lil' Friend (mye lil fren) *Pronoun* – **1.** a woman's close male friend. **2.** a woman's pet name for a young man who is too young to start a relationship with, but still a close friend. **3.** a male security guard or store clerk who has a close personal relationship with a woman. **Eg.** *"Try so leave my lil' friend alone nah? He nah no hurt ta nobody."*

My Mama (mye mah-mah) *Pronoun* – **1.** a third-person reference to one's mother. **2.** mother; mummy; mama; mom. **Eg.** *"Leon, doon' mess wit my G.I. Joes or else I gah tell my mama and you nah ga be my brudda no more."*

My Sweetums (mye swee-dum'z) *Pronoun* – **1.** a nickname for a young baby. **2.** an expression of passion or excitement for something cute; as in a young baby. **Eg.** *"Look ah my sweetums eh? I lowe he lil' pretty eyes."*

My Sweetums! This baby is so cute!

Mm

Naah (na'ah) *Adverb* – **1.** no. **2.** a negative used to express dissent, denial, or refusal, as in response to a question or request. **3.** an utterance of the word "no". **4.** to reject, refuse approval, or express disapproval of. **Eg.** *"Wah? Naah. I know it could'n ah go like daht or else I would'n be yah right now."*

Naah-Nah (nah-naaah) *Noun (informal)* – **1.** absolutely not; no. **2.** no way; no how. **3.** not at all. **4.** objection to a particular gesture or presumption. **Eg.** *"Naah-nah! Who you tink you is, messin' wit my new Benz when I jess get it?"*

Nable (nay-bull) *Noun* – **1.** one's navel; belly button. **2.** the central point or middle of any thing or place. **3.** the mark on the surface of the abdomen of mammals where the umbilical cord was attached during gestation. **Eg.** *"Aye, you doon' see yoh nable showin' ah wah? Try so go put on ah longa blouse."*

Nah (n'uh) *Adverb* – **1.** not. **2.** a word used to express negation, denial, refusal, or prohibition. **3.** in no way; to no degree. **4.** absolutely not. **Eg.** *"I guess I gah have ta try harda from now on or else I nah gah get da raise I need ta pay my mortgage."*

Nai'ema (nye-eh-muh) *Adverb* – **1.** won't even. **2.** will not. **3.** more than likely will not. **Eg.** *"If ah nudda hurricane strike Cayman, we nai'ema gah hawe worry bug nuttin' cuz we already know how deal wid it now."*

Needlecase (nee-dul kayce) *Noun* – **1.** the *Dragonfly*. **2.** any of numerous stout-bodied, nonstinging insects of the order *Odonata* (suborder *Anisoptera*), the species of which prey on mosquitoes and other insects and are distinguished from the damselflies by having the wings outstretched rather than folded when at rest. **Eg.** *"Gee! I know da way ya see ah whole pile ah needlecase."*

Nn

Neese Berry (neeze beh-reh) *Noun* – **1.** the *Naseberry*. **2.** the fruit of the sapodilla, *Manilkara zapota*. **3.** the *sapodilla* tree. **4.** an evergreen tree of the Caribbean and Central America, having latex that yields chicle and edible fruit with sweet yellow-brown flesh. **Eg.** *"Aye, come so pick me one neese berry nah? I cyah clime cuz my back hurtin' from playin' football all ah yestaday."*

Nehwah (neh-wah) *Adverb* – **1.** never. **2.** not ever; at no time. **3.** not at all; absolutely not. **4.** to no extent or degree. **Eg.** *"Daddy! You rememba da lass time you say you wah gah cyar me fishnin' n' you nehwah did it? We kin go diss Easta instead?"*

Nehwah Happin' (neh-wah hap-in) *Adjective* – **1.** no way. **2.** not now, not ever. **3.** forget it. **Eg.** *"Uh-ugh! Nehwah happin'! You tink you kin jess come in my room n' run my a/c n' I wuzz'n gah say nuttin? You muss be mad."*

Nevyew (neh'v-yoo) *Noun* – **1.** one's nephew. **2.** the son of one's sister or brother. **3.** a son of one's spouse's brother or sister. **4.** a special child. **Eg.** *"I like ta watch my lil' nevyew (nephew) sleepin' yih'see?"*

New Brand (nyoo bran) *Adjective* – **1.** 'brand new'. **2.** entirely new. **3.** completely new. **4.** a recent purchase which is in immaculate condition. **Eg.** *"Erry time dey have ah reggae concert, Kursley always gah buy ah new brand pair ah shoes ta go out wit yih'nah?"*

Newlands (nyoo-lundz) *Noun* – **1.** a sub-district of Savannah. **2.** the housing community which surrounds the International College of the Cayman Islands, and the Rackley Canal. **3.** a quiet and peaceful place to live. **4.** a great place to raise cows and horses. **Eg.** *"If you cun hitch all a way Prospect, you cun hitchin' lil furda an reach Newlands, still"* or; *"I hear dem people from Newlands lowe country music and raise cows fa fun."*

Next Man (nexx mahn) *Adjective/Slang* – **1.** the other guy. **2.** an unknown person. **3.** the competition. **4.** that guy. **5.** one who cannot be named. **Eg.** *"Dey say Burney hadda break up wit Christy, cuz he find out she wah wit nex man when he went way ta college."*

Nn

Nickas (nih-kuhz) *Noun, Pl.* – **1.** a group of small, dark gray seeds, mostly flat or odd-shaped; which become hot when rubbed against a hard surface, such as concrete. **2.** hot seeds, which young boys use to burn eachother as a practical joke. **3.** a group of gray seeds from the *Cock Spur* plant, which tend to grow in the wild thickets throughout the Islands. **Eg.** *"Miss Junilee say she gah fix Lil' Frankie fah puttin' dem nickas down in da back ah her pants suit."*

Nidda (nih-duh) *Conjunction* – **1.** neither; not either, as of persons or things specified. **2.** not one or the other. **3.** not one person or the other; not one thing or the other. **Eg.** *"Bobo tell me something? You nah gah nidda season salt we kin use ta mek 'sauce' fah deez green maiyngah's?"*

Nigga Bible (nih-guh by-bull) *Noun* – From Old People Times; **1.** a fried bun, similar to a fritter, which is usally around ¾ in. thick, and whose ingredients are; baking soda or baking powder, mixed w/water and salt, flattened and then fried in oil. The outer crust is browned according to the preference of the cook. **Eg.** *"Granny you kin make me some nigga bible diss weekend please?"*

Niggaritis (nih-gah-rye-diss) *Noun* – **1.** a sudden stroke of laziness following consumption of a large filling meal. **2.** a sleeping disorder linked to the consumption of heavy foods. **3.** a zombie-like state due to overeating. (also called: *Lazyritis*) **Eg.** *"Burney mussa get struck by niggaritis diss weekend or someting. He nah come out ta even wash he face or scratch he b'hind."*

Nip (nihp) *Noun* – **1.** a small quantity (mostly of a drink), such as a shot, of liquor. In relation to spirits it tends to refer to a small, unmeasured quantity, a third of a pint (189ml) **2.** one of the three legal sizes for draught beer glasses; formerly used for very strong beer. **Eg.** *"Sissy, I jess goin' down ta da store ta get me ah lil' nip. Da one I gah now finish out."*

Nize (nyze) *Noun* – **1.** sound, esp. of a loud, harsh, or confused kind. **2.** a disturbance, especially a random and persistent disturbance, that obscures or reduces the clarity of a signal. **Eg.** *"Aye man! Stop mekkin' nize wit dah car fa I tell yoh daddy."*

Nn

Noblin (naw'b-lin) *Noun* – **1.** having a large nob (a bulbous protrusion) on the back of one's head. **2.** a round head. **3.** a big head. **Eg.** *"Gee, look ah dah piece ah noblin you gah deh man? I know you mussa gah nuff brains, still."*

No-Nuttin' (noh nutt'n) *Adverb* – **1.** an insignificant person or thing. **2.** a nobody. **3.** unimportant, trifling, or petty. **4.** too small to be important. **5.** of no consequence, influence, or distinction. **Eg.** *"You expeck ta put one ol' no-nuttin against Manchesta n' wonda how come dey lose? You bin smokin' breadfruit leaf ah wah?"*

Norrud (naw-rud) *Noun* – **1.** to the north. **2.** a cardinal point of the compass, lying in the plane of the meridian and to the left of a person facing the rising sun. **3.** in, toward, or facing, the north. **Eg.** *"Bobo, look yah, I bin ah Sea Captain now fah twenny fiwe years, so if I say pint da boat ta da norrud, dah mean we goin' Miami. Undastand?"*

Nor'Side (nawr'syde) *Noun* – **1.** the district of North Side. **2.** one of Grand Cayman's 5 districts. **3.** the area consisting of Frank Sound, a part of Old Man Bay, the Hutland, Rum Point, Cayman Kai, and Kaibo. **Eg.** *"If yah waugh talk 'bout ah good place ta relax jess go Nor'side an chill out on da beach."*

Nor'westa (nawr-wess-tah) *Noun* – **1.** a wind or gale from the northwest. **2.** a storm or gale blowing from the northwest. **3.** a really windy storm which brings rain and high tides to shore. **Eg.** *"Anytime ya see nor'westa comin' ya bedda board up ya windows or else ya roof might blow off."*

Not ah One (nawt ah wun) *Pronoun* – **1.** none. **2.** not any, as of something indicated. **3.** zero; zilch; nada. **Eg.** *"Yestaday one woman wah cyarrin' six bag ah groceries n' not ah one ah dem menkind would try help 'er."*

No Teet (noh-teet) *Noun* – **1.** having little or no teeth **2.** a person with very few teeth. **3.** toothless. **Eg.** *"Mista Fred is da ownliss man wit one ol' no teet dog det bark wid ah lisp."*

No Way (noh whey) *Adverb* – **1.** nowhere. **2.** in or at no place; not anywhere. **3.** being or leading nowhere; pointless; futile. **4.** not the best way. **Eg.** *"I waugh go happy hour Frideh cuz I nah bin no way in monts."*

Nn

Nuff (nuh'f) *Adjective* – **1.** enough. **2.** adequate for the want or need; sufficient for the purpose or to satisfy desire. *Adverb* – **3.** an adequate quantity or number; sufficiency. **4.** fully or quite. **Eg.** *"Wahght! You gah nuff mangoes, doh. Set me up wit one ah dem nah?"*

Nuff-Nuff (nuh'f-nuh'f) *Adjective* – **1.** more than enough. **2.** exceeding the adequate amount required to fulfill one's common needs or wants. **3.** a whole lot. **4.** a inexplicable amount. **Eg.** *"I waugh see how you gah get home by 5:15 t'day, cuz it nuff-nuff cars on da road n' I hear accident up by Prospeck."*

Nuff Dollas (nuh'f daw-luzz) *Adverb* – **1.** a significant amount of money. **2.** too much money. **3.** more money than one can possibly count. **4.** too much to spend at one time. **Eg.** *"Wah yah say $50?? Yoh, dass nuff dollas ta be spendin' on woman who doon' like you."*

Nuff Man (nuh'f mah'n) *Adverb* – **1.** a lot of men. **2.** everyone. **3.** all the guys. **4.** men by the hundreds. **Eg.** *"Georgey, you bedda try so check Lily quick time, cuz I hear nuff man bin acksin' 'er fah her phone numba."*

Numbers (num-buz) *Noun* – **1.** an underground lottery, which involves several members placing bets prior to a raffle, of which one (or sometimes more than one) winner is selected. **2.** illegal gambling. **Eg.** *"Aye, you nah hear which numba play dis week ah wah? I waugh see who win da $5,000.00."*

Numb Fish (numm fish) *Noun* – **1.** a small, shell-covered fish, bearing a thick, scaley hide, covered in bumps for protection and spikes for stinging predators and prey. **2.** a really ugly fish, which burrows itself in the sand to ambush its prey and hide from predators. **3.** one of the many legends that most people in Cayman have never seen. **Eg.** *"Sweetie, watch out way you walkin' in da sea, y'hear? Somebody tell me Freddy get sting by Numbfish cupple ah weeks ago, rite in diss spot."*

Nuttin' (nuh-t'n) *Noun* – **1.** nothing. **2.** no thing; not anything. **3.** no part, share or trace. **4.** something that is non existent. **Eg.** *"Man, if you nah doin' nuttin' t'night, try so less go by Buttonwood n' shoot some pool nah?"*

Nn

Nuune (noon) *Noun* – (primarily of East End and Bodden Town) **1.** none. **2.** no one; not one. **3.** not any, as of something indicated. **4.** not at all or in no way. **Eg.** *"Doon' acks me fah money agin cuz I nah gah nuune ta ghee you."*

Nyam (nee'yahm) *Verb* – **1.** to eat. **2.** to take into the mouth and swallow for nourishment; chew and swallow (food). **3.** to consume by or as if by devouring gradually; wear away; corrode. **Eg.** *"Ya know wah? I doon' really eat fry corn beef but I stahwin' so it gettin' nyam t'night."*

Nyam Off (n'yahm awff) *Verb* – **1.** to consume every morsel as if it is the last. **2.** to eat up greedily. **3.** to eat out of house and home. **Eg.** *"Aye, who in da world nyam off all ah dem cookies I juss buy from Fosta's?"*

Nyam Out (n'yahm owtt) *Verb* – **1.** to devour completely. **2.** to swallow or eat up hungrily, voraciously, or ravenously. **3.** to consume destructively, recklessly, or wantonly. **Eg.** *"Virgil, how much times I gah tell you yih cyah juss nyam out all da food in da fridge widdout acksin' people who it fah."*

Somebody nyam out all the corn bread last night.

Nn

Oh Yaah (owe yaahhh) *Interjection* – **1.** oh yeah. **2.** oh yes.
3. you're gonna get it now. **4.** why did you have to mess
with me (or him or her or them). **5.** watch out. **Eg.** *"Oh
yaah, I know you ga get da skin beat off ah yo b'hind now.
Wah you hadda go mess wit daddy 12-guage shotgun fuh?"*

Old Cayman House (oal kay-mahn how'ce) *Noun* – **1.** a
traditional house built in the old style, and made of wattle
and daub or wood and having a zink roof. **2.** the type of
home one's grandparents might currently live in. **Eg.** *"Ta
get ta Miss LuLu house, jess go dong by Uncle Kirwin guinep
tree, turn leff, den go down chrew Misteh Larden grass piece,
and den yih gah come up ta one pink n' white old Cayman
house on piece.ah iron shore... dass Miss LuLu house."*

Old Wife (ole wyfe) *Noun* – **1.** a species of *Triggerfish*,
which tend to vary in size and pattern, and have a
roundish, laterally flat body with an anterior dorsal fin.
2. a colourful flounder-like fish, which has tender edible
meat. **3.** odd-looking looking fish, whose slender face and
lips resemble a woman's. **Eg.** *"When I wah small, one boy
name Shane from Nor'side who used ta fishnin' plenty, would
call people ah Old Wife, if dey did im sumting."*

One English Man (wun eeng-lish mahn) *Noun* – **1.** any
person whose origins lie in the United Kingdom, whether
it be from the Island of England, Scotland or Ireland. **2.**
a Brit. **3.** any man with an English accent. **Eg.** *"Man, I
hear one English man had get ketch committin' fraud on dah
Eurobank case."*

One Lil' Man (wun lill mahn) *Noun* – **1.** a really short
fellow who shows up at one's home or place of business
unannounced, while one is absent. **2.** a really short guy.
3. an individual who can only be identified by his height
and body type. **4.** a man who cannot be fully identified
by the message taker, because no name or other form of
identification was given at the time of the visit. **Eg.** *"Joy,
one lil' man juss came see you but I diddn' know way u wuz."*

Oo

One Piece (wun peece) *Prefix* – **1.** a nonspecific reference to objects, events or activities. **2.** a lot of one thing. **Eg.** *"I see dah time when Lillian had fall offa her brudda bicycle, she start one piece ah hollarin' n' errybody juss come runnin' like somebody wah dead."*

One Time (wun tyme) *Adverb* – **1.** at once; at the same time. **2.** right away. **3.** before the next thing. **4.** while time permits. **5.** right now. **Eg.** *"We miya zwell go pick up lunch one time while we out yah waitin' fah Lil' Frank ta get ready."*

One Tourist Man (wun tore-iss mahn) *Noun* – **1.** a male tourist. **2.** any male person who is new to the Islands and knows very little about its culture. **3.** a man who has the tendency of showing up in a restaurant dressed in swim trunks and no shirt. **Eg.** *"One time I see one tourist man come up in Corna acksin' fa directions ta Westin, n' da cashier tell im West End is in Cayman Brac."*

One Tourist Woman (wun tore-iss wuh'mun) *Noun* – **1.** a female tourist. **2.** any female person who is new to the Islands and knows very little about its culture. **3.** a woman who has the tendency of showing up in front of one's home asking for directions while riding on the back of a scooter. **Eg.** *"Man, if you had see dah piece ah bikini one tourist woman had on lass week, yoh eyes woulda fall outta yoh head."*

Open Wrist (oh-pin riss) *Noun* – **1.** the spraining of one's wrist, which tends to have the sensation of being separated. **2.** a common injury to the wrist joint after a fall. **3.** a really painful sensation in one's wrist which can be treated by wrapping brown paper (from paper bags) and vinegar around the area. **Eg.** *"One time when I wah still in school, I couldn' play goalie fa da football game cuz I had fall down 'n get open wrist."*

Ouk (owhk) *Adverb* – **1.** out. **2.** away from, or not in, the normal or usual place, position, state, etc. **3.** not in present possession or use, as on loan. **4.** not in. **Eg.** *"Mummy! Tell Carson ta hurry up n' come ouk ah da bahtchroom or else I gah pee-pee up myself."*

Oo
———

Out House (owt how'ce) *Noun* – **1.** a small tool shed or storage facility to the rear of a dwelling home. **2.** an old Cayman-style bathroom made of wood built over a large pit, which houses one or more crudely made toilet seats. **Eg.** *"I used to hate goin' down by my granny's cuz all she had wah one ol' out house n' I had always get stuck in deh wit no tylet paypah."*

Outta Style (ow-dah stile) *Adverb* – **1.** unfashionable. **2.** out of fashion; used; worn out; exhausted. **3.** ugly and undesirable. **4.** old and forgotten. **Eg.** *"Aye, wah you doin' wearin' dem Nike's ta school fah? Dem tings outta style bad - I know nuff people gah laff at you still."*

Ouwa (uh-wah) *Pronoun* – **1.** our; a nominative plural of 'I' used to denote oneself and another or others. **2.** a form of the possessive case of *'we'* used as an attributive adjective. **3.** belonging to us. **Eg.** *"It's ah good ting ouwa house nehwa blow down durin' Ivan cuz we wouldn' ah had no way ta stay."*

Ownliss (ooon-liss) *Adverb* – **1.** only. **2.** without others or anything further; alone; solely; exclusively. **3.** no more than; merely; just. **4.** being the single one or the relatively few of the kind. **Eg.** *"Sicily is da ownliss friend I gah det really care 'bout how I doin'."*

Cellphones go outta style quicker than they came in.

Oo

Padnah (pah'd-nuh) *Noun* – **1.** a financial partnership between two or more persons, which involves the pooling together of funds. Each person is given an opportunity to draw his/her share (the sum of all single contributions) on a specified date, whether it be weekly, bi-weekly, monthly, or bi-monthly. **2.** one of the best ways to raise a large sum of money for a particular cause. **3.** to contribute money to a shared transaction. **Eg.** *"Man, one time I jine one padnah n' draw out $8,000 one lick. Me n' my wife went France fa two weeks on dah money."*

Padnah Ground (pah'd-nuh graown) *Noun* – From Old People Times; **1.** the property - off of Elgin Avenue - which belonged to the former Racquet Club sports bar. **2.** the area on which the new Government Office is currently located. **Eg.** *"Dem times when we used ta play football up by Agriculture Field, we used ta hawe ta cut chrew by Padnah Ground ta get home ta Scranton b'fore dark."*

Padsin's (pahd-sinz) *Noun* – **1.** a small mini-market owned and operated by Cayman Farm Soldier 'O'chester *"Pad-sin"* Patterson. **2.** the best place to buy Ackee and Codfish, Mackerel or Salt Beef during the late 1960's, the 70's, the 80's and most of the 90's. **3.** one of the shantiest-looking shops ever built on Grand Cayman. **Eg.** *"Anytime I used ta drive pass Padsin's, yih could smell da mackerel n' salt beef right cross da road."*

Pah (pa'ah) *Noun* – **1.** one's father. **2.** daddy. **3.** a male guardian. **Eg.** *"Sonny, go so call ya pah fah meh nah? I waugh acks im sumting."*

Pah'ndeh (pah'n-deh) *Noun* – **1.** a pair of panties; female underwear. **2.** short underpants for women or girls. **3.** a woman's 'drawers'. **Eg.** *"Sweedeh, you cyah go out deh way people is wit yoh pah'ndeh showin' in da back."*

Pp

Palm Dale (pah'm day'le) *Noun* – **1.** a housing community off of Crewe Road near to Tropical Gardens. **3.** a neighborhood near the airport. **Eg.** *"Jeremy say as long as he live he gah represent he Palm Dale barba green like it da bible."*

Paper Towellin' (pay-pah tow-ill-inn) *Noun* – **1.** paper towel: a disposable towel made of absorbent paper. **Eg.** *"Archie, come so run by Merren shop 'n get me some Windex n' some paper towellin'."*

Pahpa (pah-puh) *Noun* – **1.** one's grandfather. **2.** an older man who has a tendency to interfere with the raising of his grandchildren. **3.** the father of one's father. **4.** a link to one's family heritage and tradition. **5.** a loving old man. **Eg.** *"I rememba when my pahpa had mek me one stool ta sit on wit he bare hands."*

Pahro (pah-row) *Adverb* – **1.** of, like, or suffering from *paranoia*. **3.** very uneasy; untrusting. *Noun* – **4.** a person suffering from *paranoia*. **Eg.** *"Boy you pahro. You cyah hear deh nah no such ting as duppy? You waugh people call you sissy ah wah?"*

Pain Up (pee'n upp) *Adverb* – **1.** physically painful or sensitive, as a wound, hurt, or diseased part. **2.** sore; tender; infected; wounded. **3.** full of aches and pains. **Eg.** *"I love workin' out in da gym y'see? Aftawords ya be all pain up, but afta ya bade it feel good."*

Painy Belly (pee-neh beh-leh) *Noun* – **1.** pain in the stomach caused by gas or cramps. **2.** an ache in the abdomen. **3.** a reason to complain through whining or moaning. **Eg.** *"Diss mornin' I had one painy belly like ah dunno wah... I taught I wah gah die."*

Park Off (pah'rk awff) *Verb* – **1.** to park in a secluded area so as to attract attention to one's vehicle. **2.** to park diagonally, taking up two parking spaces, to avoid one's vehicle being scratched by others. **3.** to place one's vehicle in a grassy area near the road for all to see. **Eg.** *"I miss da days when yah could juss go and park off by Cinema n' play music n' nobody wouldn' say nuttin' or call Police."*

Pp

Park Up (pah'rk upp) *Adverb* – **1.** filled with vehicles. **2.** congested by automobiles. **Eg.** *"Maaannnn, I hate when people have house parties on my road. Da place always be all park up and ya cyah find no way ta put ya car."*

Patty (pah-deh) *Noun* – **1.** a traditional Cayman-style meat pastry. **2.** any item of food covered with dough, batter, etc., and fried or baked. **Eg.** *"You rememba when we used ta go get ah patty n' ah pepsi from Island Taste when dey wah on da waterfront?"*

Pelt (pehlt) *Verb* – **1.** to throw (any projectile). **2.** to cast. **3.** to move an object from one location to another by throwing with excessive force. **Eg.** *"I wish I could go New York fah Christmas so me n' my cousin kin pelt snowballs at each udda all day."*

Peel Head (peel hed) *Noun* – **1.** a closely shaven hair cut. **2.** having one's hair cut too low. **3.** an army cut. **4.** a bald head. **Eg.** *"You cyah miss Arlin deez days, he gah one piece ah peel head deh, ya could spot im ah mile away in da middle ah Pirate's Week."*

Pick Picks (pik pikz) *Noun, Pl.* – **1.** a species of small, schooling fish which are colorful and close in size to *Sprats* and *Fries*, and resemble a small, slender *Squab*. **2.** a little fish which constantly picks at one's bait while fishing, but will never take the bait. **3.** a series of tiny fish which often deceive fishermen into believing that the bait has been taken, while in fact it has been lodged into rocks on the ocean floor. **Eg.** *"Anytime we go fishnin' on da ironshore I always be worry dat Pick Picks gah drag my line inta piece ah coral or someting."*

Picky Head (pih-keh hed) *Noun* – **1.** the state of one's hair which closely resembles a bush; thick and shaggy. **2.** untidy; unkempt hair. **3.** overgrown and poorly groomed hair. **Eg.** *"Aaaaahhhh!! Look ah yoh ol' picky head dog man? Way you get him from?"*

Piece ah Ting (pee'ce ah teeng) *Noun* – **1.** a piece of something **2.** a person. **3.** part of something. **4.** a fraction of a particular object. **Eg.** *"Alice May always call me one sicknin' piece ah ting wheneva I bodda her when she be makin' midnight up in dah bed."*

Pp

Pint (pynt) *Verb* – **1.** to point. **2.** to stress a particular topic or part of a story. *Noun* – **3.** a sharp or tapered end. **4.** a mark or dot used in printing or writing for punctuation, especially a period. **5.** a reason. **Eg.** *"Errytime Linford try tell ah story, Gina always gah im ta get ta da pint."*

Pirates Week (py-rutz week) *Noun* – **1.** an annual festival held in recognition of Pirates who first visited the Islands during the 17 and 1800's. **2.** a grand event, comprising of a costumed street parade, a pantomime, a street dance, a fireworks display, and lots of other activities for the whole family; held in November of each year. **Eg.** *"Dis year I dressin' up in my May Cow costume so I kin win da Pirates Week Costume Contest."*

Piss Pot (pih'ce pawt) *Noun* – **1.** a large round pot or bowl, made of porcelain or metal, which is used during urination. **2.** a portable toilet bowl. **3.** an old Cayman toilet. **Eg.** *"Watch ya? Boy if you had turn ova dah piss pot, I woulda mek you wipe up erry lass drop b'fore you go school."*

Plaitin' (plahtt'n) *Verb* – **1.** to braid or plait anything, especially thatch, coconut leaves, or straw. **2.** the act of braiding one's hair or other material. **3.** a favourite pastime for older Caymanian women. **Eg.** *"My Aunt Miriam cun do some plaitin' doh yi'nah."*

Plantain Trash Bed (plah'n-t'n trah'sh bade) *Noun* – **1.** a traditional Caymanian bed (from the late 19th and early 20th century) which bears a mattress made from the leaves of a *Plantain Sucker* tree. **2.** a mattress made of plantain leaves. **3.** a very soft bed of plantain leaves. **Eg.** *"Granny say deez new beds cyah touch da plantain trash beds she used ta mek back in her good ol' days."*

Play-Play (playe-playe) *Adverb* – **1.** fake; counterfeit; simulated. **2.** contrived and presented as genuine. **3.** a toy; sham. **Eg.** *"If you tink you kin scare me wit dah play-play gun, you bedda tink again."*

Play Fightin' (play fite-in) *Verb* – **1.** to pretend to be fighting. **2.** to imitate fight scenes which one may have seen on t.v. or in actuality. **3.** light contact fighting with a friend. **Eg.** *"Lass night, my brudda Greggy n' Harwell wah play fightin' an' Harwell accidently lick Greggy in he eye."*

Pp

Playin' Karate (play-yin kah-rah-deh) *Verb* – **1.** pretending to fight with the skills of a true martial artist. **2.** imitating key kung fu movie characters such as Bruce Lee, Jet Li or Jackie Chan. **3.** getting your butt kicked by your next door neighbor. **Eg.** *"Next time me n' you playin' karate I gah fly kick you inside yoh head fa bussin' my lip da lass time."*

Playin' Up (play-yin upp) *Adverb* – **1.** frolicking; having fun; flirting. **2.** messing around. **3.** clowning. **Eg.** *"Aye, get outta my room n' stop playin' up in people bed like it yours!"*

Play Toy (pley toi) *Noun* – **1.** one's toy. **2.** a play thing. **3.** a doll; baseball; CD; videogame; or other object used for the entertainment of oneself. **4.** an object, often a small representation of something familiar as an animal or person for children or others to play with. **Eg.** *"People mussa tink dah car is yoh play toy da way you treat it."*

Ploppas (plaw-puz) *Noun, Pl.* – **1.** ploppers; small, twisted pieces of paper filled with gunpowder, which tend to explode and release a loud plopping sound when thrown against a solid surface (wall or floor). **2.** a favourite toy amongst schoolchildren in the 1980s. **Eg.** *"Me n' Bobby had get in trouble wit Teacha Langley one time fah flingin' ploppas up in Delroy head durin' prayer meetin'."*

Plug Dat (pluh'g dah't) *Interjection* – **1.** take that. **2.** it serves you right. **4.** you deserve whatever you get. **Eg.** *"Yeah, plug dat! I tell you bout climbin' ova people barbwire fence ta try steal dey mangoes – I hope Mr. Rankin peel yoh behind wit da tamarind switch."*

Plywood Bunkey (plie wud bung-keh) *Noun* – **1.** buttocks which are as flat as a piece of plyboard. **2.** having wide buttocks which appear to be completely flat. **3.** a flat butt. **4.** no bonkey whatsoever. **Eg.** *"I hear Robby checkin' one gyal dat gah ah serious piece ah plywood bonkey boy."*

Poinciana Tree (pun-see-yah-nuh tree) *Noun* – **1.** any of several other tropical trees of the legume family, with showy flowers. **2.** a really huge tree which bears bright red-orange petals several times a year. **3.** a very messy tree to have in one's yard. **Eg.** *"I really like dah pictcha wit dem two Poinciana trees crossin' ova da road in Sawannah while dey bloomin'; dass ah nice one ta put on da wall."*

Pp

Poinsettia Tree (pun-set-ee-yah tree) *Noun* – **1.** a tropical shrub, that has showy, usually scarlet bracts beneath the small yellow flowerlike inflorences. **2.** a tree which is commonly mis-pronounced and more often mistaken with the *Poinciana Tree*, which is much larger, and more beautiful. **3.** a small, thin tree closely resembling a Poinciana, although bearing prickles (thorns) on its limbs and much smaller leaves and petals. **Eg.** *"Neva make da mistake of tryin' ta climb ah Poinsettia tree tinkin' it ah Poinciana tree; you gah regret it when you start ta get juug up wit all ah dem prickles."*

Pomp (pawmp) *Verb* – **1.** to emit, cause or produce a honk. **2.** to cause an automobile horn to sound. **3.** the blaring sound of the horn from a motor vehicle. **Eg.** *"I really don't care if you go head and pomp yo horn till kingdom come, I nah movin my car till you get yo ol' jalopy out da way."*

Pong (pawng) *Noun* – **1.** a measurement; one pound. **2.** a very foul odor; a stench. *Verb* – **3.** to strike an object by delivering blows to it from overhead; to pound. **Eg.** *"I hear Tee-Cee had get pong up by Chelsea dah time in highschool."*

Poomp (poo'mp) *Noun* – **1.** a fart. **2.** a flatus expelled through the anus. *Verb* – **3.** to break wind. **4.** to relieve flatulence and release a very foul smelling odor which is offensive to others. **5.** to make a funny sound with one's behind. **Eg.** *"Man, one time Fletch had poomp durin' ah all-school meetin' n' dey hadda clear da buildin' like it wah on fiyah."*

Poor Sufferah (pore suh-fah-rah) *Noun* – **1.** one who is currently undergoing a severe hardship. **2.** an unskilled individual who continues to try, but to no avail. **3.** one who suffers on account of principle. **Eg.** *"Look ah dah poor sufferah eh? He be tryin' still, but I don't tink he should be in construction cuz he cyah hardly eable pound ah nail inta piece ah wood."*

Pop Head (pawp hed) *Noun* – **1.** an injury to the top of the head which results in splitting of the skin and bleeding. **2.** an insult. **3.** a very painful head injury. **Eg.** *"I remember one time when Baby Frank hadda get 17 stitches ta close up he pop head."*

Pp

Pop Lip (pawp lipp) *Noun* – **1.** an injury to the mouth which results in a splitting of the skin and bleeding. **2.** the result of being punched hard, in the mouth. **3.** a swollen lip which has been injured in some way. **4.** an emotional response to an unforeseen embarassment. **Eg.** *"Ted had come school one day wid ah pop lip da size ah Cayman Brac Bluff when he Daddy slap im fah lyin!"*

Poppy Show (paw-peh sho) *Verb* – **1.** to show off. **2.** to purposely attract attention to oneself. **3.** to slave for the impression of others. **4.** to act the fool. **Eg.** *"Jason get ah poppy show dah time 'bout doin stunts on he bicycle 'n' bring up inside ah Mista Curly chicken coop. I nearly dead laffin!"*

Pose Off (pow'ze awff) *Verb* – **1.** to assume a particular attitude or stance, esp. with the hope of impressing others. **2.** to stand against a wall, well-dressed and ready to go somewhere. **3.** to stand up in such a way that others will watch. **Eg.** *"Boy, you shoulda see how Manny wah pose off in dah new suit he buy from Beltina's lass week."*

PPM (pee pee em) *Noun* – **1.** The People's Progressive Movement; a political party comprised of elected Members of the Legislative Assembly within the Cayman Islands Government and its administrative staff and followers. **Eg.** *"I hear lass election, nuff people wah runnin' rong Cayman with dey PPM t-shirts."*

Pretty Eye (prih-deh eye) *Adjective* – **1.** having very attractive eyes. **2.** having either hazel, blue, gray or light brown eyes. **3.** eyes which are magnetic and appealing. **Eg.** *"Keisha say if she decide ah go prom diss year, it gah only be wit one pretty eye boy name Harley."*

Pretty Up (prih-deh upp) *Verb* – **1.** to fancify. **2.** to dress up; embellish. **3.** to improve the physical appearance of oneself/another/something. **Eg.** *"I doon' see why erry time somebody come ova yoh house you gah pretty up fa nuttin!"*

Prickles (prih k'ls) *Noun, Pl.* – **1.** the long spikey thorns which protrude from various species of plants, as protection from animals. **2.** something to fear whenever one is galavanting in a grass piece or mango bush. **Eg.** *"Furdy, mek sure ya wear gloves when ya pullin' bush cuz dey full ah prickles n' yih kin get all juug up."*

Pp

Prickle Bush (prih-k'l buush) *Noun* – **1.** any area containing dense portions of trees and plants which are at least 60-80% covered in prickles or thorns. **2.** a dried out thicket, filled with thorns or prickles, and having very few leaves or shrubbery. **Eg.** *"Wah you hadda go up in dah prickle bush fah when I tell you not to?"*

Prickly Gut (prihk-leh gut) *Noun* – **1.** the whitish-coloured stomach of a Green Sea Turtle. The prickly gut is removed during butchering and resembles a porcupine, hence the name 'prickly'. **2.** a favourite delicacy among turtle product enthusiasts. **Eg.** *"Wheneva I used ta watch daddy cut out da prickly gut, I used ta feel like I wah goin' chrow up. It juss look nasty, man."*

Probleh (praw-b'leh) *Adverb* – **1.** probably. **2.** in all likelihood. **3.** most likely; presumably. **Eg.** *"I cyah really say 'yes', but I might probleh be able ta lend ya my car nexx weekend."*

Proudy (praow-deh) *Adverb* – **1.** drawn to self-actualization. **2.** having, proceeding from, or showing a high opinion of one's own dignity, importance, or superiority. **3.** full of vanity. **4.** stuck up. **5.** snobbish. **Eg.** *"Ol' proudy, always gah be different eh?"*

Prup Prup (pruh'p pruh'p) *Noun* – **1.** one of the many species of *Triggerfish*, which is similar to the *Old Wife* and the *Ocean Turbit*. **2.** a Flounder-like fish, having bright colourful streaks on a thick, coarse hide. **Eg.** *"Lass time I went fishnin' I ketch one lil' ol' prup-prup an I hadda chrow it back, cuz it wah too small."*

Puhpah (puh-paah) *Noun* – From West Bay; **1.** one's grandfather. **2.** an older man who constantly interferes with the raising of his grandchildren. **3.** the father of one's father. **Eg.** *"If you doon' get outta my ya'ad rike now, I gah call my puhpah on you."*

Pungkin (pung-kin) Noun – **1.** pumpkin; a large edible, thick-skinned orange-yellow fruit borne by a coarse, decumbent vine, of the gourd family. **2.** a plant bearing such fruit. **3.** a common nickname for a young baby or child. **Eg.** *"Looka my lil' pungkin, eh? She so cute!"* or; *"Mama, we gah any pungkin ta go wit diss turtle steak?"*

Pp

Pupaw (puh-pawe) *Noun* – **1.** the *Papaya* fruit. **2.** a large, yellow, melon-like fruit of a tropical shrub or small tree, *Carica papaya*, eaten raw or cooked. **3.** a large oval melon-like tropical fruit with yellowish flesh. **Eg.** *"In some places, dey call it papaya, but Caymanians call it pu-paw. I doon' care wah yah call it cuz I gah eat it same way."*

Pure Man (p'yure mahn) *Adverb* – **1.** completely populated by men. **2.** no woman in sight. **3.** all men. **4.** a massive gathering of men. **Eg.** *"Yow! I see lass week when I went Next Level; when I open dah door all yih'see is pure man up in deh n' 'bout two gyals."*

Purple Wash (purr-pull wausche) *Noun* – **1.** *Mecuricome*; a nonmetallic halogen element occurring at ordinary temperatures as a grayish-black crystalline solid that sublimes to a dense violet vapor when heated: used in medicine as an antiseptic. **2.** the purple stuff mothers put on cuts and bruises before applying a band-aid. **3.** an antiseptic solution which is often used to protect minor injuries from infection and to reduce bleeding. **Eg.** *"Anytime anybody get skin-up knees from playin' football on dah barba green, dah way ya see purple wash walkin' up n' down."*

A nice 'pupaw' is the perfect dessert after a great meal.

Pp

Quadrille (kwawh-drih'lle) *Noun* – **1.** a traditional square dance for four couples, consisting of five parts or movements, each complete to itself. **2.** the music for such a dance. **3.** a favourite dance of the fashionable French society in the late 18th century, which debuted in the ballrooms of England in the early 19th century, from where it found its way into various European dependencies, such as the West Indies. **4.** a Cayman tradition which was preserved for many years by Radley Gourzong and the Happy Boys band. **Eg.** *"At Agriculture Fair dis year, da East End Quadrille Troup had errybody all rile up n' dancin' all on top da tables n' ting; boy dah way ya see people hawin' fun."*

Quashy (k'wash-eh) *Noun* – **1.** a really insignificant person. **2.** a worthless individual. **3.** a person of little significance, importance, or one who appears to possess no skills or talents whatsoever. **Eg.** *"Daddy used ta get mad anytime he waugh watchin' wresslin' n' dey put ah ol' quashy in ta fight wit da World Champion. He say it wah ah waste ah time juss ta watch it."*

Queen's Highway (k'ween'z hi-waye) *Noun* – **1.** the road linking North Side and East End, which was opened during the Royal Visit of Queen Elizabeth II in February 1983. A plaque commemorating the event was placed at the site. **2.** one of the only places on the island where the speed limit is 50mph. **3.** a long stretch of open road that is attractive to speeders. (many fatal accidents have taken place on Queen's Highway) **Eg.** *"Anytime I hear bug ah accident, da first ting dat come ta my mind is "I betcha it happin' on Queen's Highway."*

Quenk (kweh'nk) *Noun* – **1.** a sound. **2.** the utterance or emission of a squeak or squeaky sound. **3.** any sound which can be heard. **Eg.** *"Alright you children, it bedtime now, so unnna go ta bed n' I doon' waugh hear ah quenk or else I gah bring da belt."*

Qq

Que-Que (kyoo-kyoo) *Noun* – **1.** a small quantity (mostly of a drink), such as a shot of liquor. In relation to spirits it tends to refer to a small unmeasured quantity. **2.** one of the three legal sizes for draught beer glasses; it was formerly used for very strong beer but is now rarely seen. **3.** a small hard liquor flask usually kept in the back pocket during times of celebration. **Eg.** *"Erry Christmas, pahpa hadda hawe he que-que in he back pocket so if he friends come ova he would hawe something ta drink."*

Quick Time (kweh-heh) *Adverb* – **1.** quickly. **2.** immediately. **3.** at once. **4.** right away. **5.** on the double. **6.** right now. **7.** with speed; rapidly; very soon. **Eg.** *"Less go drop diss off deez tapes ta Blockbusta quick time while dey still open nah?"*

Quincentennial (kwin-sen-ten-ih-yul) *Noun* – **1.** 2003; the 500th anniversary of the discovery of the Cayman Islands by Christopher Columbus on May 10, 1503. **2.** a very memorable year for the people of the Cayman Islands. **Eg.** *"Quincentennial year was ah really beautiful celebration for Cayman. I think Angela Martins did ah excellent job puttin' erryting tagedda."*

Quinine (kwye-nyne) *Noun* – From Old People Times; **1.** a natural white crystalline alkaloid having antipyretic (fever-reducing), antimalarial, analgesic (painkilling), and anti-inflammatory properties and a bitter taste. **2.** the antimalarial drug of choice until the 1940s, when other drugs took over. **4.** a prescription drug which was occasionally used to treat nocturnal leg cramps, arthritis. **Eg.** *"Between Quinine, Fensic, Vwicks Sahwe, n' SSS Tonic, I doon' know which one dem ol' people lowe da most."*

Qweh-heh (kweh-heh) *Adjective* – **1.** nothing at all. **2.** having no knowledge of anything. **3.** lacking proper understanding or knowledge. **4.** completely oblivious. **Eg.** *"Look yah right? Tracey Ann always try ta show me up in uwah staff meetin's but she doon' know qweh-heh 'bug Accountin' n' I almost gah my CPA."*

Qq

Racquet Club (rah-kit klubb) *Noun* – **1.** one of the first, and quite possibly the most notorious of the sports bars on Grand Cayman. **2.** a sports bar formerly located on the same property as the new Government Administration Building. **3.** the primary source of most loud music heard throughout George Town in the 1980s and 90s. **Eg.** *"I use ta wonda why dey had call it Racket Club till I hear all da nize dey use ta mek erry bloomin' night."*

Rain Fly (reen flye) *Noun* – **1.** a small brown flying termite commonly seen during or after a long rain. **2.** a harmless moth-like fly. **3.** an annoying but unoffensive insect. **Eg.** *"If ya see ah rain fly pitch on yoh pillow when ya wake up in da mornin', dah usually mean it rain hard da night b'fore."*

Ram (rahm) *Adverb* – **1.** jam-packed. **2.** full to capacity and beyond. **3.** filled to the greatest extent. **4.** overloaded. **5.** overflowing. **6.** stuffed to the gills. **7.** crammed; crowded; saturated; ready to burst at the seams. **Eg.** *"Alan couldn't get into Rumheads cuz dah whole place wah ram."*

Rate (ray'te) *Verb, Trans.* – **1.** to place in a particular rank or grade. **2.** to regard or account. **3.** to hold in high regard. **4.** to give respect; commend or support. **5.** to give acknowledgement. **Eg.** *"Man, dah Jim Carrey movie wah funny boy. I rate dah one, still."*

Rat Trap (raht traapp) *Noun* – **1.** an old, beat-up, shabby, dilapidated, tetanus infected automobile, which appears to have lived past its time. **2.** a junk-mobile. **3.** a jalopy. **Eg.** *"Cuzzy, if you had see dah rat trap way Binwurd daddy ghee him ta drive, you woulda ketch diarrhea in yo pants."*

Rebecca's Cave (rih-beh-kuhz kay'v) *Noun* – **1.** a large cave located in the West End district of Cayman Brac, where a young girl named Rebecca took shelter and died during the 1932 hurricane. **2.** a famous attraction on Cayman Brac. **Eg.** *"Dah time when dem children had skip school n' went beer drinkin' up in Rebecca's Cave, I know dey mussa get ah good beatin' dah day."*

Rr

Red Ade (rade ade) *Noun* – **1.** a bright red mixed drink, which is extremely sweet and tasty. **2.** a cheap version of the popular Kool Aid drink. **3.** powdered red drink. **Eg.** *"Yih kin always tell when somebody bin drinkin' red ade, cuz dey whole mout be glowin' red like dey Dracula or someting'."*

Red Mole (rade mowle) *Noun* – **1.** an extremely valuable and mineral-rich form of top soil, which is red in colour, and having a tendency to stain clothes with its rich pigment. **2.** really fertile top soil. **3.** the best kind of local soil for growing fruits and vegetables. **Eg.** *"If you gah red mole in yo ya'ad, you set fa life cuz you kin grow all kinda veggatebbles ta live off a when times hard in Cayman."*

Red Shank (rade shainke) *Noun* – **1.** a small land crab, having a dark shell and reddish orange and purple claws and feet. **2.** the *'Halloween Crab'*; a species of crab from the family of *Gerarcinidae*. **3.** a burrowing crab which can be found on local beaches and around Almond and Willow trees throughout the Islands. **Eg.** *"Philip say bug one time he had get bite by one Red Shank and da docta hadda cut im off wid ah laser but I doon' believe dat."*

Ress Ya'self (reh'ce yuh-self) *Adverb* – **1.** *rest yourself*; a phrase which means 'stop fooling around'. **2.** take it easy. **3.** chill out. **4.** relax. **5.** stop all the harassment. **6.** leave me alone. **Eg.** *"Man, try so ress ya'self, nah? If you doon' stop messin' wit me I nah buyin' you no birtday present again."*

Reverse Back (rih-vurce bak) *Verb* – **1.** to move in a backward direction. **2.** to move in reverse. **3.** to back up. **4.** to shift into reverse gear and proceed. **Eg.** *"Ok Sonny, just reverse back ah lil' bit, n' you should be alright."*

Rich Boy (ritch boyy) *Noun* – **1.** one who appears to have come into a significant amount of cash. **2.** the child of wealthy parents. **3.** a young man who has just been paid for services rendered, or received money as a result of an allowance, a raffle, or other means. **Eg.** *"I dunno why Trenwick always play like he nah ah rich boy when he well know he daddy own half ah Cayman."*

Rr
—

Rich Gyal (ritch gyaall) *Noun* – **1.** a snobby young lady who tends to treat others as if they are of a lower class. **2.** a young girl born to wealthy parents. **3.** a young lady/ woman who has just been paid for services rendered, or received money as a result of an allowance, a raffle, or other means. **Eg.** *"Wendy always go on like she one rich gyal when she get pay; spennin' out all ah her money on make-up n' clothes, when she well know she gah all kinda bills ta pay, an her baby fadda nah helpin' wit nuttin'."*

Righted (rye-did) *Adverb* – **1.** having a significant amount of understanding or sensibility to be considered sane. **2.** normal. **3.** in good mental or physical health or order. **Eg.** *"Miss Winnie always tell me I nah righted wheneva I go on like ah edieyut."*

Right Right Now (ryte ryte now) *Adverb* – **1.** immediately; to this instant. **2.** now. **3.** not yesterday, not tomorrow, not ten minutes from now. **4.** without delay. **Eg.** *"So you sayin' Marsha wah supposed ta come ova now right? She comin' right right now? or she gah one ah dem watches wit Cayman Time built in?"*

Rile Up (ryle up) *Verb* – **1.** to irritate or vex. **2.** to fill with anger. **3.** ready to fight. **4.** on the verge of rioting or fighting. **Eg.** *"Wheneva da gas prices go up, people get all rile up cuz dey know da light bill and wadda bill goin' up too n' dey cyah do nuttin' 'bout it."*

Rock Bun (rawk bun) *Noun* – **1.** a traditional dessert, made from vanilla extract, coconut milk, brown sugar, cinnamon, allspice, nutmeg, salt, butter/margarine, etc...; rolled into a curly shaped bun. **2.** a tasty bun, which has a solid surface on the outside and a soft, tender inside. the whole bun is sweet throughout. **3.** an excellent treat after a good home-cooked meal. **Eg.** *"I used ta help my daddy mek some good rock bun but afta Iwan flood out uwah oven, we nah really made none since."*

Rocket's (raw-kitz) *Noun* – **1.** the number one venue for afterhour 'sessions' during the 1990s. **2.** a great place to party until 5am. **3.** a pioneer of early entrepreneurship. **Eg.** *"I remember one time in '94; me 'n Marlon had went by Rocket's and when Police come, all ya see is people scattarin' like flies."*

Rr

Rock Hole (rawk hoal) *Noun* – **1.** the area of George Town, first named in the early 20th Century, when a large hole was dug into the ground to create a well; wood ash was mixed with the well water and left to settle over time and become lye, a natural detergent. women came from miles around to the 'rock hole' to get lye to use as laundry detergent. hence, the area became known as 'Rock Hole'. **2.** the neighborhood beginning at School House Road near Boosey Shop (Solomon's Grocery) and ending at School Road, next to Young World Fashions. **Eg.** *"Some people down in Rock Hole don't even go ta Annex ta watch football."*

Rong (rawng) *Adverb* – **1.** around. **2.** in a particular region or area neighboring a place. **3.** about; on all sides; encircling; encompassing. **4.** somewhere nearby. **Eg.** *"Try so moo from rong me wit dah fooshniss 'bout you love me but you 'accidentleh' kiss somebody else."*

Rosemary Broom (roze-may-reh brume) *Noun* – **1.** a homemade broom; made of twigs and leaves from the *Rosemary Tree*. **2.** a great broom for sweeping out wattle and daub houses. **3.** a multi-purpose broom used for sweeping the house, and also sweeping sand yards. **Eg.** *"Granny say her daddy use ta put ah wallopin' on her brudda Avis wit da rosemary broom wheneva he misbehave."*

Row (ruw) *Noun* – **1.** a noisy dispute or quarrel; commotion. **2.** noise or clamor. **3.** to quarrel noisily. **4.** to scold. **Eg.** *"If you mess up my pants wit dah marka my mama gah row wit me n' den I gah come lookin' fa you."*

Rubba (ruh-bah) *Noun* – **1.** a common pink eraser found in most school supply kits. **2.** a device, as a piece of rubber or cloth, for erasing marks made with pen, pencil, chalk, etc. **Eg.** *"Teacha always use ta tell me dat if I fuhget ta bring my rubba ta school I coulda always use hers."*

Rubba Tree (noh-teet) *Noun* – **1.** a *Rubber Tree*. **2.** any tree that yields latex from which rubber is produced, esp. *Hevea brasiliensis*, of the spurge family, native to South America (and also found in the Caribbean), the chief commercial source of rubber. **3.** a tall tree with long, sturdy limbs, and large tentacle-like vines. **Eg.** *"Georgey used ta lowe swingin' on dah rubba tree when we wah in Troot Fah Yoot School."*

Rr

Rubry (rubb-reh) *Noun* – From East End; **1.** rugby; a game played by two teams of 15 players each on a rectangular field 110 yards long with goal lines and goal posts at either end, the object is to run with an oval ball across the opponent's goal line or kick it through the upper portion of the goal posts, with forward passing and time-outs not permitted. **Eg.** *"Less go play some rubry since football season done now!"*

Ruction (ruck-shi'yun) *Noun* – **1.** a riotous disturbance; a noisy quarrel. **2.** a disturbance, quarrel, or row. **3.** the act of making a noisy disturbance. **4.** the noise which accompanies the dropping and crashing of many objects. **Eg.** *"My cat had knocked down some fryin' pans n' all ya hear is one piece ah ruction goin' on in da kitchen."*

Ruff Up (ruhf upp) *Verb* – **1.** to mishandle. **2.** to handle badly; maltreat. **3.** to manage badly. **4.** to deal with clumsily or inefficiently; mismanage. **Eg.** *"I feel bad fa Carwell in dem. It sad how dey went Miami fa da weekend n' get ruff up by some ol' cruffs when dey wah walkin' back ta Park Plaza."*

Rum Point (ruhm poynte) *Noun* – **1.** the peninsula at the northwesternmost part of North Side. **2.** a residential community which borders the Cayman Kai area in the District of North Side. **3.** the area where (according to legend) a boat carrying casks of liquor (thought to be rum) ran aground, giving the area its name. **4.** one of the best places to hang out, play volleyball, drink, eat, and socialize on the weekend. (also pronounced: '***Rum Pint***') **Eg.** *"I know I nah seen yah all week, but juss wait till Sundeh n' we kin go Rum Pint n' chill out."*

Run (ruhn) *Verb* – **1.** to cause an action or event to happen. **2.** to perform a particular act. **3.** to operate. **4.** to cause another person to flee or feel unwelcomed. **Eg.** *"If L.B. come rong yah again, try so ghee im two dollas n' run im bug he bizniss"* or *"When I started diss taxi twenny odd years ago, I diddn' realize how much dedication it tecks ta run ah business."*

Rr

Run Down (runn down) *Noun* – **1.** a popular Caribbean dish made primarily of ground provisions, including potatoes, yams, broccoli, etc. mixed with various forms of meat (i.e. chicken; various fish) or plain vegetables and coconut milk. it tends to be altered according to the interests of the chef and the consumer. **2.** a traditional Sunday lunch. **3.** the source of most niggaritis (see: **niggaritis**) throughout the Islands. **Eg.** *"Anytime I finish ah good bowl ah run down, jess gimme ah hummuck n' I good fah da ress ah da day."*

Runnin' Ants (ruh-nin ahntz) *Noun* – **1.** small black or dark brown ants which are harmless to humans. **2.** one of the few non-biting species of ants on Grand Cayman. **3.** picnic ants; sugar ants. **4.** ants which can be found running in circles, but appear to be going nowhere. **Eg.** *"Anytime ya see sumting spill on da ground like juice or milk or someting, and ya leff it deh fa good lil' while, dah when ya gah see dem runnin' ants comin' out all ova da place."*

Runny Belly (ruh-neh beh-leh) *Noun* – **1.** frequent and watery bowel movements. **2.** diarrhea: an intestinal disorder characterized by abnormal frequency and fluidity of fecal evacuations. **Eg.** *"Hear wah I tell you, doon' eat nuttin' Felisha cook cuz it jess gah ghee ya runny belly."*

Run Off (ruhn awff) *Verb* – **1.** to make a photographic reproduction of (printed or graphic material), especially by xerography. **2.** to photocopy. **Eg.** *"Sweetie, when you go ta work tomorrow, try so run off cupple ah ya fadda birt certificates fa meh."*

Run Two Shoe (run too shoo) *Verb* – **1.** to beat hard and persistently or to pound repeatedly. **2.** to damage by beating or hard usage. **3.** to deal heavy, repeated blows. **Eg.** *"If ya tink you man less go play some Mortal Kombat so I kin run two shoe in you wit Sub Zero. Bring any man ya waugh, cuz I gah clean im up anyway."*

Russell's (ruh-sulz) *Noun* – **1.** the venue of several afterhour 'sessions' during the mid-1990s. **2.** a fun place to enjoy reggae music in the middle of the night during the 1990s. **Eg.** *"One time deh wah so much cars down by Russell's, dat Police hadda come direct traffic so people could go home."*

Rr

Saheppmihgeezumpiece
(suh-hepp-muh-jee-zum-pee'ce) *Interjection* – **1.** so help me. **2.** listen closely, or else. **3.** if it is the last thing I do. **4.** an expression of disbelief. **Eg.** *"Sweetie, if you doon' hurry n' go bayde so we kin go shoppin' at Fosta's, saheppmihgeezumpiece, I gah mek ya go wit ya dirty skin!"*

Sail Ho (sale hoh) *Noun* – From Old People Times; **1.** a title given to the first man, woman or child to sight an arriving vessel who always raises the hail. **2.** the person responsible for notifying everyone in town that a ship is arriving. **3.** the first person to spot the heart-racing sight of an approaching ship in George Town harbor who would give the cry "Sail Ho" – the response would be hurried thronging to the dock. **Eg.** *"Way back when people used ta moo 'bout on ships, dah when ya hear people talkin' bout "Sail Ho" wheneva dem ships wah comin' een."*

Salad-ah-Kick (sah'lud-ah-kik) *Noun* – **1.** a non-traditional game of football; whereby every man is for himself, and the object is to place the ball between the opponent's legs to score. a *'salad'* indicates that one has scored, and gives permission for all players to kick the scoree in the buttocks (one time only). **2.** a good way to get injured right before class. **3.** a really fun game to play; which can become dangerous and unsafe at times. (also known as *'salad-a-root'*) **Eg.** *"Come less go play salad-ah-kick. I still owe Samuel some shoes fah kickin' me so hard lass time."*

Salads! (sah-ludz) *Interjection* – **1.** a cry of victory during the game *'salad-a-kick'*; which indicates that one has successfully placed the football between the opponents legs. **2.** the general cry of victory; permission for all individual players to kick (root) the opponent in the buttocks. **3.** a reason to run if scored upon during the game of *'salad-a-kick'*. **Eg.** *"Freddy kin cheat boy; when he had get salads diss mornin'; cuz he kin run fass, nobody had get ah chance ta kick im up."*

Ss

Sallurd (sah-lurd) *Noun* – **1.** a salad made of green vegetables and various toppings. **2.** a usually cold dish consisting of vegetables, as lettuce, tomatoes, and cucumbers, covered with a dressing and sometimes containing seafood, meat, or eggs. **3.** any of various dishes consisting of foods, as meat, seafood, eggs, pasta, or fruit, prepared singly or combined, usually cut up, mixed with a dressing, and served cold: chicken salad; potato salad. **Eg.** *"Wendy's always have da bess sallurds in Cayman."*

Salt (sawl't) *Adverb* – **1.** in serious trouble. **2.** without options. **3.** out of luck. **4.** in between a rock and a hard place. **5.** up the creek without a paddle. **Eg.** *"Ya should always try to save some money fa emergencies when ya go splurgin' in Miami. Cuz if ya miss ya flight n' yih nah gah no extra money ta stay ova night, yih gah be salt den."*

Salt Air (sawl't eere) *Noun* – **1.** an invisible mist which emanates from the sea. **2.** salty air. **Eg.** *"Anytime salt air blow on Richard car, he gah cyar it straight home n' wash it off."*

Salt Spray (sawlt sp'ray) *Noun* – **1.** the scattered particles of salt water from the ocean. **2.** the salty mist which comes from the sea during tropical storms, cold fronts and hurricanes. **3.** one of the worst things to get on one's car. **Eg.** *"Awleh! I bedda try so hurry get home and wash my car b'fore diss salt spray mess up my engine and russ out my paint."*

Same Diffrunts (sayme dih-frence) *Idiom* – **1.** a jocular colloquial phrase which dates from about 1940, meaning; the same thing. **2.** no difference at all. **3.** whatever you say; I really could care less. **Eg.** *"Aye, 'pumpkin' and 'pungkin' is da same diffrunts, it orange dah same way, it round da same way and I gah eat it da same way."*

Same Speed (seem speede) *Slang* – **1.** all the same. **2.** in any case; anyhow; nonetheless; regardless. **3.** in any way or manner whatever. **4.** no matter what. **Eg.** *"Cuz, hear wah I tell you... I sit down n' watch ah fly pitch in Lowell soup, n' my boy slop dat up same speed."*

Ss

Sand Yard (sahn ya'ard) *Noun* – **1.** the tradition of backing buckets of sand from various beaches to spread throughout one's yard. **2.** a yard full of beach sand, regardless of the proximity to the ocean. **Eg.** *"Granny say erry Christmas, widdout fail, she hadda mek sure she gah ah nice sand yard or else she couldn' sleep."*

Sanapee (sah-nah-pee) *Noun* – **1.** a common centipede. **2.** any of numerous predaceous, chiefly nocturnal arthropods constituting the class *Chilopoda*, having an elongated, flattened body composed of from 15 to 173 segments, each with a pair of legs, the first pair being modified into poison fangs. **Eg.** *"One time, ah sanapee bite my gyalfriend on her lip in da middle ah da night n' I hadda rush 'er hospital. Boy we wah scared."*

Sauce (saw'ce) *Noun* – **1.** a homemade dressing, consisting of vinegar, black pepper, salt or seasoned salt, and other spices used primarily for adding flavour to green mangoes and other fruits. **2.** a marinating liquid for green mangoes. **3.** a tangy, spicy, home-made hot sauce created by green mango lovers. **Eg.** *"It mango season now, so ya know I gah mek 'sauce' fa when I get my mangoes."*

Sauce Up (saw'ce upp) *Adverb* – **1.** drunk. **2.** impaired by an excess of alcoholic drink; intoxicated. **3.** overcome or dominated by a strong feeling or emotion. **4.** drunk and happy. **5.** liquored up. **Eg.** *"Anytime ya see Kelrick sauce up ya bedda watch im cuz he be stumblin' 'bout da place."*

Sapappah (suh-pah-puh) *Noun* – From Old People Times/From West Bay; **1.** a really bad beating. **2.** the worst beating of one's life. **3.** a demonstration of screaming and hollering while being beaten with a seemingly indestructible Tamarind Switch. **Eg.** *"Hurry up n' lemme play da PlayStation now or else I gah tell Pahpah n' he gah ghee you ah good sapappah t'night."*

Savannah Gully (sah-vah-nuh guh-leh) *Noun* – **1.** a small ravine worn away by running water, located near Pedro St. James. **2.** a low-lying area having the tendency to overflow during heavy rains; especially, during the passing of a major hurricane or tropical storm. **Eg.** *"Man, I feel sorry fa dem people in Sawannah, cuz erry time it rain too hard, da ol' gully full up wit wadda n' flood um out."*

Ss

Sawannah (suh-wah-nuh) *Noun* – **1.** *Savannah;* a community within the district of Bodden Town. **2.** the area which encompasses all parts between Spotts Newlands Road and Hirst Road, including Pedro St. James, ICCI, CountrySide Shopping Village, Savannah Meadows and Savannah Acres. **3.** the birthplace of many Cayman cowboys. **4.** Cayman's self-proclaimed countryside. **Eg.** *"I hear dem boys from Sawannah lowe horses more dun dey lowe woman."*

Schooole (s'hule) *Verb* – **1.** to water at the mouth, as in anticipation of food. **2.** to show excessive pleasure or anticipation of pleasure. **3.** to drool. *Noun* – **4.** saliva running down from one's mouth. **Eg.** *"Mama cookies so good dey mek ya schooole till ya tung fall out."*

School Pants (s'kool pahntz) *Noun* – **1.** a pair of pants of which the sole purpose of their existence is to be worn to school (and nowhere else; whatsoever). **2.** the uniform pants of a particular school. **3.** very boring looking pants, that never seem to match with casual, after-school attire. **Eg.** *"If mama ketch you climbin' dah guinep tree in yoh school pants, you gah get da biggest beatin' in yoh life."*

Scotch Bonnet Peppa (skotch baw-nit peh-pah) *Noun* – **1.** a popular brand of 'hot pepper' which has been used for decades to season fish, beef, pork, chicken and other meats. **2.** an extremely hot pepper seasoning. **Eg.** *"Child, if you don't stop mekkin' all kine ah nize 'bout goin' ova dis one house n' dah one house, I gah put some scotch bonnet on yoh tongue n' I betcha hush up den."*

Scranton (skrah'n-tun) *Noun* – **1.** the area encompassing all parts between Linwood Street and Tigris Street. **2.** the neighborhood directly behind Burke Maude Plaza. **3.** one of the best places to find someone who can cook beef and bake heavy cakes. **Eg.** *"I cyah wait till church convention come 'round dis year cuz wheneva dem ladies from Scranton cook, errybody be lickin' dey fingas cuz it taste so good."*

Scrape (s'kray'pe) *Noun* – **1.** one's crew. **2.** a collection of friends. **3.** a gang. **4.** a body of friends and acquaintances. **Eg.** *"Next time I have ah birtday party I gah hawe invite dah whole scrape from Central, Windsa Pa'ak n' Wess Bay."*

Ss

Scrounge (skraown'jh) *Verb* – **1.** to scrape for money. **2.** to borrow (a small amount or item) with no intention of repaying or returning it. **3.** to gather together by foraging; seek out. to borrow, esp. a small item one is not expected to return or replace. **Eg.** *"Anytime da ice cream truck come cross my house, dah way ya see man scroungin' up two dollas ta buy ah milk shake."*

Scruffian (sk'ruff-ee-yun) *Noun* – **1.** the combination of a *ruffian* and a *scruff*. **2.** a nasty, tough, lawless person; roughneck; bully. **3.** a person who does not observe any rules, and lacks even basic upbringing. **4.** a dirty person; unkept and ill-mannered. **5.** a scruffy ruffian. **Eg.** *"Aye man! Moo from me wit dah garlic bret, yah ol' scruffian!"*

Scummy Teet (skuh-meh teet) *Pronoun* – **1.** nasty looking teeth which are yellowing and overrun with plaque. **2.** rotten teeth, covered with a film of impure matter. **Eg.** *"Man, dah time when Trent had open he mout ta yawn, I taught I wah in Pirates ah da Caribbean when I see all ah dem scummy teet he had up in deh."*

Sea Beef (see beef) *Noun* – **1.** a hard, slug-like animal commonly found stuck to rocks on the ironshore. **2.** a parasite with a striped, stoney shell which spends it's entire life stuck to a rock, ingesting minerals from the ironshore. **3.** a tough, tiny creature which is extremely difficult to remove from the ironshore and closely resembles a *Slug* or *Leech*, with pinkish-coloured flesh underneath a tough shell. **Eg.** *"I know it nah ga be me eatin' no Sea Beef tonight."*

Sea Cutta (see cudda) *Noun* – **1.** a small, blueish coloured amphibious crab, which comes on land occasionally. **2.** a small crab, with strong snapping claws and hind fins for travel underwater. **3.** a species of sea crab. **Eg.** *"I always wonda how a Sea Cutta would taste, cuz erry time my daddy ketch one, he fling it back in da sea."*

Sea Egg (see aye'g) *Noun* – **1.** a type of *sea urchin*, usually black and covered in long prickles. **2.** one of the most painful objects to step on while walking in the sea. **3.** an ugly egg-like creature which lives in small caves beneath the ocean **Eg.** *"One time ya could jess reach in da wadda by Bob Soto's n' pick up ah hand full ah sea eggs."*

Ss

Sea Grape (see gray'p) *Noun* – **1.** *Coccoloba Uvifera*; a species of flowering plant in the *buckwheat* family (Polygonaceae), which grows primarily near the sea or large bodies of salt water. **2.** a sprawling bush or small tree that is found on beaches throughout the Cayman Islands and the Caribbean, as well as southern Florida. **Eg.** *"I wish I had ah nice sea grape tree in my yaad"*

Sea Itch (see ih'che) *Noun* – **1.** a bulbous, brownish-green floating algae (a close relative to '*Sea Weed*') which is extremely irritant to the human skin. **2.** a floating algae armed with the potency of a jellyfish, but disguised as a harmless Sea Weed. **3.** the ruination of many snorkeling trips for tourists and locals alike. **Eg.** *"Hush nah? I know you just get sting by Sea Itch, but you nah gah mek so much nize det dah whole Public Beach kin hear."*

Seb'm Mile Beach (she'b'm myle beech) *Noun* – **1.** the amazing Seven Mile Beach. **2.** a long crescent of coral-sand beach on the western shore of Grand Cayman. **3.** the most popular and most developed area of Grand Cayman. **Eg.** *"All kine ah man be tryin' check touriss woman wit dey American twang n' kin barely speak English."*

Secondary Modern School (seh-kun-deh-reh maw-dern skool) *Noun* – **1.** an early Government-funded 'middle school', established to provide education for students past the age of 11 + . **2.** a comprehensive system of secondary education during the 1960s and 70s. **3.** a precursor to the Cayman Islands High School. **Eg.** *"Daddy say if we could go back ta when he wah in Secondary Modern, he would do it jess ta show me way Cayman come from."*

Seddee (seh-dee) *Noun* – **1.** a standard living room sofa. **2.** a seat for two or more persons, having a back and usually arms and often upholstered. **3.** the family chair. **4.** the best seat in the house when the World Cup is on t.v. **Eg.** *"It hard ta believe dat my granfadda used ta sit right deh in dah seddee when he wah livin'!"*

Seet (seeet) *Noun* – **1.** pssstt. **2.** to generate a hissing sound with one's mouth as a form of flattery or communication. **3.** to call one's attention by making a hissing sound with one's mouth. **Eg.** *"sssssssttttt... sweetie yah waugh ah ride home? I kin keep yah comp'neh yih'nah?"*

Ss

Serasee (sir-see) or **Cerasee** (sare-ah-see) *Noun* – **1.** *Momordica charintia*; a climbing vine of the cucumber and pumpkin family. **2.** a popular tea bush. **3.** a tea made from the boiled leaves of the *Serasee Plant*, which is said to be good for strengthening the blood, relieving jaundice and purging and promoting healthy skin. **Eg**. *"My ahn'deh always gimme some ol' stink Serasee Tea ta drink when my belly hurtin' but I cyah stand it man."*

Session (she-shun) *Noun* – **1.** an afterhours party held on occassion during the 1990s when Cayman law prohibited nightclubs from opening past 1:00pm. **2.** an illegal party which often involved the sale of alcohol without a liquor license, disturbing the peace, littering, destruction of property, violence and trespassing. **Eg**. *"If gowament nehwa change da law ta mek nightclubs open till tree'clock, we woulda still be hawin' session all now."*

Sexxy (seck-seh) *Adjective* – **1.** overwhelmingly attractive. **2.** appealing to one's intimate desires. **3.** excitingly appealing; glamorous. **4.** sexually interesting or exciting; radiating sexuality. **Eg**. *"Mmmm!! Dat gyal is so sexxy man! If I didn't hawe a wife, a wifey, and tree babies on da way, I woulda hawe try check dat still."*

Sexxy Legs (seck-seh layg'z) *Noun* – **1.** long, slender, curvy legs which are extremely attractive. **2.** stout, muscular legs which are well defined and blemishless. **3.** perfect legs; well pigmented and appealing to the sight and touch. **Eg**. *"Dah gyal gah some sexxy legs, eh? I like da way she be walkin' rong in dem tight-up shorts n' ting."*

Shaap (sh'aaaahhp) *Adjective* – **1.** highly skilled and attentive. **2.** keen or eager. **3.** alert and vigilant. **4.** shrewd to the point of dishonesty. **5.** good looking. **6.** well dressed. **Eg**. *"Boy you shaap doh. You cyah see da sign say push n' you tryin' pull da door open?"* or; *"Max shaap when it come ta kickin' da ball way da goalie couldn' reach it."*

Shackin' Up (shah-kin upp) *Adverb* – **1.** living together. **2.** sharing a house for the convenience of maintaining a relationship. **3.** living together while in a relationship, irregardless of any plans to get married. **Eg**. *"I hear Trudy wah shackin' up wit Bradly cuz she taught she wah pregnant, but afta she fine out it wuz'n true, she moo back home."*

Ss

Shades (shay-dz) *Noun* – **1.** any pair of dark sunglasses. **2.** spectacles that are darkened or polarized to protect the eyes from the glare of the sun. **3.** a mandatory fashion accessory in today's world. **Eg.** *"Billy always gah be wearin' he shades when he cruisin' chrew town in he new Benz."*

Shame Face (sheem fay'ce) *Adverb* – **1.** bashful. **2.** shy. **3.** embarrassed. **Eg.** *"Wah ya lookin' at me all shame face fah? If ya like da gyal, go tell 'er, nah me."*

Shandy-Dandy (shah'n-deh dah'n-deh) *Noun* – **1.** a version of *dodgeball*. **2.** a game in which one player throws an inflated ball at several opponents which are lined up against a blank wall. The opponents must avoid being hit, and therefore eliminated, the winner being the one who remains unhit. **Eg.** *"I always used ta love playin' Shandy Dandy cuz all now nobody nah hit me yet."*

Sharp Up (sh'ahrp upp) *Verb* – **1.** to make oneself more presentable. **2.** to dress better; get a hair cut; buy new clothes. **3.** to become more attractive. **Eg.** *"Back in da 90's people used ta get all sharp up b'fore dey went ta ah concert', but nowadays dey doon' bizniss 'bout all dat no more."*

Sharkin' (sha'ah'r-kin) *Verb* – From East End; **1.** the process of hunting for a date with a woman, especially female tourists. **2.** attempting to get a date with a girl; any girl. **3.** laying claim to all women in a particular location, regardless of their availability or interest. **4.** 'starved out' for women. **5.** desperate to find a girl. **Eg.** *"I doon' know 'bout you, but I goin' sharkin' t'night ta look two gyal still."*

She Bad (shee bahd) *Adverb* – **1.** this (or that) is amazing. **2.** a specific reference to something that is unbelievable. **3.** something incredible. **Eg.** *"Lissin' ta my car man? She bad nah? – dah new cherry bomb I put in er sound kriss."*

Shiffin' Clouds (noh-teet) *Noun* – **1.** *Shifting Clouds*: a series of ill-shaped light coloured blotches on one's face. **2.** *Pityriasis versicolor*; a harmless skin disorder caused by a yeast, *Malassezia furfur*, which may be found on normal skin. **Eg.** *"Miss McLaughlin said Tamika didn't show up fa Graduation Practice yestaday, cuz she gah Shiffin' Clouds."*

Ss

Shiny Shoes (shy-neh shooze) *Noun* – **1.** shoes made of patent leather. **2.** a popular fashion accessory worn by the people of 1990, especially to Grafitti's Teen Nightclub, Monkey Business, and Faces Nightclub (**note:** all three clubs no longer exist). **3.** hard, glossy, smooth leather shoes, worn by MC Hammer. **Eg.** *"When I use ta dance Runnin' Man n' ting, I hadda have on my shiny shoes at all times."*

Shtrink (sh'treengk) *Verb* – **1.** 'shrink'; to contract; reduce. **2.** to cause (a fabric) to contract during finishing, thus preventing shrinkage, during laundering of the garments made from it. **3.** an act or instance of shrinking. **Eg.** *"I hate da way my clothes always come out all shtrink up afta ya wash um da first time yih'see?"*

Sick-eh (sihk-ehh) *Noun* – **1.** a pet name for a sick person. **2.** one who is always sick. **Eg.** *"Come yah, sick-eh. Lemme try so help you cuz all you gah do is cough all ova da place and mek me sick too."*

Sick Finga (sihk feeng'gah) *Noun* – **1.** an injured finger. **2.** a cut, burnt or broken finger. **Eg.** *"Daddy, I know you had waugh me go fishnin' wit you, but my sick finga hurtin' so I gah stay home."*

Sick Foot (sihk) *Noun* – **1.** an injured foot. **2.** a cut, burnt, or broken foot. **Eg.** *"Doon' mess wit me or else I gah drop one cement block on yoh sick foot."*

Sicknin' (sihk-nin) *Adverb* – **1.** very annoying. **2.** causing annoyance; irritatingly bothersome. **3.** harassing or disturbing. **Eg.** *"Geez, dah woman is so sicknin' wit dah lil' dog. All he do is leave ca-ca in people yard n' I gah be da one ta clean it up."*

Sick Toe (sihk) *Verb* – **1.** an injured toe. **2.** a cut, blistered, or broken toe. **Eg.** *"Come. Bring ya sick toe so I kin bandage it up - you poor bay-beh."*

Sick Toot (sihk tute) *Noun* – **1.** a tooth which is afflicted in some way, whether by cavity or external damage. **2.** a painful illness affecting one or more teeth. **Eg.** *"You bedda try so go dentist quick b'fore dah sick toot get worse."*

Ss

Siddown (sih-down) *Verb* – **1.** relax. **2.** to make less tense, rigid, or firm; make lax. **3.** to release oneself from inhibition, worry, tension, etc. **Eg.** *"Boy you bess try so siddown or else I gah tump you one time if you don't stop bodderin' me ova stupidness."*

Silva (sih'l-vah) *Noun* – **1.** loose change, consisting primarily of silver coins. **2.** any type of coin made of silver or a similar precious metal; excluding one cents. **3.** spare change. **Eg.** *"I hadda stop goin' by Champion House, cuz Randy always be out deh beggin' people fa dey silva."*

Silva Tatch (sih'l-vah) *Noun* – **1.** *Coccothrinax proctorii;* the Silver Thatch Palm; a native thatch tree, of which the leaves were a key ingredient in the Cayman economy up until the mid-20th Century. **2.** the leaves from a tree of the same name which are used for creating thatch products, including roofs for houses, bags, rope, hats, and bowls. **3.** Cayman's only endemic palm. **Eg.** *"On summa days like diss, juss gimme a good silva tatch hat, a hammock n' some swanky, n' I kin mek it chrew, no problem."*

Simpa Wiweh (sim-puh wy-weh) *Noun* – **1.** the Aloe Vera plant. **2.** any aloe of the species *Aloe Vera*, the fleshy leaves of which yield a juice used as an emollient ingredient of skin lotions and for treating burns. **3.** a leaf containing a puss-like liquid which can be used to correct children from using foul language. **Eg.** *"Dah time when mama ketch Shirley tellin' lies, she put some simpa wiweh on her tongue, n' she neva lie afta dat."*

Sir Turtle (sur tur-tuhl) *Noun* – **1.** Cayman's 'Uncle Sam'. **2.** the mascot of the Cayman Islands. **3.** one of Cayman's most prominent National Symbols. **4.** a pegged legged turtle which became the national symbol for Cayman Airways, when it was purchased from Suzy Soto in 1960 for $1.00. **Eg.** *"If dey eva try ta get rid ah Sir Turtle again I know it gah be pure ruction cuz errybody lowe ah Sir Turtle".*

Sittin' Room (sih-tin rume) *Noun* – **1.** a small living room, often one that forms part of a suite in a hotel, private house, etc. **2.** a room in a private house or establishment where people can sit and talk and relax. **3.** the t.v. room. **Eg.** *"Come less go in da sittin' room so we kin talk 'bout how we gah fix up da house fuh Christmas."*

Ss

Skid Out (skihdd owt) *Verb* – **1.** to burn tires when leaving a venue. **2.** to leave in a hurry. **3.** to create skid marks on pavement or gravel. **Eg.** *"I used ta lowe goin' out in da Kirk Freeport parkin' lot next ta way da camera store is now, jess so I could skid out my bicycle and play football wit my cousin."*

Skin No Teet (s'kin noh teet) *Slang* – **1.** to become cold and emotionless. **2.** never smile, or give in to charm. **3.** unrelenting; unyielding or swerving in determination or resolution, as of or from opinions, convictions, ambitions, ideals; inflexible. **4.** steadfast; determined. **Eg.** *"If it anyting about Harwell; he don't skin no teet wit none ah dem crooks dey gah in dah construction business."*

Skin Teet (s'kin teet) *Adjective* – **1.** to smile or grin a lot despite the occassion. **3.** jokey; jovial. **4.** exuberant; effusively and almost uninhibitedly enthusiastic; lavishly abundant. **Eg.** *"Look yah, ya ol' skin teet ting, stop jokin' rong n' less play some dominoes, man."*

Skinny Lee-Lee (s'kih-neh-lee-lee) *Noun* – **1.** an abnormally thin person. **2.** seemingly anorexic. **3.** a very lean or slender; emaciated person. **4.** unusually low or reduced; meager. **Eg.** *"Mummy, diss mornin' Miss Julie-Ann introduced ouwa class ta da new gyal from da states. Ah know she wuz'n ah real ol' skinny lee-lee doh yih'nah?"*

Skin Up (s'kin up) *Verb* – **1.** to give in to one's charm. **2.** to make peace, or become friends with. **3.** to smile broadly, esp. as an indication of pleasure, amusement, or the like. **4.** to smile or grin. **Eg.** *"If Renley come yah acksin' fah money, doon' skin up wid im no more, juss tell im yih nah ghee'in im nutt'n'!"*

Slave Wall (slay'v wohl) *Noun* – **1.** an incomplete wall built by slaves as the last line of defence against pirate raids. **2.** a long wall located in Bodden Town, which rises to a height of six feet in some places and meanders for about a half mile in a horse-shoe shape through the rocky backwoods of town. **3.** a wall which was allegedly cursed by the slaves who built it, one day before slavery was abolished in Cayman. (also called: **Drummond's Wall**) **Eg.** *"I use ta tink det Slave Wall wah juss ah pile ah rocks until Uncle Jimmy explain wah happen when dey build it."*

Ss

Slaw Pail (slaw payle) *Noun* – From Old People Times; **1.** a tall, bucket-like portable toilet, measuring approx. two feet tall used for gathering feces and urine. **2.** a traditional toilet. **3.** an alternative to using the 'out house' or 'back house'. **Eg.** *"Sweetie, empty da slaw pail fa granny so I kin use it."*

Sleepy Head (slee-peh hade) *Noun* – **1.** one who loves to sleep. **2.** always tired or sleepy. **3.** a constant sleeper. **4.** a really lazy person. **Eg.** *"I used ta have one sleepy head dog ya see? Yih could even pick im up n' fling im in da bed n' he would still be sleepin'."*

Slocum (slow-kum) *Noun* – **1.** a very slow person. **2.** one who may try very hard but is unable to move at the required speed. **3.** a sloth. **4.** lazy and weak. **5.** a human snail. **Eg.** *"Man, slocum, you cyah bag dem groceries no fasta dun dat?"*

Smart Alick (smah'rt ah-lick) *Noun* – **1.** a very sarcastic person who has an answer to everything. **2.** an obnoxiously conceited and self-assertive person. **3.** the person everyone wants to beat up, although no one admits it. **Eg.** *"Troy used ta be ah real Smart Aleck when we wah growin' up. Always talkin' bug how good he kin play football n' how much money he daddy had in da bank."*

Smit Barcadere (s'mitt bar-kuh-deer) *Noun* – **1.** *Smith Cove.* **2.** a beautiful cove located on South Church Street, featuring a relaxing array of tropical trees, warm, clear waters, and magnificent sunsets. **3.** a popular beach for locals and tourists alike. **Eg.** *"Any Caymanian who tell you he nehwa went n' go bayde in da sea at Smit Barcadere is a liyud. Errybody bin deh."*

Smoke Pan (smoke pahn) *Noun* – From Old People Times; **1.** a one gallon paint can with a wire handle, half full of sand, with holes above the level of the sand to increase air flow. **2.** an empty paint can filled with burning dried cow dung or black mangrove wood to ward off mosquitos. **3.** a crude but inexpensive mosquito repellant. **Eg.** *"Man, if I hadda walk rong wit ah smoke pan deez days, I wouldn' be able go ta work, cuz it would be so stink."*

Ss

Smude (s'moood) *Adjective* – **1.** smooth. **2.** free from projections or unevenness of surface; not rough. **3.** easy and uniform, as motion or the working of a machine. **4.** free from or proceeding without abrupt curves, bends, etc. **5.** careful; skillful; exact; precise. **Eg.** *"I like how Jordan used ta play basketball yih'see? Sometimes he wah so smude wid it, nobody couldn' eable touch im yih'nah?"*

Snobbish (snaw-bish) *Adjective* – **1.** mightier than thou. **2.** two-faced; having the tendency to disregard one's affiliation with people of a lower class, when in the company of wealthy or high-positioned persons. **3.** of, pertaining to, or characteristic of a snob. **4.** the act of pretending to be rich or cultured, to impress others. **Eg.** *"Afta Ivan, nobody wah actin' snobbish cuz errybody wah starwin', n' errybody had need help from somebody's else."*

Soap Powda (sope pow-dah) *Noun* – **1.** powdered soap used for washing clothes or scouring dishes. **2.** detergent powder. **3.** powdered laundry detergent. **4.** the best kind of detergent to use in industrial washing machines. **Eg.** *"One time when Pookeh had run out a tootpaste, he use he mama soap powda ta bresh he teet."*

Soffy Soffy (saw-feh saw-feh) *Adverb* – **1.** really soft. **2.** yielding readily to touch or pressure; easily penetrated, divided, or changed in shape; not hard or stiff. **3.** out of condition; flabby. **Eg.** *"Eva since I stop goin' gym, people say my muscles get soffy soffy"* or; *"Doon' leave diss bag ah mangoes in da sun or else dey gah turn soffy soffy."*

Soft Boy (sawf boy) *Noun* – **1.** one who lacks the assertiveness to defend himself, verbally or physically. **2.** one who is afraid of violence, and succumbs to bullying. **3.** a person easily stirred to sentiment or tender emotion. **4.** a wimp. **5.** one who lacks strength of character. **Eg.** *"Dem bad boys always like ta pick on Leelan, cuz dey know he ah lil' soft boy n' he doon' fight back."*

[Aunt] Sookie (ah'nt sooh-kih) *Noun* – **1.** one half of the comedic duo known as 'Sookie and Zekiel'. **2.** a prominent Caymanian entertainer. **3.** a former Member of the Legislative Assembly and local real estate agent. **Eg.** *"I used ta lowe goin' Harquail jess ta watch some good Sookie and Zekiel skits. Dey wah da hardest, boy."*

Ss

Soldier Crab (sol-jah krahb) *Noun* – **1.** the *Hermit Crab*. **2.** a burrowing crab of the genus *Gelasimus*, of many species. the male has one claw very much enlarged, and often holds it in a position similar to that in which a musician holds a fiddle, hence the name. (also called: *Calling Crab*, and *Fighting Crab*) **Eg.** *"Anytime Miss McField wrap up her head in ah bun, it always look like ah soldier crab."*

Some Lil' Way (sum lill wey) *Adverb* – **1.** in some way or another. **2.** however possible. **3.** the easiest and quickest way without going to an extreme. **4.** somehow; with the help of a miracle. **Eg.** *"Dah time when we had get stuck in Alaska wit no money, my Daddy hadda find some lil' way ta send us two dollas cuz da bank wuz'n open."*

Some Sorta How (sum sawr-da haow) *Adverb* – **1.** somehow. **2.** in some way not specified, apparent, or known. **3.** somehow or other, in an undetermined way; by any means possible. **4.** one way or another. **Eg.** *"Dah nah really da right way I wanted it ta be, but at least I fix up da garage some sorta how."*

Some Sorta Way (sum sawr-da wey) *Adverb* – **1.** in some way, someways. **2.** in some way or another; somehow. **3.** in some unspecified way or manner; or by some unspecified means. **Eg.** *"You coulda at least try ta call me back some sorta way even if yoh cell wuz'n wurkin' right."*

Sometimish (sum-tyme-ish) *Adverb* – **1.** unreliable. **2.** neither here nor there. **3.** liable to be erroneous or misleading. **4.** not worthy of reliance or trust. **5.** unstable and unpredictable. **Eg.** *"Don't try ta hold Mia ta nuttin' cuz she too sometimish n' she gah mek make ya look stupid."*

Sore Up (soh're upp) *Adverb* – **1.** full of aches and pains due to soreness; tenderness. **2.** fatigued in the muscles. **Eg.** *"When I wah small, my granfadda used ta leave uwah bunkey all sore up when me n' my brudda wah misbehavin'!"*

So-So (soh soh) *Adverb* – **1.** about average. **2.** indifferent; neither very good nor very bad. **3.** in an indifferent or passable manner; indifferently; tolerably. **Eg.** *"Even doh I feel kine-ah so-so t'day, I still goin' gym, cuz I waugh lose 27.75lbs. by da enna da munt."*

Ss

Sound Road (song rode) *Noun* – **1.** North Sound Road. **2.** the road which begins next to Reflections Liquor 4 Less, passes next to A.L. Thompson's Home Depot, Paramount Carpets, Public Works, CUC, and runs into the North Sound. **3.** the quickest route into Industrial Park from Shedden Road. **Eg.** *"Sound Road be so congested sometimes, especially when dey hawin' sump'm at Welly's."*

Sour Sop (suh-wah sawp) *Noun* – **1.** a broadleaf flowering evergreen tree native to the Caribbean, Central and South America. It is in the same genus as the *cherimoya* and the same family as the *pawpaw*. **2.** a fruit which is somewhat difficult to eat, as the white interior pulp is studded with many large seeds, and pockets of soft flesh are bounded by fibrous membranes. The soursop is therefore usually juiced rather than eaten directly. **Eg.** *"Gimme some good soursop juice n' ah piece ah Cassava cake, n' I do anyting ya waugh tomorrow."*

Sour Tap (suw-ah tapp) *Noun* – **1.** a very painful strike or blow to one's body. **2.** a beating, by hand or with an instrument. **3.** a licking. **Eg.** *"Cuz, when Foggy ghee him one sour tap yih'see? Even ta he dead granny mussa feel it."*

Space Out (s'pay'ce-owtt) *Adverb* – **1.** spaced out; daydreaming. **2.** dreamily or eerily out of touch with reality or seemingly so; spacey. **3.** absentminded dreaming while awake. **Eg.** *"I used ta be space out in class erry day cuz it wah borin' n' Ms. Lorna diddn' know how ta teach Social Studies."*

Spanish Rock (spah-nish rawk) *Noun* – **1.** an area in Bodden Town which is approximately north-west of the Guard House. **2.** an area of Bodden Town first inhabited by Christian Moors in 1632 when they were outcast from Spain. They inhabited the island for forty years until their young men were lured into the effort to recapture Jamaica for the King of Spain. Spanish Rock was deserted by 1672. **Eg.** *"When I use ta hear my daddy talkin' ta Mista Fred 'bout Spanish Rock, I taught it wah ah type ah music."*

Spar (spah'rr) *Noun* – **1.** a close friend or acquaintance. **2.** a friend of a friend who is worth having around. **3.** the younger companion of an older friend or sibling. **Eg.** *"Yow, Freeburn, hook my lil' spar up wit some popcorn nah?"*

Ss

Sparrin' Partnah (spah'rr-in pahrt-nuh) *Noun* – **1.** one's partner-in-crime. **2.** a close personal friend; best friend. **3.** a relationship whereby one individual cannot be found far from the other. **4.** partners in mischief. **Eg.** *"Man, me 'n my sparrin' partna Georgie goin' check some football down by Annex diss weekend."*

Splinta (splih-nah) *Noun* – **1.** a common wood splinter. **2.** a small, thin, sharp piece of wood, bone, or the like, split or broken off from the main body. **Eg.** *"One time I had get one splinta up in my foot, it felt like it wah two feet long. Boy, dah had hurt."*

Spoily (s'poyle-eh) *Noun* – **1.** one who is childish and spoiled. **2.** juvenile. **3.** rude and unruly. **4.** full of contempt for rules. **5.** determined to have one's way. **Eg.** *"Wathcha spoily nah? He face always gah be screw up like somebody tryin' kill im."*

Spotts Straight (spawt'z stray'te) *Noun* – **1.** a straight road, originating from the end of *Old Prospect*, and ending at the *Spotts Dock*. **2.** the venue of many fatal car accidents. **3.** one of the longest stretches of straight road on Grand Cayman. **Eg.** *"Cuz, you shoulda see how I had sink da clutch n' pop 'er in fiff gear up by Spott's Straight. It wah sweet man."*

Sprats (s'pratz) *Noun, Pl.* – **1.** *Spratelloides robustus*; also known as *blue bait, blue sardine* or *blue baitis*. **2.** a genus of small oily fish of the family *Clupeidae*, commonly fried and eaten whole in Cayman cuisine. **3.** small, blueish-silver fish, which are best used for bait, and must be caught with a net because of their size. **4.** the best bait to use. **Eg.** *"If yah chrow out yoh fishin' net an' it come back wit nuttin' but sprats, dah mean it nah no big fish in da area."*

Sprawl Out (s'praw'l owt) *Verb* – **1.** to sit or lie in a very compromising position with one's limbs spread out carelessly or ungracefully. **2.** to be stretched or spread out in an unnatural or ungraceful manner. **3.** to compromise one's personal privacy while lying or sitting. **Eg.** *"Watcha how Treecia always sprawl out afta she finish runnin' track, nah? I tell her she gah meck sure no boys nah watchin' when she layin' down like dat."*

Ss

Spray Rain (s'praye reen) *Noun* – **1.** intervals of light rainfall and windiness. **2.** drizzle. **3.** a very light rain. **Eg.** *"If you wauh get ta yoh car, ya bedda run quick, cuz it juss spray rain out deh now but it gah get worse dun dat."*

Spult (spul't) *Adverb* – From West Bay; **1.** spoiled; having the character or disposition harmed by pampering or oversolicitous attention. **2.** rude and unruly. **3.** full of contempt for rules. **4.** of the impression that one's own self-interests are predominant over all others. **Eg.** *"David always be goin' on spult cuz he cyah get he way all da time."*

Spult Behind (spul't buh-hine) *Adjective* – From West Bay; **1.** extremely spoiled. **2.** completely oblivious to the interests of others. **3.** narrow-minded. **4.** dissatisfied with everything that does not match with one's primary objectives. **Eg.** *"Dat stink mout ting ah Calbert is ah real ol' spult behind y'see. If he cyah get ta smoke he cigarette, he always gah mek trouble fa errybody's else."*

Spulteh (spul-teh) *Noun* – From West Bay; **1.** one who is extremely spoiled. **2.** an annoying person. **3.** a selfish and inconsiderate individual. **Eg.** *"Awright, ya ol' spulteh. I gah ghee ya some ah my guineps so stop bawlin'."*

Spultfulness (spul't-full-niss) *Noun* – From West Bay; – **1.** unruliness. **2.** unjustified pettiness. **3.** an allergic reaction to inconvenience. **Eg.** *"Swee-deh if you gah go on wit yoh spultfulness erry time I leave you in da car ta go shoppin', I nah ga cyar you no way wit me no more."*

Spyla (s'pye-lah) *Noun* – **1.** spoiler. **2.** an aerodynamic attachment to the trunk, which assists with speed while driving. **3.** a device for changing the airflow past a moving vehicle, often having the form of a transverse fin or blade mounted at the front or rear to reduce lift and increase traction at high speeds. **Eg.** *"I know why dey call it spyla, cuz when ya put it on ya car, it spyle da way it look."*

Spyle (s'pile) *Adverb* – **1.** spoiled. **2.** having the character or disposition harmed by pampering or oversolicitous attention. **3.** greedy; selfish. **Eg.** *"Stop bein' so spyle or else I nah cyar-in' you no way wit me."*

Ss

Spyle Up (s'pile upp) *Verb* – **1.** to ruin; to devastate. **2.** to destroy the integrity of an object. **3.** to sabotage one's integrity. **Eg.** *"I used ta have ah nice dress ta wear ta church, but it had get spyle up wit green mango."*

Squab (skwob) *Noun* – **1.** a species of *Parrotfish*, which are mostly tropical, perciform marine fish of the family *Scaridae*. **2.** a bottom feeding fish which is partly responsible for the production of beach sand, caused by the digestion and excretion of coral and other rocks. **3.** a beautifully coloured fish, with tender, almost boneless meat. **Eg.** *"Lass night, I had ah good lil' piece ah fried Squab from Mr. Wellington birtday party."*

Squat (skwot) *Verb* – **1.** the process of lowering one's car. **2.** a car which has been *lowered*, usually by altering the suspension system to make it sit closer to the ground. **Eg.** *"Gee-doh, look ah Big D car man, boy she squat low, doh."*

Squinch Up (skwintch upp) *Adverb* – **1.** to squeeze together or contract. **2.** to bring in. **3.** to draw together. **Eg.** *"Lisa, I know it nah much room in dis lil' car, so you gah have ta squinch up by Burton, even doh ya say he smell frowsy."*

Sstchyuppid (stch-yupp-idd) *Noun* – **1.** stupid. **2.** characterized by or proceeding from mental dullness; foolish; senseless. **3.** a stupid or foolish person. **4.** having no sense, whether common or uncommon. **Eg.** *"I wonda how come some people could be so stchyuppid as ta leave dey car runnin' wit da keys in it."*

Stall Out (stawl owt) *Verb* – **1.** to receive an insult so terrible, it stops one from moving. **2.** to stop moving; die; as in a vehicle. **3.** a fatal, unexpected embarassment. **Eg.** *"You shoulda see when Clarence went go acks Renee ta prom; I know he nah get ah stall out when she tell im Brinwell had already acks 'er from lass year"* or; *"I cyah believe my car stall out n' leff me on da side ah da road in Nor'side."*

Stan Up (stah'n upp) *Noun* – **1.** a standing position; stance. **2.** the position or bearing of the body while in an upright position. **3.** standing posture. **Eg.** *"Look ah dah piece ah stan up she puttin' on deh, like she ah mannequin or someting."*

Ss

Star (stah'r) *Noun* – **1.** 'friend'. **2.** my boy. **3.** good buddy. **4.** brethren. **5.** a substitute when one's name does not come to mind. **Eg.** *"No star, it don't go like dat. I wah walkin' down da street, n' yoh wife almost run me off da road. If I diddn' had jump in da bush, she woulda wipe me out."*

Starve Out (stah'rve owt) *Adverb* – **1.** really greedy. **2.** having a strong or great desire for food or drink. **3.** excessively or inordinately desirous of wealth, profit, etc.; avaricious. **4.** keenly desirous; eager. **Eg.** *"People always used ta tell me I wah starve out ta play Mortal Kombat at Pops' game room when we wah youngah."*

States (stay-t'z) *Noun, Pl.* – **1.** an abbreviation of the United States of America. **2.** a republic in the Northwestern Hemisphere comprising 48 conterminous states, the District of Columbia, and Alaska in North America, and Hawaii in the North Pacific. **3.** the best place to get away for shopping on a long weekend. **Eg.** *"If I eva get tiyud ah Cayman I kin always go live wit my cousins in da States."*

Stateside (stay-t'-syde) *Noun* – **1.** being in or toward the continental U.S. **2.** any city in Florida (especially: Miami, Tampa or Orlando), or New York City. **3.** America. **Eg.** *"Kilburn went stateside dis weekend an bring back one big time American chick ta show off wit."*

Steef (ss'teef) *Verb (slang)* – **1.** a combination of the words 'steal' and 'thief. **2.** to take (the property of another or others) without permission or right, esp. secretly or by force. **3.** to commit or practice theft. **4.** to get or take secretly or artfully. **5.** to steal and thief at the same time. **Eg.** *"Aye, you like steef too much man..., who tell you you kin come up in people room an tek dey cd's like it yours?"*

Steely (stee-leh) *Noun* – **1.** a child's playing marble made of stainless steel. **2.** a small steel bearing taken from construction or mechanical equipment, which can be cleaned and used as a marble. **3.** the best marble to use when you're trying to 'sack' your competition. **Eg.** *"Boy, when Devon pull out dah big ol' steely he gran-fadda ghee him fuh Christmas, errybody wah worried about losin' all ah dey marbles."*

Ss

Stick-Up (stik upp) *Noun* – **1.** a profane use of the middle finger. **2.** to use profanity through sign language. **3.** to 'flip the bird'. **Eg.** *"Ahh-haah! Dah wah ya get fa showin' people stick-up. Ya shoulda get more dun two weeks detention."*

Still (stih'l) *Adjective* – **1.** a common suffix to any sentence or statement. **2.** the last word in a statement, regardless of context or connotation. **3.** a word that is often stressed to emphasize other parts of a sentence. **Eg.** *"Deez new Jordans look kine-ah kriss, still."*

Stilt House (stihl't howce) *Noun* – From Old People Times; **1.** a traditional *Old Caymanian House*, built on a series of stilts (3-5ft. above ground) to avoid flooding during severe storms (i.e. Nor'westers, Hurricanes, etc...). **2.** a classic Caymanian house. **Eg.** *"When Mr. Artha turn he stilt house inta ah store, some people tell im he wah crazy."*

Stink (steenk) *Adverb* – **1.** the state of one's well being; uncomfortable; irritated. **2.** the appearance of a particular person or object. **3.** the look of something. **4.** the feel of an object. **5.** a behavior. **Eg.** *"If anyting, just call me when ya see Brenton, cuz he be goin' on stink sometimes when ya acks im ta do someting"* or; *"Man, dah new dress Shirley juss bought look stink on her boy; she should cyar dat back."*

Stink Out (steenk owt) *Adverb* – **1.** to wreak with a horrid stench; as in a room or entire building. **2.** to carry a bad smell throughout a large area. **3.** to leave a room smelling really bad. **4.** to pass gas amongst a multitude in a poorly ventilated area. **Eg.** *"I hate goin' in da baffroom afta granfadda yih'see? He always stink out da whole room."*

Stoopidness (stoo-pid-niss) *Adverb* – **1.** pure foolishness. **2.** annoyances and irritatants; trouble. **3.** really outrageous. **4.** uncalled for. **5.** making no sense whatsoever. **Eg.** *"I tink it's pure stoopidness ta go rent movies when I jess pay $1,599.00 fah ah new DSS system."*

Straight Leg Pants (strate laig pahntz) *Noun* – **1.** a pair of pants often being the same size from the hip straight down to the ankle. **2.** baggy-free pants. **3.** the kind of pants a school principal may wear. **Eg.** *"Boy, I doon' know how Mr. Hardell kin wear dah chocolate brown cod'roy suit wit dem straight leg pants and tink it still in style."*

Ss

Street Dance (street dahn'ce) *Noun* – **1.** any party, festival, concert, or musical demonstration that includes the gathering of people around a deejay or band, for the purpose of dancing in the street. **2.** a party that is held in the middle of the street, of which both ends are cordoned off to vehiclular traffic. **3.** a great place to enjoy reggae and soca music, find someone to dance with, and leave cheerful and sweaty, while singing the last song that was played. **Eg.** *"If I could bill ah time machine, I would go back ta '91, when Batabano used ta hawe da bess street dances eva."*

Strickleh (strik-leh) *Adverb* – **1.** exactly; of course. **2.** precisely; only. **3.** need I say more? **Eg.** *"Come man... I know you deal strickleh wit one barba, but I jess waugh you come wit me ta get my hair cut."*

String Up (streeng upp) *Adverb* – **1.** goofy looking. **2.** ridiculous; silly; wacky; nutty. **3.** to hold someone off of their feet or compromise their footing. **Eg.** *"Mr. Parley say dah guy had look all string up when he come in he shop lass week."* or; *"If you don't stop messin' rong wit dem bad boys you gah get string up by Police one ah deez days."*

Striker (stry-kah) *Noun* – **1.** a twenty-foot long stick, made from a *Cherry* tree, and having a hole carved out of the tip, to insert a pair of metal 'prongs' for grabbing. the striker is used when fishing for conch and/or lobster, from the comfort of a small boat in waters which are 20ft. deep or less. the fisherman generally uses a 'water glass' to find the catch, and 'strike' the animal carefully with the prongs. **2.** a long stick, similar to a fruit picker, used to collect lobster and conch from the ocean floor. **Eg.** *"One time my Uncle Charley had drop he striker in da wadda n' hadda go diwe it up quicktime b'fore it wash way."*

Stubby Toes (stuh-beh toze) *Noun* – **1.** really short nub-like toes. **2.** chubby, short toes. **3.** baby-like feet. **Eg.** *"Kurt always used ta tell Tania she had stubby toes, n' she say he's look like cigarette butts."*

Stupid Eediyut (stoo-pidd ee-dee-yutt) *Noun* – **1.** a real fool. **2.** a buffoon. **3.** a person of little intelligence or common sense. **Eg.** *"Doon' say nuttin' more ta me ya stupid eediyut! I jess cyah tek da way you go on sometimes yih'see."*

Ss

Stush (stoosh) *Adverb* – **1.** snobbish. **2.** of, pertaining to, or characteristic of a *snob*. **3.** having the character of a snob. **4.** befitting or resembling a snob; pretentious. **Eg.** *"Hi Lisa, I saw you at Rumheads lass week, but you had look too stush in yoh new clothes n' ya new boyfriend so dah why I diddn' say nuttin'."*

Style (stile) *Noun* – **1.** the current trend or fashion. **2.** the thing to do. **3.** a mode of living, as with respect to expense or display. **4.** a mode of fashion, as in dress, esp. good or approved fashion; elegance; smartness. **5.** something to be followed. **6.** a cause for people to dress up in unorthodox garments and accessories, claiming that anyone who does not appreciate their attire is obsolete. **Eg.** *"I don't care wah nobody say. I nah runnin' around in dem sissy slippers and bug eye glasses just ta be in style."*

Sucka Tree (suh-kah tree) *Noun* – **1.** a Banana or Plantain tree. **2.** any of several tropical and subtropical tree-like herbs of the genus *Musa* having a terminal crown of large leaves and usually bearing hanging clusters of elongated fruits. **3.** a banana sucker. **4.** a plantain sucker. **Eg.** *"Ah good way ta practice darts is ta pelt um at ah sucka tree in da back yard when nobody nah ah'rong."*

Suck Finga (suk feeng'gah) *Noun* – **1.** the digit of the hand that is favoured during finger sucking, usually the thumb. **Eg.** *"Caroline, get dah suck finga outta yoh mout right now!. You's ah big ten year-old gyal now so you cyah be doin' dat no more."*

Sugar Head (shuh-gah hed) *Noun* – **1.** a funny looking afro which consists of red, brown and blonde hair; usually found on light-skinned persons. **2.** a fluffy multi-pigment afro. **3.** a very dry-looking afro which holds its shape, even when wet. **Eg.** *"Tell me something? Who dah sugar head boy you wah long wit yestaday? I waugh acks im who he belongs ta."*

Sugga Rugga (suh-gah rug-ah) *Noun* – **1.** having nappy, unkept, stringy hair. **2.** long hair, tangled and knotty; overgrown. **3.** bushy hair. **Eg.** *"Boy try so go run ah comb chroo dah piece ah hair you gah deh. Yoh head look like ah real ol' sugga rugga now."*

Ss

Sumpm'n (suhm'p'm) *Noun* – **1.** something. **2.** some thing; a certain undetermined or unspecified thing. **3.** a person, place, thing, time, or location, which has not been clearly specified. **Eg.** *"Man, sumpm'n doon' feel right about Leroy comin' ta pick me up wit my ex-husband in da car."*

Surrud (suh-rud) *Adverb* – From Old People Times (seafaring navigation) **1.** to the south. **2.** a cardinal point of the compass lying directly opposite north. **3.** lying toward or situated in the south; directed or proceeding toward the south. **Eg.** *"Dey say if ya house facin' ta da surrud, ya might get good prewailin' winds in da affanoon."*

Swamp (swawe'hmp) *Noun* – **1.** an overly congested neighborhood located on Grackle Road, directly behind the Old Godfrey's Enterprises Building and Green Thumb Nursery (respectively). **Eg.** *"One time, I used ta cyar all ah my new pants ta one Spanish lady down in swamp ta get um hem up."*

Swanky (swaieng-keh) *Noun* – **1.** a special treat made from a *Civil Orange (sour orange)*, brown sugar and water which is mixed or blended into a drink similar in taste to lemonade. **Eg.** *"Man, when summa be hot, gimme ah good glass ah swanky n' ah hummuck n' I good ta go."*

Sweet Boy (s'weet boy) *Noun* – **1.** a young man who is always well-dressed and immaculately groomed, especially when in the company of females. **2.** the guy everyone teases for being too effeminate, despite his ability to impress women with his attention to detail. **Eg.** *"Mm-mmm! Look ah dah sweet boy man? He always gah be combin' he hair all da time n' even when he playin' basketball he gah on about 10 pongs ah cologne."*

Sweet Sop (sweet sop) *Noun* – **1.** *Annona squamosa;* (*Sugar-apple, Sweetsop or Custard Apple*) a species of *Annona* native to the Caribbean and the tropical Americas **2.** a semi-evergreen shrub or small tree reaching 6-8 m. tall. the fruit flesh is edible, white to light yellow, and resembles and tastes like custard. the seeds are scattered through the fruit flesh; they are blackish-brown, 12-18 mm long, and hard and shiny. **Eg.** *Durin' Hurricane Ivan, I watch one sweetsop hold on ta da tree fa dear life, n' it made it chrew... jess like me n' you."*

Ss

Sweetums (swee-dumz) *Noun* – **1.** one's heartstring. **2.** the object of one's affection. **3.** a favourite child or baby. **Eg.** *"My sweetums, look ah how Lacey growin' up wit her lil' white boots man? She so cute!"*

Sweet Up (swee-dup) *Verb* – **1.** to brown-nose. **2.** to curry favour; behave obsequiously. **3.** to play on one's emotions for personal gain. **4.** to spray cologne, lotion, or any other odorous substance on oneself. **Eg.** *"Well, diss how it go. Anytime I waugh sleep ova by Cristy house, I juss go n' sweet up my daddy n' he meks me get my way"* or; *"Carden comes ta work all sweet up erry mornin' cuz he tryin' get Molly Ann ta like 'im."*

Sweety Pie (swee-deh pye) *Noun* – **1.** sweetheart. **2.** a person loved by another person. **3.** one's heartstring. **4.** the object of one's affection. **5.** a boyfriend or girlfriend. **6.** a lover, a wife, or a husband. **7.** a crush. **Eg.** *"Please doon' say nuttin' about Johnny, cuz dat's my sweety pie, n' I would kill anybody who gah sump'n bad ta say about 'im."*

Swell Head (sweh'l hed) *Adverb* – **1.** full of ego. **2.** pertaining to or characterized by egotism. **3.** given to talking about oneself; vain; boastful; opinionated. **4.** looking after one's own self interests. **5.** full of excitement as a result of having impressed or inspired envy of; others. **Eg.** *"Erry time Lily tell Brandon dat he dress sexy, he be walkin' rong wit one swell head da size ah George Town."*

Swipe (s'wype) *Verb* – **1.** to strike an object by brushing across it. **2.** the technique used in delivering a strike with a *Tamarind Switch*. **3.** to make a sweeping stroke. *Noun* – **4.** a lashing. **Eg.** *"If Kurney come back fassin' wit you, swipe im two times wit dah rasta belt you got on, n' run like duppy chasin' ya."*

Switch (s'witch) *Noun* – **1.** a slender, flexible shoot, rod, etc., used esp. in whipping or disciplining. **2.** an act of whipping or beating with or as with such an object; a stroke, lash, or whisking movement. **3.** the limb of a tree; usually either *Tamarind* or *Birch*, which is used for disciplining young children. **Eg.** *"Charley always say if he had he Tamarind switch wid im, errybody would have watch out."*

Ss

Tally Wappin' (tah-leh wah-pin) *Noun* – From Old People Times; **1.** a really bad beating. **2.** to have one's credibility destroyed as a result of losing a fight. **3.** to have one's butt kicked. *Slang* - **4.** to get kicked to pieces. **Eg.** *"I doon' know how chrew it is, but dey say Randal ghee Freddy ah good tally wappin' fah steppin' on he Jordan's."*

Tamarind (tahm-rinn) *Noun* – **1.** the pod of a large, tropical tree, *Tamarindus indica*, of the legume family, containing seeds enclosed in a juicy acid pulp that is used in beverages and food. **2.** the tree from which the notorious 'Tamarind Switch' is made. **Eg.** *"Lemme tell ya something, if somebody mek ya da real Caymanian Tamarind Jam, you gah lick yoh fingas off when you taste it."*

Tamarind Switch (tahm-rinn switch) *Noun* – **1.** a large branch, freshly picked from the *Tamarind Tree* for the specific purpose of disciplining a child. **2.** the most feared word in a child's vocabulary. **From Old People Times** – **3.** a stick and leaves from the *Tamarind Tree*, used to discipline unruly, disrespectful children. **Eg.** *"If yoh Daddy eva sen ya fah ah Tamarind Switch, ya know somebody gettin' beat n' it might even be you."*

Tar Baby (tar bay-beh) *Noun* – **1.** a derogatory term for a really dark-skinned person. **Eg.** *"Dah time when Selbert call Michelle ah tar baby, she kick im so hard between he legs, I know he mama mussa felt it."*

Tatch (tah'che) *Noun* – **1.** *Thatch*; a material, as straw, rushes, leaves, or the like, used to cover roofs, grain stacks, etc. **2.** the leaves of various palms that are used for thatching. **3.** something resembling thatch on a roof, esp. thick hair covering the head. **4.** a material used for plaiting various household items, including hats, fans, brooms, and plates. **Eg.** *"My Aunt Miriam kin mek anyting outta tatch if ya tell 'er wah ya waugh."*

Tt

Tatchin' (tah-chin) *Adverb* – From Old People Times; **1.** *Thatching*; the process of weaving, twisting, tying, or by any other means, working with thatch leaves and thatch products. **2.** an early occupation for many of the poor families throughout the Islands, who would work tirelessly to create thatch products such as ropes, twine, hats, plates, brooms, etc. for sale at local and overseas markets. **3.** the process used in creating large projects, such as the traditional 'thatch roof'. **4.** an endangered Cayman tradition. **Eg.** *"Anytime ya see Granny Linette doin' some tatchin' dah mean she in ah bad mood."*

Taw (taugh) *Noun* – **1.** one's favourite shooter in a game of marbles. **2.** the one marble that must be protected [at all times] against the opponent's shooter during a game of marbles. **Eg.** *"I hadda tell Devon I couldn' play marbles wid im t'day cuz I loss my favourite taw n' I cyah play good widdout it."*

Teck (tek) *Verb (used with object)* – **1.** take; to get into one's hold or possession by voluntary action. **2.** to hold, grasp, or grip. **3.** to receive or be the recipient of. **4.** to convey in a means of transportation. **Eg.** *"Ransford say if Wilson doon' stop messin' wid im, he gah teck back dah new Playstation game he jess buy im fah he birtday."*

Tee-Dee (tee-dee) *Noun* – From West Bay; **1.** a close personal friend, usually female. **2.** reference to someone without using their real name. **Eg.** *"Aye Tee-Dee, pay attention nah? You cyah see people tryin' talk sense in yoh head?"*

Teef (teef) *Noun* – **1.** a thief. **2.** one who steals, esp. secretly or without open force; one guilty of theft or larceny. *Verb* – **4.** to take (the property of another or others) without permission or right, esp. secretly or by force. **Eg.** *"Lissin' yah man: You cyah hear I nah gah no money ta lend you cuz somebody teef my wallet lass night?"*

Teefishness (teef-ish-niss) *Noun* – **1.** the act or practice of thieving. **2.** having the ability to rob, steal or vandalize the property of others. **3.** inclined to commit thievery. **Eg.** *"Aye, try so moo frum yah wit yah teefishness nah? You always waugh eat out people chips and doo waugh buy none back."*

Tt

Tee-Tee (tee-tee) *Noun* – From West Bay; **1.** a close personal friend, usually female. **2.** reference to someone without using their real name. **Eg.** *"Awww... how ya doin' tee-tee? I nah seen you in so long."*

Teets (teetz) *Noun* – **1.** a common nickname for someone who loves to smile and grin a lot. **2.** pl. of tooth. **3.** the group of instruments designed for biting and chewing one's food. **Eg.** *"I gah ah cousin name 'Teets' but he leff Cayman when he wah small n' I nah seen im since."*

Tee-Wee (tee-wee) *Noun* – **1.** 't.v.'. **2.** a common household television of any size, shape or brand. **3.** a man's favourite piece of technology. **Eg.** *"Wheneva World Cup football be on, errybody be bringin' tee-wee ta work, n' dey boss doon' even say nuttin' cuz dey waugh watch it too."*

Templeton (tem-pull-tunn) *Noun* – **1.** *Templeton Pine Lakes;* the housing community located directly behind the George Town Hospital. **2.** the neighborhood to the East of Windsor Park, which is low-lying, and prone to flooding due to various swamps and a large pond. **Eg.** *"Dis week I gah hawe go check Renny down in Templeton or else he gah disown me."*

Tereckleh (tuh-reck-leh) *Adverb* – **1.** later. **2.** the not-so-distant future. **3.** a future time to come. (also pronounced: 'ereckleh', 'dereckleh', or 'areckleh' in some areas) **Eg.** *"Lemme know wah ya doin' tereckleh so I kin plan ma day bedda."*

Tenna (teh-nah) *Noun* – **1.** any person of East End origin or descent. **2.** one who lives in East End, the easternmost district on Grand Cayman. **3.** an East Ender. **Eg.** *"It might be biased since my family from East End but I know dem tennas is some ah da bess fishaman een da Caribbean!"*

The Firm (duh furm) *Noun* – **1.** the first official Hollywood movie to be filmed in the Cayman Islands. **2.** an early 1990s movie starring Tom Cruise, Gene Hackman and Jeanne Tripplehorn. **3.** one of the first American movies to feature Caymanians as extras. **Eg.** *"If you look good, yih kin see my face in The Firm."*

Tt

The Juice (duh joo'ce) *Noun* – **1.** the latest gossip. **2.** juicy gossip; fresh news. **3.** the latest talk of the town. **Eg.** *"Aye, hurry up so gimme da juice nah? I waugh know wah happen while I wah in Hialeah."*

The '32 Storm (duh tir-deh too stawrm) *Noun* – **1.** a massive hurricane which struck the Sister Islands in November 1932, claiming the lives of 108 persons, including 29 children under age 10. **2.** the worst storm in the history of the Cayman Islands. **3.** the 'killer storm' which left many dead and others either injured or mourning on Little Cayman and Cayman Brac, where houses were ripped to shreds and trees were left completely bare. **Eg.** *"My granny say if we wah livin' when da '32 storm had hit, we woulda know wah real disasta is."*

The Republic (duh rah-pubb-lick) *Noun* – **1.** the district of West Bay. **2.** the place where West Bayers are kept. **3.** Weh Bay. **Eg.** *"Aye, watch wah ya sayin' bug West Bay rong Arnold; he from the Republic."*

Truppance (thruh-puntz) *Noun* – From 'Old People Times'; **1.** the threepence coin; a denomination of currency, used by various jurisdictions in England, Ireland, Scotland and Wales, until decimalisation of the pound sterling and Irish pound; usually pronounced either "thripp'nce", "thrupp'nce" or "threpp'nce", the distinction perhaps being geographical. **2.** an odd-shaped bronze coin. **Eg.** *"Back in my gran-fadda days, dey used'ta feel rich if dey get couple'ah truppance fah ah days work."*

The Wife (da wyfe) *Noun* – **1.** one's wife or girlfriend. **2.** a longtime girlfriend who assumes the duties of a wife. **3.** a girlfriend who behaves as if she is a wife. **4.** a fiance'. **Eg.** *"By da time I get back home I hadda acks the wife ta juss fix me some dinna so I could tek my med'sin n' go sleep."*

Tick (tik) *Adverb* – **1.** thick. **2.** having relatively great extent from one surface or side to the opposite; not thin. **3.** measured, as specified, between opposite surfaces, from top to bottom, or in a direction perpendicular to that of the length and breadth. **4.** a measurement of one's girth. **Eg.** *"Way back when, Cayman used ta be tick wit miskittas"* or *"Deez jeans so tick, ah bullet couldn' eable go chrew um."*

Tt

Tick Dope (tik doap) *Noun* – From Old People Times;
1. a really toxic chemical (shampoo) which was used to remove ticks and other insect from cows. **2.** a flea bath for cows. **3.** a tick repellent. **Eg.** *"If dey hadda keep usin' dah tick dope on dem cows, we woulda nehwa had no beef on diss Island. I hear dem farmas used ta use too much ah it n' kill off all da cows."*

Tightas (ty-duz) *Noun, Pl.* – **1.** clothes which are untrendy to teenagers due to lack of bagginess. **2.** unattractively close-fitting clothing; usually t-shirts or jeans. **3.** a guaranteed reason to be teased in school. **Eg.** *"Gee, I doon' know how Kerwin kin wear dem tightas ta school. Dey would cut off my blood flow."*

Tights (titez) *Noun, Pl.* – **1.** any piece of clothing which is either too small or made of skin tight material. **2.** a skin-tight, one-piece garment for the lower part of the body and the legs, now often made of stretch fabric, originally worn by dancers, acrobats, gymnasts, etc., and later made for general wear for adults and children. **3.** really tight clothes. **Eg.** *"Laura doon' seem ta like wearin' tights ta P.E. on Fridays."*

Timeto Point (tih-mee-doh poynt) *Noun* – **1.** the area located between the Papagallo Restaurant and Barkers National Park in West Bay. **2.** the dikes past Papagallo Restaurant. **3.** a pile of mosquito bush and mangroves in West Bay. **Eg.** *"If ya know wah good fa you, doon' ride bicycle chrew Timeto Point afta dark cuz dem miskittas is tick as molasses n' dey will bite da skin offa yoh backside."*

Ting (ting) *Noun* – **1.** *thing*; a material object without life or consciousness; an inanimate object. **2.** some entity, object, or creature that is not or cannot be specifically designated or precisely described. **3.** a fact, circumstance, or state of affairs. **Eg.** *"It's a good ting I neva had buy dah house I wah plannin' to cuz one big ol' cook'nut tree had fall on top ah it durin' Iwan."*

Tired Out (ty-urd owt) *Adverb* – **1.** extremely exhausted to the point of dehydration and delirium. **2.** enervated, tired, exhausted, fatigued **2.** weary of struggling against misfortunes. **Eg.** *"I be so tired out afta I finish playin' football det I cyah barely liff my hand ta feed my face."*

Tt

Tiyud (tye-udd) *Adjective* – **1.** lacking the ability to move forward with energy or enthusiasm. **2.** sluggish. **3.** weak and futile. **4.** unable to compete against stronger forces, due to one's lack of assertiveness, drive, and will. **5.** undesirable. **6.** worn out. **Eg.** *"Dean say he hadda get rid ah dah ol' tiyud Lexus he had cuz it wah always on da bum."*

Tobacca (ta-bah-kuh) *Noun* – **1.** tobacco; any of several plants belonging to the genus *Nicotiana*, of the nightshade family, esp. one of those species, as *N. tabacum*, whose leaves are prepared for smoking or chewing or as snuff. **2.** the habit of smoking tobacco. **3.** tobacco products, including: cigarettes, chewing tobacco and cigars. **Eg.** *"Chewin' tobacca is one real nasty habit dat my Granfadda couldn' give up no madda how hard he try."*

Toe Peak/Toe Punch (toh peek/toh puntch) *Noun* – **1.** a really powerful kick in the game of football where the player uses only his/her toes to launch the ball to the other side of the field. **2.** the wrong kick to use for close range targets. **Eg.** *"If you see Boggy comin' runnin' fass fass fass, he gah chrow one toe peak and miss da ball. He do dat all da time n' den be blamin' da grass 'bout it too long or somebody spill wadda on it."*

Tom Fool Day (tawm-fool dey) *Noun* – **1.** April 1st of each year. **2.** the day of which one may become the victim of a practical joke or trick; also known as 'April Fools' Day'. **3.** a day of pranks and gags, which, while fun at times, can also lead to public deception, lies and unjustified trickery. **4.** a day to avoid playing games with others where possible. **Eg.** *"Erry Tom Fool Day, Renton always come wit da same ol' tricks n' be gettin' on people nerves."*

Tong (tawng) *Noun* – **1.** town. **2.** a contraction of 'George Town'. **3.** the capital district of Grand Cayman. **Eg.** *"Aye, tanks fah ghee'in me ah liff ta Tong yih'hear? My car nah workin' n' I nah had no money ta ketch no bus."*

Too Controllin' (too kuhn-chroh-linn) *Adverb* – **1.** manipulative. **2.** skillful in influencing or controlling others to one's own advantage. **3.** artfully subtle or shrewd; crafty; sly. **Eg.** *"I love my sista Lisa ta dett, but she kin be too controllin' sometimes. Ta da point way nobody doon' waugh be rong 'er n' dass bad."*

Tt

Top Lip (tawp lipp) *Noun* – **1.** the upper lip **2.** the uppermost part of one's mouth. **3.** the part of the lip which is located directly beneath the nose. **Eg.** *"Anytime somebody say dey smell someting funny in Keisha car, she always tell um dey muss be smellin' dey top lip."*

To the Tee (ta duh tee) *Adverb* – **1.** to the extreme; above and beyond; super. **2.** reference to one's clothing; to be immaculately dressed. **3.** overdressed and inappropriate. **4.** dressed in high-fashion attire. **5.** wearing expensive clothes. **Eg.** *"I doon' know if it chrew, but my friend tell me some people use ta always dress up to the tee on Fridays n' go watch planes come in at da airport."*

Touch I (tutch eye) *Verb* – **1.** verbal encouragement to show respect by touching one's fist against that of another. **2.** to show one's appreciation to another by touching his/her hand. **3.** to empower an individual through a simple touch of the hand. **Eg.** *"Yeah man, touch I nah? I diddn' tink you would get chrew wit yoh license, but it work out still."*

Tourisses (toh-rih-siz) *Noun, Pl.* – **1.** one or more persons who have travelled to the Cayman Islands for pleasure and exlploration. **2.** a group of tourists. **3.** visitors to the Islands who may arrive either by plane or by cruiseship. **4.** very friendly visitors who are always welcome to the Cayman Islands. **Eg.** *"Lass week I see one whole pile ah tourisses walkin' dong North Church Street. I taught I wah in da middle a Pirate's Week or someting."*

Towna (taow-nuh) *Noun* – **1.** a '*George Towner*'; one whose origins and upbringing lie in George Town, the Capital district of Grand Cayman. **2.** any person from the district of George Town, which includes (but is not limited to); Scranton, Bell Bell, Swamp, Central, Harlem, Windsor Park, Palm Dale, Tropical Gardens, Spotts, Dog City, Bodden Road, Templeton and Monkey Town. **Eg.** *"It gah always be competition between districts, so I don't see no harm in respeckin' ah towna fa representin' my district."*

Tt

Towin' (toe-yin) *Verb* – **1.** the act or an instance of towing. **2.** the condition of being towed. **3.** the act of carrying a second individual on either the handlebar, crossbar or rear pegs of a bicycle. **4.** giving someone a lift on a bicycle. **5.** pulling a car with another car or truck. **Eg.** *"One time when Daniel wah towin' me, we accidentally fall down in one pothole and he run he face right in dah ground."*

Tree (tree) *Noun* – **1.** 'three'; a cardinal number, 2 plus 1. **2.** a symbol for this number, as 3 or III. **3.** being one more than two. **Eg.** *"I doon' know way Tommy get all ah diss money from but I hear he gah 'bout tree cars in he yard park off ketchin' duss."*

Trifles (try-fullz) *Noun* – **1.** a renown ice cream shoppe; formerly located in Elizabethan Square. **2.** a popular place to hang out on a Sunday during the 1980s. **3.** a landmark business formerly located in the heart of George Town. **Eg.** *"Aye Boosey, you rememba when me n' Harwell used ta always ride ouwa bicycles out by Trifles jess ta get grapenut ice cream?"*

Tropical Gardens (traw-pi-kull gar-dinz) *Noun* – **1.** a large housing community located off of Crewe Road, near to the airport and having access to the North Sound. **2.** a warm, friendly neighborhood in which to raise children and/or retire. **3.** the neighborhood to the West of the Lion's Centre. **Eg.** *"I hear Tropical Gardens had get flood out bad durin' Ivan."*

Tryin' Play Hero (try-inn play hee-roh) *Adverb* – **1.** committing to bravery for the impression of others. **2.** to immerse oneself in danger erratically. *Noun* – **3.** a failed act of bravery or courage. **4.** a stupid stunt. **Eg.** *"Yeah, dah wah yah get fa tryin' play hero. I dunno why you would try ta triple jump ova Ms. Molly-Ann barbwire fence."*

Tuh Dat (tah daatt) *Adverb* – **1.** unlike most other people. **2.** hardly. **3.** not that often; seldomly. **4.** only just; almost not; barely. **Eg.** *"SUSAN: Sissy, yah wah some milk wid yoh tea ah wah? SISSY: No, sweedeh, I doon' really drink tea tuh dat so juss mek it black fah meh nah?"*

Tt

Tun (tuhn) *Verb* – **1.** turn. **2.** to cause to move around on an axis or about a center; rotate. **3.** to reverse the position or placement of. **Eg.** *"Chee! I hear one car jess tun ohwah comin' rong by Linford Pierson highway n' one pregnant woman stuck een da car."*

Turn-eh (turn eh) *Noun* – **1.** a mango which is currently at the beginning stage of the ripening lifecycle, but is still somewhat green. **2.** an almost ripe mango. **3.** an in-between ripe and green mango. **4.** a great mango to eat with 'sauce'. (see also: **Turn Mango**) **Eg.** *"Anytime we share up da mangoes you kin tek as much green ones as you waugh, but doon' mess wit my turn-eh."*

Turn Mango (turn maing-goh) *Noun* – **1.** the stage in the ripening lifecycle of a mango in which the fruit has begun to ripen, but is still somewhat green. **2.** an almost ripe mango. **3.** an in-between ripe and green mango. **4.** a great mango to eat with 'sauce'. **Eg.** *"Fah some reason I seem ta like turn mangoes bedda dun ripe ones sometimes cuz dey be nice n' firm."*

Turtle Head (tur-tull hed) *Noun* – **1.** having an abnormally long neck and a knobbly head, resembling that of a turtle. **2.** one whose head resembles a turtle. **3.** a long-necked person. **Eg.** *"Sometimes it good ta play wit udda people, but Randy went too far when he call Minwell ah turtle head in front ah he gyalfriend."*

Turtling (tur-tull-eeng) *Noun* – **1.** turtle fishing; to hunt for turtles, especially as an occupation. **2.** one of the most prominent occupations responsible for the growth and development of the Cayman Islands during the early to mid 20th Century. **Eg.** *"Gran-fadda always used ta lowe tellin' stories 'bout how he used ta go turtling, spear fishnin' and pongin' conch on da iron shore."*

T.V. Room (tee vee rume) *Noun* – **1.** a room set aside for viewing television. **2.** a living room or den. **3.** the room where the family television is located. **4.** a man's favourite hang-out spot. **Eg.** *"Sweetie, when Charley come ova, jess tell im come chrew ta da t.v. room. I gah be up in deh watchin' cricket."*

Tt

Twang (twaingh) *Noun* – **1.** to formulate or imitate the accent of a foreign country knowingly, but without regard. **2.** to speak with an American, Spanish, English, Jamaican or other accent, despite having never lived in any of those countries. **3.** to surrender one's liguistic heritage for the sake of sounding different. **4.** to embarass oneself unknowingly by putting on an accent. **Eg.** *"I hate ta hear how some Caymanians go way fa couple days n' come back speakin' wit ah twang, yih'see?"*

Twinny (twih-neh) *Noun* – **1.** any object which consists of two similar parts or elements joined or connected. **2.** a single guinep having two seeds in the same shell. **3.** the most coveted guinep in any bunch. **Eg.** *"Trisha always seems ta waugh da twinny even doh I do all da work by climbin' da guinep tree n' pickin' off all da leaves."*

Twiss Foot (twiss foot) *Adverb* – **1.** lacking the ability to kick a football in a straight line. **2.** badly coordinated feet. **3.** having a really wobbly step while walking. **4.** an injured foot. **Eg.** *"We coulda win da five-a-side game still, but ol' twiss foot Bingum hadda go kick da last ball ova da goal post."*

Twissin' Strand (twih-sin strahn) *Verb* – From the Mid-20th Century; **1.** the traditional art of twisting and weaving thatch into a rope. **2.** a technique which was used to create thatch rope for various uses, including; tying cows, latching houses during inclement weather, etc. Twisted strand ropes were also used to barter for goods at various stores throughout the islands. **Eg.** *"My mama say Granny n' her fiwe sistas used ta be twissin' strand erry Friday night, so dey could do some weekend shoppin' on Satdehs."*

Twiss Toot (twiss toot) *Noun* – **1.** having one or more teeth which are either twisted, ill-shaped or irregular in size. **2.** having bad teeth. **3.** a reason to get braces. **Eg.** *"Elrick used ta check one twiss toot gyal, but he hadda stop cuz her daddy diddn' like im."*

Tt

UDP (yoo dee pee) *Noun* – **1.** The *United Democratic Party*; a political party comprised of elected Members of the Legislative Assembly within the Cayman Islands Government and its administrative staff and followers. **Eg.** *"Man, lass election, dah way ya see people runnin' rong Wess Bay wit dey UDP t-shirts."*

Um (uh'm) *Pronoun* – **1.** them. **2.** those. **Eg.** *"Aye, if ya waugh me peel dem sweet padaydas yih gah bring um ova yah way I is."*

Unna (uh-nah) *Pronoun* – **1.** you all. **2.** you guys. **3.** the lot of you. **4.** a reference to two or more persons as a collective. (see also: *unneh* – used by select districts) **Eg.** *"If unna don't stop teasin' me I gah tell my daddy."*

Unneet (uh'n-eet) *Noun* – **1.** underneath. **2.** below the surface or level of; directly or vertically beneath; at or on the bottom of. **3.** at a lower level or position; on the underside. **Eg.** *"Sweetie, go so look unneet da seddee n' see if yih kin find dah blasted t.v. remote."*

Unneh (uh'n-eet) *Pronoun* – **1.** you all. **2.** you guys. **3.** the lot of you. **4.** reference to two or more persons as a collective. (see also: *unna*) **Eg.** *"I hear unneh nah get ta go Miami again cuz Michael cuss out yo daddy."*

Up'na-bush (uh'p'nuh bush) *Noun* – **1.** into the bushes. **2.** into a grassy area, overgrown pasture, or thicket. **3.** advancement into an area overgrown by weeds and grass and having many tall trees and wildlife. **Eg.** *"If ya waugh go up'na-bush wit me ta look mangos, mek sure ya wear ah long sleeve shirt n' long pants so ya doon' get bite by ticks n' miskittas or rub up on piece ah Maiden Plum."*

Urr (erh) *Pronoun* – **1.** our. **2.** the nominative plural pronoun. **3.** a form of possessive case of *'we'* used as an attributive adjective. **Eg.** *"Diss is urr country, nobody cyah tell us wah ta do unless we mek um get 'way wid it."*

Uu

Uwah (uh'wah) *Pronoun* – **1.** our (a form of the possessive case of *'we'* used as an attributive adjective). **2.** belonging to us. **Eg.** *"Less have ah party so we kin have fun wit uwah friends nah?"*

A morning trek up'na-bush is a great way to connect with nature.

Uu

Veggatebbles (vedge-ah-teb-ulz) *Noun, Pl.* – **1.** *Vegetables.* **2.** plants which are cultivated for an edible part such as the root of the beet, the leaf of spinach, or the flower buds of broccoli or cauliflower. **3.** ill-tasting foods which are healthy, but not as tasty as fruits. **Eg.** *"I heare Hurley's always gah da bess selection ah veggatebbles."*

Video Max (vid-ee-oh mackz) *Noun* – **1.** one of the first tapeclubs on Grand Cayman to feature pre-recorded *Beta* and *VHS* tapes. **2.** a popular tapeclub during the 1980s. **3.** a tape rental facility (formerly) located in The Village Shopping Centre. **Eg.** *"One time I had rent one movie from Video Max, kepp it fa 17 munts, n' dey nah even know I had it. Da funny ting is I wah still rentin' udda tapes same time."*

Voylent (voye-lent) *Adjective* – **1.** a mis-pronunciation of the word 'violent'. **2.** acting with or characterized by uncontrolled, strong, rough force. **3.** having or showing great emotional force. **Eg.** *"I keep tellin' Sherry det if she don't stop messin' wit my curlin' iron, one ah deez dayz I gah get voylent."*

Vwicks-Sahwe (vwikz-sahwhe) *Noun* – **1.** the ointment known as '*Vicks Salve*'. **2.** an old wives remedy for any ailment. **3.** a special ointment used for treating the common cold, aches and pain. **Eg.** *"Even if ya head doon' hurt too bad, still try so rub some vwicks sahwe on it and it might feel bedda."*

Vwe (v'w-ee) *Noun* – From West Bay; **1.** the letter 'v' - pronounced with a strong Caymanian accent. **2.** the 22nd letter in the common alphabet. **3.** the letter before 'w' and after 'u'. **Eg.** *"P, Q, R, S, T, U, Vwe."*

Vv

Wah (wuh) *Adjective* – **1.** what. **2.** used interrogatively as a request for specific information, or to inquire about the character, occupation, etc., of a person. **3.** used interrogatively to request a repetition of words or information not fully understood, usually used in elliptical constructions. **4.** was. **Eg.** *"I dunno wah you doin', but I nah stayin' yah tonight."*

Wah'henameis (wuh-hee-neem-iz) *Pronoun* – **1.** an unclear reference to a male person who cannot be named. **2.** that guy. **3.** the man. **4.** him. **Eg.** *"Uncle Albert, wah'henameis out deh lookin' fah you again."*

Wah'hernameis (wuh-hur-neem-iz) *Pronoun* – **1.** an unclear reference to a female person who cannot be named. **2.** she. **3.** her; that woman. **4.** your friend. **Eg.** *"When I go back ta work tomorrow, wah'hernameis bedda nah be sittin' by my desk again or else it gah be me n' her."*

Wah'itnameis (wuh-itt-neem-iz) *Pronoun* – **1.** a nonspecific reference to someone or some thing, without giving any useful description whatsoever. **2.** that thing. **3.** the object; the place; that guy. **4.** someone or something which cannot be described in any way. **5.** the object or person which cannot be named. **Eg.** *"Mummy, way da wah'itnameis? I waugh show Silvia wah I got fah Christmas."*

Wahoo (wah-hoo) *Noun* – **1.** *Acanthocybium solandri*; an elongated, dark blue scombrid fish found in tropical and subtropical seas. **2.** a popular fish among deep sea fishermen. **3.** a fish, having flesh that is delicate and white and regarded as very good in quality. **Eg.** *"Some people say Wahoo is da Cayman dolphin, n' some say dey diffrunt. I doon' care cuz dey goin' in my belly same way."*

Wyahcallit (wy-ah-kawl-it) *Adverb* – **1.** that thing. **2.** whatever it is. **3.** the object. **4.** the thing that cannot be described at this time. **Eg.** *"Purnell, go so tell Randy muss bring da wyahcallit from out my tool shed please? Da satellite gone out again."*

Ww

Wayahsayin? (wy-yih-say-in) *Adverb* – **1.** what's up. **2.** how are you today. **3.** an informal greeting to someone familiar, but yet unknown. **4.** a form of acknowledgement between males. **Eg.** *"Wayasayin' man? I neva know dah wah you det had dah new Civic wit dem kriss out rims."*

Wadda Ball (wauda bawl) *Noun* – From the Eastern Districts; **1.** the sport of Volleyball. **2.** a game for two teams whereby the object is to keep a large ball in motion, from side to side over a high net, by striking it with the hands before it touches the ground. **3.** the inflated, spherical ball used in the game of Volleyball. **Eg.** *"Turney wah mad when he fine out det Richard wah usin' he wadda ball ta play football wit."*

Wadda Knee (waugh-dah nee) *Noun* – **1.** *water on the knee*; a general term used to describe excess fluid that accumulates in or around the knee joint. **2.** knee effusion. **3.** a traumatic injury to the knee which is most dreaded by athletes, especially football players. **Eg.** *"Bobo, anytime ya go kick ah football, mek sure ya doon' miss, cuz yih gah dihwellup wadda knee n' ya doon' waugh dah."*

Wah Part (wah pahrt) *Noun* – **1.** where. **2.** in or at what place, part, point, etc. **3.** a place; that place in which something is located or occurs. *Slang* – **4.** where the most exciting, prestigious, or profitable activity or circumstance is to be found. (also used as: *which part* or *way part*) **Eg.** *"Tell me someting? Wah part ah "you nah goin' no way wit dah boy t'night" you doon' undastand?"*

Wampa (wawm-puh) *Noun* – From Old People Times; **1.** a sandal made from old automobile tires lashed with palm fibers between the toes and around the heel. **2.** a very comfortable traditional Caymanian shoe. **3.** the name teenagers give to any shoe that is not current or trendy. **Eg.** *"If I had ah dolla fa errytime my Granny talk 'bout how she miss her wampas, I would be ah zillionairre."*

Warp Up (worp upp) *Adjective* – **1.** to change or distort; to warp. **2.** to bend or twist out of shape, esp. from a straight or flat form, as timbers or flooring. **3.** to curve or bend. **Eg.** *"Look yah man? Errytime I lend Lisa a CD, she leave it in her car n' it get warp up in da hot sun. She gah do bedda man!"*

Ww

Wash Out (waush owt) *Noun* – **1.** an old wives solution to any form of illness that is not immediately apparent. **2.** to purge one's digestive system via a laxative. **3.** of, pertaining to, or constituting a laxative; purgative. **4.** to administer a laxative of some sort, whether it be natural, over-the-counter, or clinical. **Eg.** *"Mel say anytime she feel bad, her mama would tell 'er she need ah good wash out."*

Washova Gold (waush-owah gole) *Noun* – **1.** a gold wash. **2.** cheap gold plating. **3.** a yellowish gold covering which is washed onto a cheaper metal to simulate real gold. **Eg.** *"I doon' care wah nobody say. Dah ol' washova gold chain det Garvin wah wearin' lass night had look like somebody spray paint it on."*

Wash Rag (waushe-rag) *Noun* – **1.** a standard washcloth. **2.** a small cloth for washing one's face or body. **3.** any small rag, kerchief, or hand towel that is used to bathe oneself or wash hands while doing dishes, laundry, etc. **Eg.** *"Mama, pass me ah wash rag please? It nah nuttin' in yah ta dry my hands wit."*

Water Glass (waugh-dah glah'ce) *Noun* – **1.** a makeshift wooden box (around the size of a milk crate) which is built into a frame (approx. 8-10 in.) around a small glass window (the lens), which serves as a portal in waters which are 20ft. deep or more. the 'water glass' is partially submersed into the water to magnify the contents of the ocean floor, allowing the fisherman to select an area to drop anchor, and also to pick lobsters and conch effortlessly, with a 'striker' (see *Striker*). **2.** a glass-bottom box used for fishing. **Eg.** *"Ol' Pah say whenevea he had he water glass wid im' he used ta bring back all kinda fish n' lobstas n' conch n' ting."*

Wattle n' Daub (wot-ul-n-dawb) *Noun* – From Old People Times; **1.** a system of building materials used in constructing houses. **2.** a woven latticework of wooden stakes called *wattles* is *daubed* with a mixture of clay and sand and sometimes animal dung and straw to create a structure; it is normally whitewashed to increase its resistance to rain. **3.** the materials from which most early homes in Cayman were built. **Eg.** *"It look like National Trust would pay good money ta preserve ah ol' wattle n' daub house juss ta keep Cayman heritage goin'."*

Ww

Waughhh! (waugh) *Interjection* – **1.** an expression of excitement and amazement. **2.** a word used to express one's enthusiasm or interest in what he or she is seeing or hearing. **3.** a verbal salute. **Eg.** *"Waughhh!! I neva know you had get yoh new Civic! It look KRISS doh."*

Way Back When (witch pahrt) *Noun* – **1.** a long time ago. **2.** decades ago. **3.** sometime in the past. **Eg.** *"I rememba way back when my mama used ta tell me how granfadda used ta ride donkey ta work."*

Way Part (way pahrt) *Noun* – **1.** where. **2.** in or at what place, part, point, etc. **3.** a place; that place in which something is located or occurs. **4.** where the most exciting, prestigious, or profitable activity or circumstance is to be found. (also used as: **which part** or **wah part**) **Eg.** *"I dunno way part Lisa Lee get dah ol' ugly dog from."*

We (wee) *Noun* – **1.** the letter 'v' - pronounced with a Caymanian accent. **2.** the 22nd letter in the common alphabet. 3. the letter before 'w' and after 'u'. **Eg.** *"P, Q, R, S, T, U, We..."*

Wear Out (wear owt) *Adverb* – **1.** the state of being wasted or diminished gradually by rubbing, scraping, washing, etc. **2.** fatigued; exhausted. **3.** to make or become unfit or useless through hard or extended use. **4.** to dress in new clothes for a special occasion at a special place. **Eg.** *"Cindy had borry my new miniskirt ta wear out ta one reggae concert n' get drink spill on it."*

Weebles (wee-bullz) *Noun, Pl.* – **1.** a series of small brown worms, often found in fiber-rich products such as flour, grain, corn meal, corn flakes and oats. **2.** a very pesky disappointment to have in one's breakfast cereal. **3.** little worms that love corn meal. **Eg.** *"Mummy look yah, my Lucky Charms fulla weebles again."*

Weed Fly (weed fly) *Noun* – **1.** one who smokes all things marijuana. **2.** any person who cannot resist the temptation to smoke marijuana. **3.** a fan of all things related to marijuana, including its products, memorabilia, and merchandise related to the culture. **4.** a ganja man. **Eg.** *"Even doh errybody know Simon ah weed fly, dat bugga is smart as Einstien when it comes ta maths."*

Ww

Weed Head (weed hed) *Noun* – **1.** any person who has an addiction to smoking marijuana or any of its products. **2.** a marijuana addict or fiend. **3.** one who smokes a lot of marijuana. **4.** a weedaholic. **Eg.** *"I tink Sherry still goin' out wit dah weedhead guy but I could be wrong, still."*

Weekend 'Merican (wee-ken mear-ih-kun) *Noun* – **1.** a local person who has visited the United States for less than a week, and returns behaving as if he/she is a resident of that country. **2.** an individual who went up to the 'States' on Friday and returned on Sunday speaking like an American. **3.** someone who wants to be an American so badly, they behave as if they were born in that country. **Eg.** *"I juss love when I go airport n' hear all ah dem weekend 'mericans twangin' like dey bin deh fah years, even doh dey only went fah tree days."*

Wee-nuhs (wee-nuhz) *Noun, Pl.* – **1.** vienna sausages. **2.** a brand of small bite-size sausages packed in a tin can. **3.** an essential item in any hurricane preparedness kit. **Eg.** *"Anytime hurricane comin, I go Hurley's n' pack up ah cart full ah wee-nuh's. I nah gettin' ketch widdout no food again like Iwan."*

Wee-Wee (wee-wee) *Verb* – **1.** to expel waste fluids from one's body through urination. **2.** to eliminate urine. **3.** to take a leak. **4.** to 'pee'. **Eg.** *"Thelma always gah wee-wee at da worst possible time, especially when we watchin' ah good movie."*

Weh Bay (weh bay) *Noun* – **1.** the District of *'West Bay'*. **2.** one of the most densely populated districts on Grand Cayman. **3.** the place where *"West Bayers'* live. **4.** a great place to find a sea captain, a fisherman, or a seafood chef. **Eg.** *"Some people say Weh Bay too far ta be drivin' ta work, but wah 'bout dem people det gah ketch bus from all ah way East End?"*

Werry (weh-reh) *Adverb* – **1.** Caymanian pronunciation of the word 'very'. **2.** in a high degree; extremely; exceedingly. **3.** true; genuine; worthy of being called such. **Eg.** *"Franklin is ah nice guy sometimes, but uddatimes he kin be werry annoyin'."*

Ww
—

West Bay (wess bay) *Noun* – **1.** one of Grand Cayman's five voting districts. **2.** the northernmost area of Grand Cayman. **3.** where '*West Bayers*' were born. **4.** a great place to find a thatchmaker, a prominent politician, or a Justice of the Peace. (also called: **Weh Bay**) **Eg.** *"Dah time when Prince Edward had come West Bay ta open Barkers Park, I diddn' get ah autograph cuz he security wah too tight."*

West Bay Spanish (wess bay spah-nische) *Noun* – **1.** really bad Caymanian slang. **2.** words that cannot be understood in any language. **3.** the native slang of West Bay. **Eg.** *"Anytime Tisha can't undastand wah I sayin', she always say I talkin' West Bay Spanish."*

Wetchrun (weh'chrun) *Noun* – **1.** a veteran: a person who has had long service or experience in an occupation, office, or the like. **2.** having had service or experience in warfare. **Eg.** *"Jerry always call Bobby ah wetchrun cuz he gah nuff experience wit chattin' up woman."*

Wex (wexx) *Adverb* – **1.** vexed to the point of nuclear status. **2.** extremely irritated; annoyed; provoked. **3.** in need of a pillow to scream in, so as to avoid a criminal record. **4.** red in the face with anger and malice. **Eg.** *"Anytime ya see my daddy come outside in he short pants n' no shirt, dah mean he 'wex' an' somebody gettin' beat."*

Which Part (witch pahrt) *Adverb* – **1.** where. **2.** in or at what place, part, point, etc. **3.** a place; that place in which something is located or occurs. (also used as: **Way Part** or **Wah Part**) **Eg.** *"Mama, which part my football shoes is?"*

Whist (wiss't) *Noun* – **1.** really bushy, dry hair. **2.** malnutritioned hair; extremely dry and coarse. **3.** a head full of 'brillo pad'. **Eg.** *"Boy, why you doon' try doo someting bug dah whist you gah deh? I know you nah gah get no woman wit daah."*

White Holes (wyte holez) *Noun, Pl.* – **1.** large patches of skin or close-shaven hair, following a really bad haircut. **2.** the result of a bad haircut done at home by a relative or close friend. **3.** a terrible hair cut which usually results in the person having to bald their entire head to save face. **Eg.** *"Waaaahhhh! Look ah all ah dem white holes, man! Yoh barba wah drunk when he cut yoh hair ah wah?"*

Ww

White Marl (wyte mahrl) *Noun* – **1.** the soft, white-ish coloured dirt often used as padding when paving a new road. **2.** a soft, loose, earthy, material that consists of varying amounts of calcium carbonate, clay and silt-size material formed primarily in freshwater conditions. **3.** the worst type of soil to get on a new pair of black pants. **Eg.** *"I hope you know we gah hawe fill up all ah dis land wit white marl since it so much swamp"* or; *"You shoulda see dah time when Chris had pelt Junyah in he head wid ah piece ah white marl."*

White Pork (wyte pohrk) *Noun* – **1.** a child's nickname for mocking a clear-skinned friend. **2.** a disrespectful nickname for a clear-skinned person. **Eg.** *"When me n' Joel used ta be playin' lass lick, I used ta say 'cyah ketch meh ya ol' white pork' n' he would chase me all ova da place."*

Whitey (wye-deh) *Noun (slang)* – **1.** a clear-skinned person. **2.** a nickname for a very dark-skinned person. **3.** discoloured or bleached. **Eg.** *"You probleh nah old enough ta know, but back in my days, Whitey wah da bess track n' feel runna in Cayman."*

Whitey-Whitey (wye-deh wye-deh) *Adjective* – **1.** having white marks or dye on one's clothing, usually from old paint or white marl. **2.** dry skin (usually elbows and knees) which appears lighter than the rest of the body. **Eg.** *"Mummy ya gah any lotion? I waugh wear my new shorts but my knees look all whitey-whitey."*

Wholesome Bakery (hole-sum bay-k'reh) *Noun* – **1.** a.k.a Norberg's. **2.** the ever-popular wholesome bakery, famous for its freshly baked breads, patties, pastries, milkshakes and other treats. **3.** a landmark cafeteria and bakery which was located on the waterfront of George Town during the 1980s and 90s. **4.** arguably the best bakery ever in Cayman. **Eg.** *"I almost cried tears when dey closed down Wholesome Bakery yih'nah. I used ta kill off some serious milkshakes and patties up in dah place yih'see?"*

Wicked (wik-id) *Adverb* – **1.** amazing. **2.** of overwhelming surprise or sudden wonder; astonishing. **3.** flattering. **4.** wonderful; great; masterful; deeply satisfying. **Eg.** *"Yeow! Dem new Jordans look WICKED man! How much you pay fah dem?"*

Ww

Wifey (wy-feh) *Noun* – **1.** a woman with solid values, who appears to be the marrying type, and is up to standard with one's family. **2.** a longtime girlfriend. **3.** someone to spend quality time with. **Eg.** *"Erry Valentimes I gah send flowas ta my wifey or else she gah tink I doon' lowe 'er."*

Wihkayshun (wih-kay-shunn) *Noun* – **1.** vacation; to go on holiday. **2.** a period of suspension of work, study, or other activity, usually taken for rest, recreation, or travel; recess or holiday. **3.** leisure time away from work devoted to rest or pleasure. **Eg.** *"I hate dah way Troy always be goin' on wikayshun y'see? All he do is brag 'bout way he bin."*

Wild (wyle) *Adjective* – **1.** Slang for 'extremely attractive'. **2.** having the quality of attracting attention. **3.** hot. **4.** pleasing to the eye or mind; charming. **Eg.** *"I don't usually mess wit Hondas but dah new Acura look kinda wild still."*

Windsor Park (win-zah park) *Noun* – **1.** the housing community located off of Walkers Road, directly to the East of Vigoro Nursery. **2.** the neighborhood to the southwest of Templeton Pine Lakes. **Eg.** *"Dah time when I used ta live down in Windsor Park, I use ta watch dem boys playin' basketball erry day like it wah nuttin'."*

Winwud (win-wudd) *Noun* – **1.** windward. **2.** toward the wind; toward the point from which the wind blows. **3.** pertaining to, situated in, or moving toward the quarter from which the wind blows. **4.** of or on the side exposed to the wind or to prevailing winds. **Eg.** *"Bobo, try so see way da stink fish scent comin' from? I tink it comin' from da winwud, but I nah sure, since it nah no wind blowin' now."*

Wit (witt) *Preposition* – **1.** Caymanian pronunciation of the word 'with'. **2.** accompanied by; accompanying. **3.** in correspondence, comparison, or proportion to. **Eg.** *"Doon' mess wit me or else I gah tell my daddy."*

Wiyah Wiss (wy-ah wiss) *Noun* – **1.** a wild green-coloured vine covered entirely in prickles and medium-sized leaves. **2.** a strong, barbwire like vine, which grows in the wild thickets throughout the Islands. **3.** a type of prickly bush. **Eg.** *"Chummy say Misteh Harley land so full up wit wiyah wiss yih kin hardleh get ta da mangoes n' guineps he gah deh."*

Ww

Womit (waugh-mit) *Verb* – **1.** to vomit. **2.** to throw up. **3.** to eject the contents of the stomach through the mouth; regurgitate; throw up. *Noun* – **1.** the matter ejected in vomiting. **Eg.** *"Juss da smell ah fish cookin' meks me feel like I gah womit."*

Wored Out (wore'd owt) *Adverb* – **1.** dog tired; utterly exhausted; worn out **2.** dehydrated; drained of energy or effectiveness; extremely tired; completely exhausted. **Eg.** *"I diddn' believe it b'fore but now I undastand wah granny mean when she use ta talk 'bout how she wah wored out from all da runnin' up n' down."*

Work Friend (werk fren) *Noun* – **1.** a close colleague or co-worker, with which one has developed a personal relationship. **2.** a friend from work. **3.** someone to share life stories and other secrets with, while at work. **Eg.** *"My mummy work friend used ta come ova on Satdays, but afta Daddy n' her ketch up in one fight ova he t.v. watchin' chair, she neva come back."*

Wowla (wow-lah) *Noun* – **1.** a really shady individual. **2.** a really sneaky person who can't be trusted and must be watched at all times. **3.** a backstabber. **4.** a treacherous person. **5.** a sneak; a snitch; a conniver. **6.** a species of snake which has been known to live in Cuba and Honduras. **7.** a loud/uncouth invidual. **Eg.** *"Watch dah ol' wowla eh? He juss always gah be in da middle ah erryting."*

Wrinkle Up (reeng-kul upp) *Verb* – **1.** to cause wrinkles (a temporary slight ridge or furrow on a surface); to crush; fold; distort. **2.** to become wrinkled. **3.** to form wrinkles in; corrugate; crease. **Eg.** *"Erry time when Gary come school wit he clothes all wrinkle up, Miss McField always use ta send im home ta iron um but he nehwa use ta come back."*

Wum (wum) *Pronoun* – **1.** them. **2.** the objective case of *'they'*, used as a direct or indirect object. **3.** people in general. **Eg.** *"Uh-angh! I tell you you could have one or two chips, but I diddn' tink you woulda tek all ah wum!"*

Wush (wuh'sh) *Noun* – **1.** extremely untidy, unkempt hair. **2.** having a very bushy head. **3.** a very embarrassing state of one's hair. **Eg.** *"I always gah be tellin' Alric ta comb he wush or else termites gah start livin' up in deh."*

Ww

Wussa (wuh-sah) *Adjective* – **1.** worse than one would ever think possible. **2.** bad or ill in a greater or higher degree; inferior in excellence, quality, or character. **3.** with more severity, intensity, etc.; in a greater degree. **Eg.** *"I doon' know which wun wussa; me tryin' lose weight n' eatin' chips, or you tryin' gain weight n' missin' meals."*

Wutless (wutt-liss) *Adjective* – **1.** worthless. **2.** without worth; of no use, importance, or value; good-for-nothing. **3.** low; despicable. **4.** lacking in usefulness or value. **Eg.** *"Lass night, my neighbah call her husband ah wutless man, cuz he loss he job in den went out drinkin' wit he severance pay."*

Wylent (wy-lehnt) *Adverb* – **1.** violent. **2.** marked by, acting with, or resulting from great force. **3.** marked by extreme intensity of emotions or convictions. **Eg.** *"Look yah man? Gimme da Playstation remote or less I gah have get wylent up in deez people house."*

A traditional Cayman kitchen made of wattle.

Ww

Xtra (eks-trah) *Adverb* – **1.** excessive in nature. **2.** too much. **3.** to carry oneself in a flamboyant way. **4.** to behave extravagantly. **4.** eccentric and misunderstood. **Eg.** *"I cyah stand da way Darcy go on when she get rong Mandy n' da crowd ah dem – dey jess too xtra man."*

Some people go on 'xtra' during Pirates Week as part of the festivities.

Xx

Yaad (yah'd) *Noun* – **1.** the place of one's residence. **2.** the ground that immediately adjoins or surrounds a house, public building or other structure. **3.** the residence of one's parents. **Eg.** *"When ya finish watchin' tee-wee jess come pick me up by my yaad. I nah gye'n no way."*

Yaah'ndah (y'aah'ndah) *Adverb* – **1.** yonder. **2.** being in that place or over there; being that or those over there. **3.** being the more distant or farther. **4.** at, in, or to that place specified or more or less distant; over there. **Eg.** *"Mama I goin' up yaah'ndah ta see if Cootsy waugh come ova fa dinna awright?"*

Yabba (yah-buh) *Noun* – **1.** one's mouth. **2.** the source of conversation. **3.** a talkative mouth. **Eg.** *"Wah? Gyal try hush yoh yabba, talkin' bout you see my friend drinkin' beers down by Mr. Early grasspiece."*

Yah (y'ah) *Adverb* – **1.** here. **2.** to or toward this place; hither. **3.** in or to this very spot. **Eg.** *"Aaanhh, huuhhhh... Come yah! Way you tink you goin? Ya lil' brute."*

Yalla Tail (yah-lah tayle) *Noun* – **1.** slang for *Yellow Tail*; a specific reference to the Yellow Tail Snapper. **2.** any of several other fish with a yellow caudal fin. **3.** *Ocyurus chrysurus*; a small West Indian snapper. **Eg.** *"Next time I go fishnin' I cyar'in my big line cuz lass time one big ol' yalla tail had bite off dah ol' flimsy one I had deh."*

Yeow! (y'owh) *Slang* – **1.** what's up? **2.** hello my friend. **3.** how's it going? **4.** oh my gosh! is that really you? **Eg.** *"Yeow wah goin' on? Erryting kriss ah wah? I nah see you since we graduate John Gray."*

Yih'nah (yih-nuh) *Slang* – **1.** you know. **2.** can you believe it? **3.** a conversational filler, equivalent to "um" and occasionally repeated over and over. **Eg.** *"Gee, she diddn' eable gimme time ta mek up my mind yih'nah; She juss run up'na bahtchroom ta wash her hair so she kin go look man."*

Yy

Yoh (y'oh) *Pronoun* – **1.** your. **2.** a form of the possessive case of YOU used as an attributive adjective. **3.** one's own. (used to indicate that which belongs to oneself or to any person). **Eg.** *"Cuz, dah yoh football rong da back deh?"*

Yonda Hill (yawn-dah hihl) *Adverb* – **1.** a hill not far from here. **2.** a nearby hill. **3.** the closest hill. **Eg.** *"I lowe it when I kin ride up yonda hill cuz it be fun goin' down on da udda side."*

You Boy (yoo boy) *Pronoun* – **1.** you there. **2.** an interjection directed at a particular male person, without using a given name. **3.** hey you. **4.** reference to an unknown individual. **Eg.** *"Aye you boy, you cyah see my dog nah gah mess wit you if you don't mess wit him? Why you hadda go kick afta im fah? He shoulda eat ya alive"* or *"Wah ya doin'? Try so doon' open up dem fiyahworks in da publics you boy."*

You Gah Go (yoo gah goh) *Adverb* – **1.** you're crazy. **2.** something is wrong with you. **3.** you're embarrassing. **Eg.** *"So tell me someting. You tink I gah do all deez dishes when it wah you who chrow da party lass night? You gah go! I nah doin' it n' ya bedda nah tell nobody bug I lazy needa."*

You Gone (yoo gawne) *Adverb* – **1.** go right ahead. **2.** proceed at your own risk. **3.** if I were you, I would think that through a little more first. **4.** things are really not what they seem. **Eg.** *"You gone tryin' play hero. If Rolanda ketch ya eatin' out her Wendy's, she gah mek ya buy it right back."*

You Gyal (yoo g'yull) *Pronoun* – **1.** you there. **2.** an interjection directed at a particular female person, whose name is currently unknown. **3.** an indirect reference to one's female friend; from the 2nd person. **Eg.** *"Psssstttt, you gyal. You cyah pass meh some choong gum ah wah?"* or; *"You gyal look yah one minute. I waugh acks ya sump'm 'bout uwah mahts homework."*

Youngy (yung-eh) *Noun* – **1.** a common nickname for an immature mango. **2.** the youngest one. **3.** one which has not reached its maturity. **Eg.** *"I teachin' my nephew 'bout all da types ah mangoes, includin' turney, youngy, scruffy, etc. so he kin know wah dey name when he grow up."*

Yy

Yuh Faywah (yuh fay-wuh) *Interjection* – **1.** a sarcastic remark, interjected in reference to a close resemblance of something (or nothing at all) **2.** you must be kidding. **3.** are you for real? **4.** were you born yesterday? **Eg.** *"Wah? Yuh faywah! I nah cyarrin' you all ah way East End jess tah tek ah pitcha ah Blowholes fa yoh pen pal. Ya bedda try sehn 'er ah postcard."*

Many people travel up yonda hill as a daily commute to home or work.

Yy

Zee (zee) *Noun* – **1.** the 26th letter of the alphabet, a consonant. **2.** a written or printed representation of the letter *Z* or *z*. **3.** any spoken sound represented by the letter 'Z'. (also pronounced: **zed**). **Eg.** *"I doon' care wah you say, the word is 'zee' not 'zed'. Yoh teacha mussa nah learn ya nuttin' in school."*

Zed (zed) *Noun* – **1.** the last letter in the alphabet. **2.** another way of pronouncing the alphabet known as 'zee'. **3.** the 26th letter of the English alphabet, a consonant. (also pronounced: **zee**) **Eg.** *"Dey say some people say 'potayto' n' udda people say potah-to. Well den nobody bedda na say nuttin' ta me fa sayin' 'zed' when I talkin' 'bout ah 'zee'."*

Zekiel (zee-ki-yell) *Noun* – **1.** one half of the comedic duo known as 'Sookie and Zekiel'. **2.** a prominent Caymanian comedian and cultural enthusiast. **Eg.** *"I used ta lowe goin' Harquail jess ta watch some good Sookie and Zekiel skits. Dey wah da hardest boy."*

The letter 'Z' spelled with Poincianna seed pods.

Zz

BONUS MATERIAL

The following pages contain useful information
on the Cayman Islands

BASIC CHRONOLOGY

....

1503:   Discovered by Christopher Columbus.

Named *"Las Tortugas"* (The Turtles) after the numerous sea turtles.

1586:   First recorded English visitor, Sir Francis Drake re-names the islands *"Cayman Islands"* after the Spanish term *'Caiman'* which means crocodile.

1587-1699: Islands remained uninhabited.

1670:   The Islands, along with neighbouring Jamaica were captured then ceded to England under the Treaty of Madrid.

1700:   Isaac Bodden (born on Grand Cayman), became the first recorded permanent inhabitant of the Cayman Islands. It is said that he was the grandson of the original settler named *Boden* who arrived in Cayman via Jamaica in 1655.

1962:   Jamaica wins independence from England. Cayman Islands become a separate British Overseas Territory.

1972:   First ever Constitution allows election of a local government, granting greater autonomy to pursue its own goals.

2003:   Quincentennial Celebrations mark 500 years of growth and prosperity.

Sources: www.gov.ky and Cayman Islands National Archive

BASIC FACTS

....

Capital: George Town, Grand Cayman.

Demonym: Caymanian

Government: British Overseas Territory
- **Monarch:** Queen Elizabeth II
- **Governor:** HE Duncan Taylor, CBE
- **Premier:** McKeeva Bush, OBE, JP

Legislature: Legislative Assembly

Establishment: British Overseas Territory (1962)
Current Constitution (Nov. 2010)

Area: **Total:** 264 km^2 (206th) / 102 mi^2
Water %: 1.6

Population: 2010 Census Estimate: 58,878
Density: 212/km2 (57th)
549/sq mi

GDP: 2009 Estimate:
- **Total:** $2,541.56 million
- **Per Capita:** $46,278.00

Currency: Cayman Islands Dollar (KYD)

Internet TLD: .ky

Calling Code: +1.345

Time Zone: - UTC-5)
- Summer (DST)

THE CAYMAN ISLANDS

A British Overseas Territory located approximately 480 miles southeast of Miami, Florida.

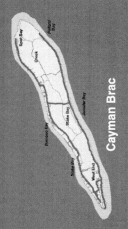

Cayman Brac

Spot Bay
Creek
Pollard Bay
Stake Bay
Aerostar Bay
Kanoon Bay
Stake Bay
West End

Little Cayman

Calabash Spot
Mary's Bay
Wells Bay
South Hole Sound
Owen Island
Blossom Village
Blondy Bay

Grand Cayman

North Sound
Little Sound
North Side
Old Man Bay
Frank Sound
East End
Bodden Town
George Town
West Bay
Seven Mile Beach
Conch Point
North West Point
Boatswains Bay

BELOVED ISLE CAYMAN

as composed by Leila Ross-Shier - June, 1930.

1. O land of soft, fresh breezes,
Of verdant trees so fair
With the Creator's glory reflected ev'rywhere.
O sea of palest em'rald,
Merging to darkest blue,
When 'ere my thoughts fly Godward,
I always think of you.

Chorus
Dear, verdant island, set
In blue Caribbean sea,
I'm coming, coming very soon,
O beauteous isle, to thee.
Although I've wandered far,
My heart enshrines thee yet.
Homeland! Fair Cayman Isle
I cannot thee forget.

2. Away from noise of cities,
Their fret and carking care,
With moonbeams' soft caresses,
Unchecked by garish glare,
Thy fruit and rarest juices,
Abundant, rich and free,
When sweet church bells are chiming,
My fond heart yearns for thee.

(Chorus)

3. When tired of all excitement,
And glam'rous worldly care,
How sweet thy shores to reach,
And find a welcome there,
And when comes on the season,
Of peace, good will to man,
'Tis then I love thee best of all,
Beloved Isle, Cayman!

DAYS AH DA WEEK

Key: 'Deh' = Day (all words represent the local dialect of the Cayman Islands)

Sundeh	Mundeh	Chewsdeh	Wensdeh	Tursdeh	Frideh	Satdeh
	1	2	3	4	5	6
7	8	9	10	11	12	13
14	15	16	17	18	19	20
21	22	23	24	25	26	27
28	29	30	31			

MUNTS AH DA YEAR

Pronounced: 'Munts ah da yare'

CAYMANIAN	STANDARD
Jannarerry	January
Febarerry	February
Maarch	March
April	April
May	May
Joon	June
Joo-lye	July
Aweguss	August
Septemba	September
Ocktobah	October
Nohwembah	November
Deesembah	December

Special Thanks from the Author

"I would like to thank everyone who contributed to this project in any way as your input is not only invaluable to Caymanology but to the Cayman Islands as a whole.

First, I would like to thank my wife, Leticia Goring for her encouragement and support, my parents Ted & Inez Goring, brother Kurt Goring, sisters Tania Ebanks (nee Goring) and Sarah V. Goring and brother-in-law Avons Ebanks for word contributions, fact checking, marketing advice, editing and proofreading.

Many thanks to all Testimonial Contributors and Supporters (too many to name) and my two year-old son, Nolan Goring, for being the inspiration and purpose for this publication (you are the future). May God bless you all."

-- Kevin M. Goring

Credits
The Cayman Islands National Archive - (research and definitions for words in its reference library directory)
  - especially; *Bush Med'sin; Cayman-made Boats; Crabbin'*
  - some info has been paraphrased throughout this
    publication and may not be recognised immediately.
Gov.ky - (general info about the Cayman Islands)
Eso.ky - (statistical information)

Photo Credits
All photos provided by the author, Kevin M. Goring, except those that appear on the following pages: 12 (american football), 13 (barbecue chicken), 33 (burning paper), 54 (calculator), 68 (clock), 100 (turtle), 118 (baby), 124 (empty plate), 127 (cell phones), 197 (gift box). The aforementioned photos were all found on various public domain websites or purchased by the author for promotional use.

BE A PART OF THE EXPERIENCE

Are you interested in contributing to the Cayman Islands Dictionary© or future products of the Caymanology© Collection?

All residents are welcome to submit words or phrases that are unique to the Cayman Islands. Please be sure to eliminate any words that are already a part of this published edition.

All submissions are subject to review for confirmation of authenticity and feasibility of use. Entrants who submit 50 or more unique words will receive credit in a future edition and enter a raffle to win a free copy of this publication.

All entries should be mailed to:

CAYMANOLOGY©
c/o GapSeed
P.O. Box 1142
Grand Cayman KY1-1101
CAYMAN ISLANDS

For more information visit **caymanology.com** or email: **info@caymanology.com** to learn more about our ongoing developments.

CAYMANOLOGY

EDUCATE. ENTERTAIN. INSPIRE. **EMPOWER.**